For Some Strange Reason

I cannot explain, there has always been a tendency during times of great seismic disturbances (and cometary appearances) for man to rise up against his fellow creatures with sword and ax, gun and bomb, and now in this age, with horribly sophisticated systems of mass destruction. If ever there was a reason for men to dissolve all the artificial barriers that separate us—be they racial, religious, national, ideological or political—this is that time. Just to visualize the armies of Sennacherib hacking their enemies to pieces and vice versa, as the Earth quaked all around them, and to realize how typical and universal such behavior is, suggests a common geo-electrical-chemical "trigger."

I suggest that the trigger is extraterrestrial in origin. Moreover, I suggest that the first in a series of devastating weather and seismic events has begun . . .

Books by Joseph F. Goodavage

OUR THREATENED PLANET
MAGIC: SCIENCE OF THE FUTURE
THE COMET KOHOUTEK
THE GREAT AQUARIAN REVOLUTION
ASTROLOGY ALMANAC
GENUS TERRAN
WRITE YOUR OWN HOROSCOPE
ASTROLOGY, THE SPACE-AGE SCIENCE
THE BIRTHDATE BOOK
STEEL CITY

PUBLISHED BY POCKET BOOKS NEW YORK

POCKET BOOKS, a Simon & Schuster division of
GULF & WESTERN CORPORATION
1230 Avenue of the Americas, New York, N.Y. 10020

Published by arrangement with Simon and Schuster
Library of Congress Catalog Card Number: 77-14118

ISBN: 0-671-81640-3

First Pocket Books printing October, 1980

10 9 8 7 6 5 4 3 2 1

Printed in the U.S.A.

To the memory of
GEORGE J. McCORMACK,
Astrometeorologist

ACKNOWLEDGMENT

Anyone who stands by you, offers encouragement when everything seems to go wrong, and has faith in what you're doing is a friend. It's something more than friendship to work unstintingly, without apparent hope of any reward whatever, when you seem to be the only one alive who believes in what you're trying to do. I am deeply grateful to Evelyn Goodavage for having had something more than faith. My thanks also to Ben Bova, John H. Nelson, Larry Ashmead and Dorothy Hughes for their support—and to the future astrometeorologists.

CONTENTS

PART TWO

AUTHOR'S FOREWORD

YOUR FUTURE AND mine is determined by climatic and other geological conditions that mankind has been trying to understand (or do something about) for more than a thousand years. Scientists now realize that something new, strange and perhaps frightening is happening to the earth's weather, and that every man, woman and child on the planet is being affected. Yet there is no viable system of predicting large patterns of weather on a long-range basis—i.e., months, entire seasons, even *years* in advance.

No scientifically *accepted* system, that is.

By mid-1976, the American Central Intelligence Agency issued a chilling report that changes in climate will instigate new political alignments—agreements forced by the necessity of feeding more and more people with less and less food as the "detrimental global climatic change brings famine and starvation to many areas of the world, which is now too densely populated and politically divided to accommodate mass migrations to areas that are more productive agriculturally. The economic and political impact of major climatic shifts is almost beyond comprehension," the CIA report said.

While the State Department negotiated grain deals with the Soviet Union, India and China, the Department of Agriculture encouraged increased wheat production in the United States to take up the slack expected by shortages of Canadian grain and corn.

Meanwhile, the CIA—its credibility damaged by a series of internal revelations of wrongdoing—tried to convince us that the entire world is in for a hell of a time. "Climate is now a critical factor. The politics of food will become the central issue of every government."

At the same time, the first in a worldwide series of natural disasters began with an intensification of seismic activity.

What *is* happening? And what, if anything, can man do about it? It's this writer's opinion that the theory of Uniformitarianism, or slow evolutionary change, is wrong, and that in order for mankind to survive during the remainder of the century, we will be forced to revolutionize our wholly materialistic concepts about the earth's interior and exterior functions, and especially its relationship with the cosmic environment, including the Sun.

As Immanuel Velikovsky, author of the controversial best seller *Worlds in Collision,* wrote (in his subsequent book, *Earth in Upheaval*), the planet on which we all travel was subjected to great tribulations in prehistoric *and* historical times. The rocks, bones and stones of the Earth are mute witnesses of terrible catastrophes of past ages.

> They testify by their own appearance and by the encased contents of dead bodies, fossilized skeletons. Myriads upon myriads of living creatures came to life on this ball of rock suspended in nothing and returned to dust. Many died a natural death, many were killed in wars between races and species and many were entombed alive during great paroxysms of Nature in which land and sea contested in destruction. Whole tribes of fish that had filled the oceans suddenly ceased to exist; of entire species and even genera of land animals, not a single survivor was left.

> The Earth and the water without which we cannot exist suddenly turned into enemies and engulfed the animal kingdom, the human race included, and there was no shelter and no refuge. In such cataclysms the land and the sea repeatedly changed places, laying dry the kingdom of the ocean and submerging the kingdom of the land.

While Velikovsky spoke of the past, the object of this book, the first modern work on astrometeorology, is to attempt to predict *future* cataclysms of weather and earthquake—by focusing attention on the activity of the Sun and the forces that *cause* this activity. There will be charges of hubris leveled against a nonscientist for daring to point out that which should have been obvious to scientists for several centuries—but that's a small price to pay if the ideas contained in the final pages of this book are put to the crucial test and used constructively, because I'm convinced that more—much more—than mass human starvation and earth changes will occur during the 1980s. Within the limits of time, space and ability given to one man, I've tried to predict the times and places where some of these cataclysmic changes will happen.

More important, I've tried to convey the basic principles with which any reasonably intelligent human being may learn the art and science of astrometeorology. We're going to need every one we can find in the very near future.

♂

"The farther backward you can look, the farther forward you are likely to see."

WINSTON CHURCHILL

INTRODUCTION

IT'S DIFFICULT TO avoid thinking of our local star—the immense sphere of nuclear fire that gives us life—as something "alive." Yet everything we are and all we know owes its existence to it. Solar astronomers, however, suspect that something ominous and mysterious may be happening to the Sun. "There are signs that the Earth's weather patterns—caused by solar activity—are undergoing dramatic changes," said one.

Long ago, men successfully predicted weather according to the positions of the planets and their effect on our local star. But never in modern times has there been a rational, objective presentation of the rules governing the ancient study of astrometeorology. Until now, the "key" to accurate planetary weather forecasting has been a jealously guarded secret of the few who know how to apply it.

The keystone of this system is the Sun; if its fires ever "went out" there'd be no weather on the Earth because the atmosphere would lie frozen solidly on the bare, dead surface of the planet, which, except for the feeble light from distant stars, would be enveloped in total darkness and the absolute zero of space. This temperature would bring all molecular activity to a halt; forests would die and there'd be no tides, no oceans, lakes or rivers.

Directly or indirectly all energy is derived from the Sun. Primitive cultures use solar energy less directly than do more sophisticated ones. The more advanced and sophisticated a technological civilization becomes, the more directly it relies on the forces of solar energy. Energy consumption increases as societies develop from the level of wood-burning tribes to coal-burning early-industrial city states to petroleum-consuming middle-industrial cultures, then to the use of atomic power reactors by later middle-technological civilizations, and finally—direct conversion of solar energy on an exponential basis.

Although we have less than two centuries of industrial and technological growth to look back on (out of approximately 8,000 years of loosely recorded history) we can only try to extrapolate the general direction of scientific advancement for the next thousand years. Chances are that ancient man has been where we are today and that in truth there's "nothing new under the Sun."

The details of such scientific/technological development, however, are often curiously difficult to anticipate. For example, after motion pictures had been developed, how could Thomas Edison have foreseen that the flickering images passing through a sequential series of transparent photographs and cast on a screen by an arc light would eventually be developed into a small magnetic card scanned by a laser beam (directed through a microscope) to produce three-hour, full-color, sound motion pictures on a home television set? Genius that he was, even Edison's mind would have boggled at this.

At this writing no human being has so much as set foot on another planet (by definition the Moon is not a planet). Even so, the minds of several world-famous scientists are already speculating about taking apart the planets of the solar system and using the material to enclose the Sun in a shell in order to trap and use all of its radiated energy. Paradoxically, many of these same people refuse to believe that the planets they presumptuously plan to dismantle may have some as yet undiscovered effect on the Sun and the Earth.

Arthur C. Clarke, author of *2001: A Space Odyssey, Childhood's End, The Sentinel,* and other science fiction stories, developed three noteworthy laws:

1. *When a distinguished but elderly scientist says something is possible, he's almost always right; when he says something is impossible, he's almost always wrong.*

2. *The only way to find the limits of the possible is to go beyond them to the impossible.*

3. *Any sufficiently advanced technology is indistinguishable from magic.*

By combining Clarke's first law with what we know from our relatively brief written history, some light may be cast on the long-range future of the human race; such an exercise may reveal some rather astonishing information about mankind's remotest prehistorical periods. The future we're (ostensibly) planning in space may actually be a biological response to the stimulus of our environment—or—a racial memory of something that happened eons ago! Freeman J. Dyson, an Anglo-American professor of physics, predicts that within the foreseeable future mankind will have colonized all the habitable areas of the solar system. He describes in detail the growth and expansion of human civilization and the ever-increasing demand for greater and greater sources of energy.

"We will completely restructure the entire planetary system, just as a new tenant decorates and furnishes an apartment to suit his needs. As we enlarge our living space, the sources from which we extract energy will expand. Our present consumption of all forms of energy will increase by a factor of hundreds of billions during the next century."

Dyson's argument is that the advanced nations of the world now manage to eke out a rather high standard of existence compared, say, to the nation-states of the Middle Ages. As an example, in spite of his wealth and power, Napoleon would have envied the luxuries possessed by some of the poorest people now living in rural America or the nation's inner cities.

Will man eventually utilize the full, supercolossal, mind-staggering power of the Sun's total radiation? Why not? Less than forty years before Neil Armstrong set foot on the Moon many of the "outstanding authorities" in rocketry, astronomy and planetary physics declared that space travel in *any* kind of vessel—either manned or robot-controlled—"is forever impossible."

"The experts," says Clarke, "are always good at spotting all the difficulties, but they lack the imagination or vision to see how they may be overcome. The layman's ignorant optimism turns out, in the long run—and often in the short run—to be nearer the truth."

How far *can* man go in controlling and shaping his expanding environment? We can already see the long-range results of the second (electronic) Industrial Revolution by the burgeoning number of nonproducing (as far as food and raw materials are concerned) people in our cities. Fewer and fewer people are needed to operate the computerized superfarms of the advanced nations (notably Canada and the United States) or turn out finished steel or run the vast, computerized transportation networks.

One Soviet astrophysicist, N. S. Kardashev, took a long, hard look at the incredible growth of the world's cities and came to the conclusion that large urban areas would probably be the fundamental characteristic of any and all civilizations—not just in human societies, but among distant alien cultures living on planets orbiting giant stars elsewhere in the galaxy.

Dr. Kardashev drew a line between industrial technological advancement and the consumption of energy, which, he says, should be the same among intelligent beings anywhere in the universe. Societies can be classified, he reasons, by their size and energy use. This is precisely the sort of thing that terrifies environmentalists. In about three decades America (and probably every other nation) will be irreversably entangled in an energy crisis of such stupendous dimensions, they believe, that it boggles the minds of world political and industrial leaders whose job it is to prevent such a catastrophe.

(Without the stimulus of war or at least the competition/cooperation of large-scale space exploration, it's conceivable that civilization could slip backward into a new Dark Age of ignorance and superstition.)

Kardashev proposed three distinct types of civilizations:

Type One: These control the energy sources of their entire planet. As the (presumably) dominant life form on Earth, mankind has yet to master controlled thermonuclear fusion, but will, probably by the year 2000.

Type Two: These large aggregates were first discussed by Freeman Dyson, whose name they bear. Such societies use a large fraction of the radiant sunpower of their parent star.

Type Three: There's just no hyperbole capable of dealing adequately with these civilizations. They control the energy output and resources of *an entire galaxy!*

One might propose a Type Four super-supercivilization wherein clusters of one or two hundred galaxies are controlled and exploited. If this were the case, such beings would be infinitely superior—even compared to our present concept of the God of Genesis. Like Him, they would undoubtedly be capable of creating planets, planetary systems and possibly great stars like our Sun!

Professor Dyson however, calculates the standard operational difference between any of these proposed three types is a factor of about *ten billion*—in the efficient use of energy. He estimates that any society expanding at the fairly moderate rate of only 1 percent per year (terrestrial reckoning of time) will graduate from Type One to Type Two in less than 2,500 years, give or take a century, and allowing for the destruction of a moon or two in the process of relocating them—or perhaps utterly destroying planets. Manipulating energy on such incredible levels is about as close to godhood as the human mind can conceive.

For all we know there may be hierarchies of such godlike creatures. Dyson estimates that graduation of a civilization from Type Two to Type Three couldn't be accomplished in anything less than 100,000 years. Other civilizations may have advanced even more during great stretches of time that we usually equate to geological epochs—*hundreds of millions of years.*

A pre-Type One civilization such as our own can be detected through our radio emissions and laser beams. We're now consuming at a crude but rapid rate the available energy resources of our home world—in the form of depletable resources, coal and oil, which absorbed solar energy when they were trees and animals billions of years ago. We use water lifted by solar heat into the atmosphere to drive hydroelectric power stations. Because of the uneven distribution of the sun's heat, winds are born and set in motion, so windmill power is indirect solar energy. By converting this solar power into electricity, new homes in the United States, Australia, Israel and New Zealand are now tapping sunlight to heat and cool their interiors and to power tools and appliances.

It is estimated that the petroleum resources of the entire planet will be exhausted sometime between 30 and 100 years from now. Coal will last three to four times longer, but this is calculated for our *present* rate of consumption, which is increasing exponentially: the average German consumes the energy equivalent to 12,000 pounds of coal each year. In Denmark, it's 13,000, in Czechoslovakia and Sweden it's 14,000, in Canada, 20,000; and for us Americans to heat the water we use to shave, shower, and boil our eggs in, to cool our homes in summer, to heat them in winter, and to continue to use the electrical conveniences we've come to regard as necessities, each of us burns the equivalent of 12 tons (24,000 pounds) of coal each year. To add to the rapid depletion, most of the underdeveloped nations have been increasing their energy consumption in order to try to keep up.

Atomic energy is not the final solution, either. The available uranium in the planetary crust will also be used up in less than three centuries—*considerably* less. Fission fusion reactors transform uranium and hydrogen into usable energy. After running out of the store of uranium on dry land we'll turn to the oceans in order to create fusion energy by "burning" a specific hydrogen isotope. At *present* levels only, this would sustain our power needs for over a hundred centuries. Sooner or later we'd face the prospect of trying to tap the only other source of energy left—the Sun.

Applying rules of this order to advanced alien civilizations indicates that after supporting a moderately growing technology for something like 100,000 years such beings would also be forced to tap their own local suns for energy. The energy-emission rate of any sun in the galaxy seems to be the "ultimate" limit on how far an intelligently directed technology can go. Until direct physical contact is made with alien beings and we learn otherwise, these rules seem to apply equally well to Homo sapiens as well as to the inhabitants of planets circling Arcturus, Vega or Betelgause. When cultures exist into stretches of time as long as tens of thousands of years, no power source other than the local star can meet their steadily increasing demand for more energy.

The awesome power of the almost eternally blazing Sun hammers at our consciousness—an insistently recurring theme. The greatest of all the wonders of the ancient world—the pyramid of Cheops—seems to have been a Sun-oriented structure. We know almost nothing about this enigmatic artifice from a vanished age; it could be a survivor of the time when human beings had achieved a Type Two civilization—an era before everything was destroyed in a disaster that engulfed the entire world. Some engineers estimate that this structure couldn't be duplicated with the technology that exists today.

A Type Two civilization is characterized by an almost endless supply of energy-collecting cells in solar orbit to capture most of the Sun's energy. But there just isn't enough of the proper material on or in the Earth to do a respectable job of manufacturing that many solar-energy collectors. A prohibitively enormous swarm of large, complex electronic instruments would be needed to orbit the Sun in order to collect most of its light and heat. This band of man-made "particles" orbiting the Sun beyond Mars, would be widened through the centuries until it formed a kind of "shell" almost enclosing our star. Every so often, the orbit of one of these solar energy-collector/transmitters would decay and the unit would plunge sunward—something like a minor comet. (Astronomers today know that there are hundreds of billions of comets slowly orbiting the Sun in the farthest reaches of interplanetary space—beyond the known planets. At this writing, there's no conclusive proof of what a comet actually is. We won't know the truth until a space probe lands on one, sends back closeup television pictures of it, analyzes its composition and perhaps brings back some pieces of it.)

A Type Two civilization would be capable of dismantling several large planets and constructing an enormous swarm of these solar energy-collectors measuring anywhere from one to ten miles on a side. Billions of these cells, orbited so as to form a thin spherical shell surrounding the Sun, would be what we now call a "Dyson Sphere." They would, of course, also be the greatest engineering feat of all known time.

Columbus would have balked at the "impossible" notion of a jet aircraft carrying two or three hundred passengers (eating, drinking, enjoying music and watching movies) crossing the Atlantic in just a few hours. We tend to take this miracle pretty much for granted; yet we are closer to dismantling the planets to create a Dyson Sphere around the Sun than Columbus was to the reality of Transatlantic jet travel.

As long as it's both economically and technologically feasible, nature doesn't limit the size or scale of activity of a dynamic, expanding technological civilization. We don't know *what* limits we'll run into between three centuries to 3,000 years from now. But some scientists believe that even if only a fraction of the societies of intelligent beings in space choose the Dyson-type answer to their own peculiar energy needs, we should be able to see them. (*Their* name for this sphere may be something unpronounceable—or unthinkable—to us.) The vast swarm of energy-collecting cells orbiting their star would create a damping effect that should be detectable to astronomers; the entire sphere of cells would heat up and radiate like a tar roof on a hot summer's day. As the photons (visible light) strike the surface of the solar cell, they are absorbed and reradiated as infrared or heat. As far as we know, there's no way of avoiding this reradiation, so we'd be able to detect their waste heat with an infrared telescope. Their local sun would appear to us as an intense infrared object and would indicate the presence of any civilization riding an unbridled technology.

On the other hand, a Type Three civilization would be

the exact opposite of Type Two and therefore much easier to find. According to Freeman Dyson, looking for a Type Three civilization would be about as easy as "searching for evidence of technology on Manhattan Island."

The exploitable energy and matter available in just about any galaxy is almost infinitely vast, and certainly beyond present human comprehension. Type Two civilizations would eventually create so many infrared sources (suns whose total energy has been dammed) that it would be all but impossible to miss them.

But because of the vast stretches of time required for a Type Two to coalesce into a true "Galactic Foundation" or Type Three civilization, chances are that such a culture would be directed and run by machines. Vast "societies" of such coldly intelligent self-perpetuating devices would be ruthlessly efficient in their use of energy, and therefore glaringly obvious to our instruments. According to Dyson, they'd never allow stellar energy to burn off and radiate wastefully throughout the universe.

The entire Earth intercepts less than two billionths of all the energy radiated by the Sun. Any small variation in this infinitely small amount of intercepted energy, however, has life and death implications for humanity. Changes in solar output are accompanied by corresponding changes in the world economy—and therefore in politics and all other human institutions. These same fluctuations in solar-energy radiation are known to be related to the Sun's retinue of planets and their angular relationships to each other.

Astrometeorology—the art and science of forecasting floods, volcanic eruptions, earthquakes, hurricanes, deep freezes and droughts—is the oldest known system of organized knowledge. It is mainly an accumulation of observational data going back thousands of years. If ever there were civilizations like our own in dimly remote times, these observations and measurements of the forces involved might have been made with advanced instrumentation.

All too often, however, modern (particularly solar) technology is regarded as an end instead of a means to an end. We rely so much on magnetographs, heat-measuring devices, spectroscopes, barometers, seismographs and other instruments that we accept knowledge of "what's happening now" instead of anticipating the future.

But under our present social system, when one man armed only with pencil and paper proves—in a series of forecasts published months in advance—that he can succeed at that which trained experts are paid millions of dollars to do, but can't, something is wrong with the system. Historically the establishment has tried to silence the innovator, make him recant or simply disappear and kindly stop annoying it. This kind of arrant suppression is a fact of scientific history, a chronicle of unsung Galileos who were persecuted or hounded, often to their very graves.

I once knew such a man. He wasn't a "scientist" in the accepted, orthodox sense. But when I first met him he had been quietly out-predicting the whole United States Weather Bureau (as an avocation) for nearly half a century. You couldn't help but be impressed by his sincerity and absolute dedication. He could have made a respectable fortune any time he wanted to, but his aspirations were different. There was a childlike purity about him. The value of his work was so obvious and intellectually challenging that I soon found myself working with him to prepare a series of very long-range weather forecasts for publication in *Analog* magazine. Thousands of readers quickly caught on to the Crucial Experiment series and avidly followed the old man's clear and lively forecasts. His hits and misses were scored against subsequent actual weather reports, and when it was over, the verdict was 93 percent accuracy for his planetary weather predictions. Naïvely, he presented his life's work to the chief of the Weather Bureau and respectfully offered to submit to any test the Bureau could devise.

But they sneered at his deferential attitude and Victorian manner. Whether it was through inertia, contrariness or despotism, they strung him along for a time and then abruptly rejected his gift because "he couldn't give a satisfactory explanation of the mechanics of his system." A Weather Bureau spokesman echoed the old refrain of astronomers: "Hell, the planets are too far away to influence anything on Earth."

Full of years when the door was slammed in his face, the astrometeorologist died before he could explain why global temperatures had been falling since 1955.

The Farmer's Almanac does an infinitely better job of forecasting than the Weather Bureau. With its global network of satellites and sophisticated computers (plus balloons, aircraft, rockets and thousands of ground observers, stations and scientists), the Weather Bureau can only report what the weather is *currently* doing. By its own admission, all attempts to *predict* weather begin to deteriorate within six hours and worsen with each succeeding hour. At best, its predictions are educated guesses; yet the Weather Bureau is the only branch of the Federal bureaucracy that always gets more Congressional appropriations than it requests. Increases are rarely questioned and never cut. Its operating revenue is greater than that of half the nations of the world.

Still . . . with all that going for it, the Weather Bureau can't even begin to cope with a request for a seasonal forecast for Minnesota in 1989. Will it be clear in Bangor on August 17, 1991? Will there be an earthquake in Los Angeles on Christmas Eve? Such questions are bizarre to an orthodox meteorologist, but they're perfectly legitimate to an astrometeorologist who uses planetary positions as his baseline for predicting terrestrial weather. Since their orbits are known with almost absolute precision (thanks to the work of the early astrologers), it's no more difficult for him to predict a blizzard at International Falls on February 3 than it is to look up the weather records for Miami Beach on the night the Titanic sank.

The underlying theory is simple. The Sun rules the weather *constitutionally* and is, in turn, yanked around gravitationally by its retinue of planets, causing magnetic storms and solar flares which affect terrestrial weather. Because we know exactly where the planets will be at any given moment in the future, their indirect influence on terrestrial weather can be predicted with uncanny accuracy.

Ancient man first noticed that when the constellation

Orion climbed higher in the skies of the northern hemisphere the weather grew colder, and for a time this led to the erroneous belief that Orion itself *caused* seasonal changes. But by about 900 B.C., Greek and Arab astronomers had long known about the tilt of the Earth's axis and the angle of solar radiation.

Solar astronomers are now concerned about the violent activity and unprecedented X-ray emissions of our star's recent hyperactivity. Information relayed by scores of satellites monitoring the interplanetary field indicates that *something new is happening on and in the Sun,* and that this has already begun to affect earthly weather, crops, the world economy, and the entire social and political future of our world. The Earth seems to be growing colder, and by late 1975, weather experts were warning of a new Ice Age.

Probably because the Sun accounts for over 98 percent of all the matter in the solar system, it is inconceivable to orthodox meteorologists that the planets could influence terrestrial weather—or anything else on Earth, for that matter. From Aristotle and Hipparchus to Kepler and Newton, natural scientists who thought otherwise backed up their belief with accurate long-range predictions. Kepler first achieved recognition because he accurately predicted the bitterly cold winter in Styermark, Austria, in 1593. Newton forecast the worst series of earthquakes and "airquakes" (hurricanes) ever to hit London; they struck exactly on the date he predicted—23 years *after* his own death.

The most successful modern weather forecaster is maverick meteorologist Dr. Irving P. Krick, who was convinced that the ever-shifting center of gravity of the solar system is the basic cause of solar activity, which, conversely, influences weather and quakes on *all* the planets. This was recently given additional support by American and Soviet studies of lunar seismic activity. More recently, two scientists announced that when all the planets align on the other side of the Sun in 1982, the San Andreas fault from Los Angeles to San Francisco will respond to the gravitational tug and slip just enough to cause one of the most disastrous earthquakes (in terms of lives and property lost) the world has ever known.

But after careful study of the solstice and equinox charts (calculated for the longitude and latitude of Los Angeles only) and all the aspects formed among the planets that you'll find at the end of this book, it is painfully clear that we're not dealing with an isolated phenomenon. Simple transposition of these solar ingress maps from one point to another on the globe clearly indicates a ubiquitous series of events.

There is nothing to be gained from alarmism. There is positive, cool and objective scientific evaluation to be made. One man alone cannot possibly erect and interpret an astrometeorological chart for every two hours for every populated point on the terrestrial globe. But even skipping through the solstice and equinox charts for one geographic area over a period of six or seven years (using the available rules of astrometeorology found in the latter chapters), a series of increasingly intense seismic activity is evident. It will not be a single confined event or series of minor aftershocks that have characteristically followed great earthquake disasters in the remembered historical past.

For some strange reason I cannot explain, there has always been a tendency during times of great seismic disturbances (and cometary appearances) for man to rise up against his fellow creatures with sword and ax, gun and bomb, and now in this age, with horribly sophisticated systems of mass destruction. If ever there was a reason for men to dissolve all the artificial barriers that separate us—be they racial, religious, national, ideological or political—this is that time. Just to visualize the armies of Sennacherib hacking their enemies to pieces, and vice versa, as the Earth quaked all around them, and to realize how typical and universal such behavior is, suggests a common geo-electrical-chemical "trigger."

I suggest that that trigger is extraterrestrial in origin. Moreover, I suggest that the first in a series of devastating weather and seismic events has begun, and that it will reach its first crescendo immediately after March 20, 1980, with a mighty wrench that will then be seen as the first supercolossal earthquake in modern times. With prior warning, international cooperation on a scale previously undreamed of, and the use of the greatest network of computers ever assembled (to analyze and distill the kind of data presented here), it is within our means to transform our machines of war into instruments of mercy. I have always regarded the compassion of one human for another as the highest, most godlike attribute of the human spirit.

There is no longer any place for a high priesthood in any area of human activity—least of all, in the sciences.

PART ONE

1

STORM ON THE SUN!

THERE MAY BE hundreds of millions of planetary systems in our galaxy—some like ours, others strange and alien. Every century about twenty of these star-suns explode, utterly destroying their planets and all life within their systems.

We live in a violent, unpredictable universe, and the familiar Sun is probably no exception to the rule. It may seem improbable that our life-giving star could adversely influence terrestrial life, but new scientific studies indicate that it may be showing early signs of instability.

During the Apollo flights, lunar samples returned by the astronauts (as well as closeup pictures of the Moon's surface) revealed fused, glazed particles from the topmost layer of lunar crust—a condition that is ubiquitous on the Moon. During some remote, brief period of instability, the Sun is estimated to have blazed with 100 times its normal heat and energy. Some scientists have fixed the time of this near-catastrophe at about 1500 B.C., thus inadvertently contributing to the controversial evidence cited by Immanuel Velikovsky of an interplanetary disaster in his monolithic book *Worlds in Collision.*

The Sun's symbol—a circle with a dot in the center

—is also the chemical symbol for hydrogen, the most abundant element in the universe—*and also in the Sun.* The mystery is that the symbol is so ancient. If the *normal* course of stellar life consists of cycles of violent activity, it may be that surviving scientists from the dim mists of antiquity had once use the same symbol. The Sun does seem to experience *periodic upheavals,* some of which result in (or are caused by) changes in magnetic polarity. This may account for the interruption of history and the interplanetary disturbances Velikovsky described in such vivid detail.

In early August 1972, during what was supposed to be the lowest ebb of the 11-year sunspot cycle, the Sun erupted in a violent series of flares and major magnetic storms. Astronomers classified them as the most severe ever recorded. There was some speculation about the possibility that the Sun was changing its magnetic polarity.

In immediate, numerous and complex ways, the Earth responded to the solar upheaval. The Aurora Borealis, previously visible only in the polar regions, was seen in the United States as far south as Richmond, Virginia. Radio communications were garbled and disrupted as the highest reaches of the Earth's atmosphere were ripped apart by storms of unprecedented intensity. Later recurrences of the same phenomenon caused some of the world's leading scientists to suspect that something strange and foreboding was happening to the Sun. They were baffled by the star's unprecedented outburst of radio broadcasts and X-rays.

Exactly one month after this stellar upheaval, radio astronomers in Canada and the United States who had been observing a binary star called Algol were surprised by two extremely interesting flares. But because of bad weather, astronomer Philip C. Gregory figured he would check out an object in Cygnus that was known for its radio bursts as well as X-rays.

Within our galaxy, he tuned in to a star called Cygnus X-3 but could hardly believe his own senses. There was a rapid increase of 220 times as much radio emission from Cygnus—something that had never been seen before.

"At first I thought something had gone wrong with the

receiver," Gregory said, "and I had to keep turning the sensitivity down." Within an hour he alerted Robert Hjellming of the U.S. National Radio Observatory at Greenbank, West Virginia.

"Would you believe an increase of 220 times more flux units from Cygnus X-3?" he asked incredulously. Before the night was over they had confirmation from Greenbank, West Virginia, as well as from astronomers at the University of Toronto and Queens University (also Toronto).

"What makes this even more spectacular," Hjellming said, "was that only the night before, emissions from Cygnus X-3 had dropped to *below* the lowest they had ever been! We're sitting on reams of unpublished data and are frankly puzzled." Totally unaware of what was yet to come, he said, "We've never seen anything like this outburst!"

The subsequent galvanic activity was reminiscent of a science-fiction film. By the following Sunday morning, scientists were vigorously investigating and had alerted six observatories. Astronomers in charge of orbiting telescopes in space were also alerted to make observations over the entire radio spectrum.

"In a celestial event as violent or abrupt as this—and at such high temperatures—we'd expect to detect brightness temperatures as high as ten million degrees Kelvin," Gregory said. Paradoxically, astronomers at Mount Palomar Observatory said they saw "nothing obvious" in the visual range of Cygnus X-3.

"This is a very, very strange object," Gregory admitted. "The outburst is as hot as a nova or supernova, but we'd expect to see some optical brightening from such an explosion."

Astronomers E. R. Seaquist and P. P. Kronberg of the University of Toronto have suggested that flare stars (such as our sun), X-ray and other stars, experience cycles of much longer duration than those recorded since the birth of modern observational astronomy.

Early in 1973 the X-ray satellite Uhuru confirmed that Cygnus X-3 was indeed an X-ray source. In June, it was also discovered to be a radio source. "It's compact and very powerful and behaves very erratically," says Riccardo Giacconi, the foremost investigator of the Uhuru data.

On September 7, astronomer Chi Chao Wu of the University of Wisconsin discovered still further evidence of anomalous stellar-energy outbursts. With raw data from OSO2 (Orbiting Astronomical Observatory 2) he reported a remarkable increase in the output of ultraviolet rays from Cygnus X-3—enough to press the latest orbiting telescope, Copernicus, into service to help solve the unnerving Cygnus X-3 mystery.

Why all this fuss over the violent activity of a distant star? Was it possible that whole groups of blazing suns in line with our own undergo regular pulsations in sequence, like some colossal string of Christmas-tree lights?

"All we know right now," says Riccardo Giacconi, "is that something very weird is going on." Since that announcement, the astronomical community as a whole has become increasingly reticent about making public statements concerning the immediate fate of the Sun. All they are willing to admit is that "we need more study and observation to find out exactly what is happening."

The eruption of the normally quiet Sun on August 7, 1972, was the most severe ever recorded up to that time. According to David McLean of the Space Environmental Sciences Center at Boulder, Colorado, "The exceptionally large (centimeter-wave) radio bursts that accompanied the unexpected flares indicated that this was the most extraordinary solar event ever recorded. The August 7 flare ran the X-ray sensors right off the scale!"

It's generally known that the Sun's gravity holds all the planets, comets and other bodies of the solar system in strict orbits, and that sunlight is the ultimate source of energy stored in food and coal. This energy is used by green plants in the process called photosynthesis. It is also the source of the energy of weather and the movement of air because its heat sets up convection currents. Because of the evaporation and condensation that occur in the water cycle, even falling water owes its energy to the Sun.

As astronomy graduated from visual observation of the

stars to the study of cosmic emissions from other parts of the electromagnetic spectrum, the variety and incidence of ever stranger mysteries has increased. These mysteries have raised new questions about our own local star. In mid-August 1975, for example, the British satellite Ariel 5 detected a flare source in the constellation of Orion; astronomers had known of such flare sources for more than a decade. They flash up suddenly and then abate just as quickly; between flares they just perk along at low energy levels.

Kitt Peak's McGraw-Hill Observatory, which was set up to make optical studies of X-ray sources, took a series of pictures of the target with its 52-inch telescope. "We looked and found something amazing to behold," said one astronomer. "Here was an object more than 1,000 times brighter than what the Palomar Sky Survey detected 20 years earlier . . . a truly stupendous stellar achievement." (If our Sun did anything like that, we wouldn't have to worry about X-ray sources or anything else ever again.)

During the next few days astronomers got four spectrograms, which only served to screw up their astonishment several more notches. They were totally different from the absorption lines usually found in the spectra of distant suns. Forrest I. Boley, chairman of Dartmouth's physics and astronomy department, said: "This indicates that we're looking at a most unusual thing. Such a spectrum suggests it is made from something of incredible heat intensity, a ball of something or other burning with a high temperature, but with no part of it hotter or cooler than any other part. Here we have a star of undetermined characteristics," said Boley, " a star of some kind that we have not yet been able to model—which has actually changed its mode of life." A thermally homogenous sun is a most unusual kind of star indeed. On the biological level it's almost as if a shark had changed into a rabbit—or vice versa.

Less than a week after the discovery of the mysterious thousandfold increase of the light, heat and X-radiation from the star Orion, a Japanese astronomer became the first of hundreds to report that a previously invisible star rose to naked-eye brilliance within 24 hours. The star—

called Nova Cygni 1975—reached *a peak brilliance of better than second magnitude,* even brighter than Polaris, the polestar. According to Italian astronomer P. Tempesti of the Collurania Observatory in Teramo, "This is brighter than all but 30 stars in the entire sky."

At peak brilliance the nova had risen 19 magnitudes—possibly more. This means it had flared to *at least 40 million times its former brightness!* (Each change of one magnitude multiplies brightness 2.512.) It was the greatest rise in brightness ever recorded for any nova in history. In 1942 Nova CP Puppis rose 16.5 magnitudes, a then staggering *four millionfold increase in brilliance and heat!*

Once a sun goes nova it usually takes years before it drops to its former brilliance. When it reaches the point where it started, the cycle may begin again. It can range anywhere from 40 years or so for novas that fluctuate only a few magnitudes to 10,000 or 100,000 for those like Puppis 1942 or Cygni 1975.

On July 2, 1975, another massive flare erupted on the Sun, causing new consternation among solar physicists who were still studying data from the 1972 eruption. Not long afterward, a star 1,000 light-years off in the galaxy flared into spectacular brilliance and fury—this one apparently a true supernova, i.e., a sun that totally destroys itself and everything in its vicinity. If it had happened to Alpha Centauri, the star closest (four light years) to the Sun, it would have vaporized the Earth and all other planets in the solar system, which is what would happen if our own Sun went nova.

Astronomers and solar physicists have always believed, however, that the Sun would remain completely stable for millions, if not billions, of years to come. But in July 1975, Lowell Observatory astronomers reported to the National Science Foundation that this was not the case at all. In fact, our local star actually "flickers," and there's no scientific understanding of this phenomenon at all.

By comparing sunlight reflected from one of the outer planets with the light of a reference star nearby, they found that the Sun's brilliance varies in the visible spectrum by as much as 2 percent. This doesn't seem very significant at first glance, but it must affect the Earth's energy balance and the dynamism of the entire atmosphere, which also affects agriculture and world food production.

This came as a dreadful shock to A. J. Meadows, of Britain's Leicester University, who has been meticulously relating solar activity (sunspots, magnetic storms and solar flares) to changes in the Earth's weather. Anything that happens on or in the sun has a direct relationship to all life on Earth, and—as we'll see later—short of causing it to go nova or supernova, the angles formed among the planets are intimately related to all solar activity.

As Pioneer 10 sailed toward its rendezvous with Jupiter on August 7, 1972, it was rocked by a solar blast packing more energy than the entire United States could consume in 100 million years. Then, in early 1974, Skylab astronauts watching for the comet Kohoutek photographed an incredible 300-million-mile-in-diameter "bubble" of solar plasma erupting on the other side of the Sun. Within minutes every orbiting satellite was affected, and within hours, every planet.

Like the Earth and every other cosmic body, the Sun rotates on its axis. Its diameter is 865,400 miles and its volume is about 1,300,000 times that of the Earth. Its mass is almost 700 times the total mass of all other bodies in the solar system and 332,000 times that of the Earth.

Since the most ancient times, men have pondered the mystery of the strange "fire" that causes the Sun to radiate such enormous amounts of heat energy and light without becoming noticeably cooler. Only during the past couple of decades have scientists deduced the nature of the forces that cause the Sun to "burn." In "design" and "purpose" our local star seems perfectly engineered to provide energy, heat and light specifically to support increasingly complex life processes on the Earth—and possibly other worlds of our local system.

Yet by its very nature, our life-giving Sun could also be a treacherous harbinger of mass human extermination.

Like all stars, the Sun *must* maintain its equilibrium in order to radiate. It does this by converting hydrogen (the most abundant element in the universe) into helium. Astronomers figure that this process has been going on in the Sun for about five billion years.

Only recently, scientists still believed that this atomic process would continue indefinitely—or for at least another ten billion years—before all the hydrogen was used up and the Sun shrank to white dwarf size, less than 15 miles in diameter. Under these conditions the atoms' electron shells at the core of the shrunken star would be compacted together and crushed. The escaping radiation from such a supercompacted dwarf star would not be enough to support the molecular activity essential to all Earthly life.

Not long afterward, spectroheliographic analysis revealed that almost half the Sun's store of hydrogen has *already* been used up! They estimated then that the Sun would "burn out" in only *five* billion years instead of ten! However, as new data keeps flowing into NASA's computer banks from orbiting planetary platforms and solar observatories, a strangely disquieting picture is emerging. The Sun is beginning to behave in odd and unpredictable ways. Instead of gradually growing cooler over a period of billions of years, the critical state of Sol's existence could be reached very quickly when the amount of hydrogen is balanced by the helium produced in the nuclear fusion process at its superhot, superdense core. This may be far sooner than anyone had previously suspected. One chilling estimate was *anywhere from a century to a few hundred thousand years.* In cosmic terminology a million years is a mere blink of the eye, which could mean that a solar catastrophe is frighteningly imminent!

Every star must have equilibrium. If the energy generated at the core exceeds the amount being radiated into space from the photosphere, one or two things can happen: the Sun's great volume will shrink *or* expand in a sudden increase of light, heat and energy. This could be up to a *billion* times its former output. The Sun would explode into nova or even supernova violence.

Gravity is the main clue to solar activity. It varies. Scientists can describe what it does, but no one knows exactly what it *is,* except that there are periodic changes in the Sun's gravitational activity. At times gravity is very intense in one area of the Sun, and very weak at others. Because we depend for our very existence on its steady, uninterrupted heat, light and energy, any disturbance, however slight, in the Sun's internal mechanism is an alarming prospect.

Astronomers admit they know very little—almost next to nothing—about this source of all life. More than 90 percent of what they do know has been learned since 1955. Almost all of *that* knowledge, moreover, has been learned during the past seven years.

Until the odd coincidence between the great solar eruptions of 1972 and 1975 and the discovery of the outburst from Cygnus, it was universally conceded that (with the exception of occasional magnetic storms, flares and sunspots) the Sun was a stable, main-sequence star.

But like so many recently overturned scientific beliefs, the serene picture of the Sun as a changeless nuclear-energy mechanism is in for a drastic overhaul.

To understand something about the function of the Sun—about what might be happening, and why—the best approach is to compare it with others of its kind. The various classifications of stars—white dwarfs, blue giants, Cepheid variables, pulsars, red giants, double-eclipsing stars and great globular clusters of gigantic suns—appear to be as unique as any human being singled out from the total population.

Any great change in temperature or variation of the Sun's magnetic or gravitational activity would mean the end of all life on Earth. A drastic upheaval might conceivably signal an impending nuclear chain reaction that could convulse the star and trigger a nova. Such an event would, of course, mean the destruction of every planet in the solar system. But there are other, less dramatic solar mechanisms—possibly undiscovered cycles that could bring on still another ice age or, worse, turn the Earth, from the equator to the poles, into a burning, lifeless desert.

There are strange properties to the kind of energy we receive from the Sun. For example, if it were physically possible to immerse your arm in the Sun's *kinetic* temperature, you could come into contact with temperatures as high as 20,000° without even blistering the skin. On the other hand, if the Sun's *radiant* temperature suddenly became equal to the kinetic, all the inner planets could be vaporized!

In spite of everything astronomers have learned, the Sun remains largely a mystery. Within a range of 93 million miles we have a splendid specimen of a main-sequence star which should have been studied more intensively, but many astronomers prefer to use existing technology to concentrate on distant stars and galaxies.

Few laymen are aware that the Sun (surprisingly) possesses an atmosphere—and *clouds!* These enormous gaseous formations of metallic gases, calcium vapor and hydrogen float anywhere between 15,000 and 30,000 miles above the Sun's visible surface. They often last for weeks. The Sun rotates in approximately 27 days, but due to inertia, its polar regions spin faster than the equatorial region which lags by about ten days per revolution. Oddly enough, the Sun's axis is also tilted (like the Earth's) from the plane of the ecliptic, but the inclination is only about seven degrees.

No one knows *why* the Sun rotates or even why it shines. We've only recently learned *how*. There's almost no scientific agreement about *why* the Earth spins on its axis. This professed ignorance is probably due to the survival of the dogma by nineteenth-century scientific materialists that the solar system—in fact the entire universe—is a vast *accident* and that its seeming order and reason exist only in man's mind.

But to assume that the cosmos is an accident, it must logically follow that "all is chaos."

The Sun's light, heat and energy almost seem to be *specifically engineered* to provide the most hospitable environment for the generation of life. "The Sun appears," said Teilhard de Chardin, "to be a great engineering achievement."

The Earth seems to rotate for pretty much the same reason. If it didn't, the dark side of the planet would be almost constantly exposed to lifeless cold and ice, and the sunlit side would be just as sterile from the ceaseless intensity of the solar furnace.

Our local star functions through the power of nuclear fusion, which is how it generates electricity and magnetism. This energy spreads from its fantastically dense core to the Sun's visible surface by conduction, i.e., through physical contact between the energy particles.

Still, there is almost nothing material in the near-vacuum of space between the Sun and the Earth. The Sun's life-giving energy is transmitted through space by *convection,* where no material contact is necessary between the particles. To maintain its critical balance, the escape of heat energy from the photosphere has to be *exactly equal* to the amount of energy being generated at the Sun's core. Although the solar core is a gas, it is far denser than the hardest and densest metal on Earth and has a temperature range of *between ten million and 70 million degrees* (as compared to the 3,000 to 10,000° at the surface)!

The atoms of this gas are under such enormous pressure that their outer electron shells are smashed and the atomic nuclei swarm together. Although a cubic inch of this stuff weighs somewhere in the neighborhood of 30 tons, it is still a *gas.*

The reflecting or reversing layer of the Sun's atmosphere is absorbed by the chromosphere (the reddish layer of incandescent gases seen surrounding the Sun during an eclipse) and the corona (the Sun's halo, also visible only during eclipses of the Sun).

The rest of the energy radiates through space, and by the time it reaches the Earth it is further filtered by the thick layer of ionized gases in the highest reaches of the atmosphere (the ionosphere), which absorbs most of the ultraviolet rays.

The Earth's breathable atmosphere is only about 12 miles high while the Sun's atmosphere extends for millions of miles. Up to about 3,000 miles, the solar temperature is the same as its photosphere, but instead of becoming cooler with increasing altitude, its atmospheric temperature starts to climb! At a height of 5,000 miles it reaches 20,000°.

In the highest reaches of the chromosphere (at an altitude of 9,000 miles) the temperature rises to 100,000°!

In the corona itself, the heat goes as high as a million degrees or more. The *kinetic* temperature alone rises to many millions of degrees.

As it is, X-rays and ultraviolet radiation from the highest and lowest parts of the corona are responsible for the different layers of the Earth's atmosphere. Photographs taken during eclipses of the Sun clearly show the spikes of plumes generated by the Sun's colossal magnetic field radiating from the north and south poles. In other magnetic fields, a bar magnet, for example, the field is roughly circular. Iron filings reveal oval rings around the magnet that connect the field. The same condition is manifested by the Earth's magnetic field, as evidenced by the doughnut-shaped Van Allen belt of charged particles trapped in the high reaches of the geomagnetic field spiraling in and out of the magnetic north and south polar areas.

Until very recently, the *super*-magnetic field of the Sun did not seem to bend or come together at any point. It was so distant that it could not be detected with then-existing technology. At the very least, it extends to the farthest reaches of the solar system (wherever that may be). About 50 years ago, the Sun was thought to be the center of everything, and the extent of the "universe" was considered to be the 10,000 to 50,000 stars visible with a telescope on a good night. No one had any idea of the shape of our Milky Way Galaxy until the American astronomer Harlow Shapley put forth the most remarkable theory since Copernicus rediscovered that the Earth moves around the Sun. (The ancient Greeks had known this.)

Every so often astronomers observe a brilliant flare of light inside our galaxy where there was previously only a faint pinpoint of light. Because they were once thought to be new stars, they were called "novas." On rare occasions these distant suns explode in an even more brilliant pyrotechnic display that dazzles the heavens. Only about four nearby supernovas are observed each century. Some are so brilliant that they can be seen with the naked eye in broad daylight. Some actually rival the sun itself in brightness.

The first documented supernova was described by Chinese astronomers in A.D. 1054. Indian drawings in

Arizona show this supernova rising beside the crescent moon about an hour before dawn on the morning of July 5, 1054. It was the most stupendous explosion ever witnessed by man. Chinese, Japanese, Indian and European records are in complete agreement about the time and place of this great exploding star.

Such a supernova produces more light, heat and energy than all the other stars in the galaxy *combined*! After almost a thousand years, that explosion is still visible—expanding outward—as the Crab Nebula in Taurus. Although it is 4,000 light-years distant, it is still expanding at a speed of 680 miles per second, and has now reached a diameter of five light-years.

In November 1572, the famous Danish astrologer Tycho Brahe discovered another exploding star. At its period of maximum brilliance it too could be seen in full daylight. In 1604, Tycho's pupil, Johannes Kepler, discovered still another brilliant nova. There wasn't a notable stellar explosion near our Sun until 1918, when an extremely brilliant star destroyed itself in the constellation of Aquila.

At least 20 stars explode every year within our Milky Way Galaxy, but supernovas are 10,000 times more powerful than ordinary novas and exceed the brilliance and energy output of the sun by a factor of several billion. So far, 25 well-established examples of supernovas have been detected.

According to science writer and astronomer John Rublowski, *"Our own Galaxy is just about due for another of these spectacular displays."*

No one can guess which star will face utter destruction. Astronomers theorize that stellar anomalies should become fairly obvious to any inhabitants of the planets that lie within the "life" zone (i.e., past the orbit of Mars) of the star before it goes nova. One of these anomalies is increased activity, especially on or within a flare star like our own. What other clues indicate that such a star is due for a supernova explosion?

The Italian physicist Enrico Fermi, who played such an important role in the development of the atomic bomb, was the first man to investigate pre-supernova conditions existing at the core of a star. He proved that it takes at least 150,000,000 pounds of pressure per square inch at the Sun's center for the atoms to collapse into this electronic state. In this condition there are no "elements" as we know them, only shattered atoms—electrons, protons, neutrons, etcetera, all whirling around each other. At this pressure, atoms collapse and become what is now called Fermi gas. The Earth's internal pressure is only about 22,000,000 pounds per square inch. The entire weight of the planet isn't heavy enough to crush a single atom.

Due to the fantastic pressures at the Sun's neutrino core, hydrogen is constantly being changed into helium, thus balancing the energy being generated by the energy being radiated into space through the photosphere.

Now that the Sun's hydrogen, which provides the fuel for its nuclear chain reactions, has been almost half-consumed, its equilibrium may be drastically tipped much sooner than scientists once believed. Judging from the Sun's recent dramatic eruptions and the corresponding changes in terrestrial weather (record-breaking rainfalls, floods, summer hailstorms, the drop in global temperature, etcetera) we may well be facing an imminent decline in the energy being produced by the Sun.

It once seemed natural to assume that as the Sun's fuel was used up, its production of heat energy would decline very gradually, and that in a few hundred million to a few billion years our local star would die a slow death, becoming colder and dimmer by the century until the blazing nuclear fire would exhaust itself.

This seems logical enough, but happens to be wrong. Dr. George Gamow, professor of physics at the University of Colorado, has discovered that *the exact opposite* would happen. Instead of becoming dimmer and colder as its supply of hydrogen reaches the critical stage of depletion or, as some astronomers now fear, *half-depletion,* the Sun will act up dramatically, with an increase in flares, magnetic storms and great sunspots which are out of phase with its 11-year cycle. Under these conditions, the Sun will grow larger, hotter and brighter. As the hydrogen decreases and the supply of helium *increases,* the difference in the amounts of these gases will produce even greater changes.

The helium in the Sun is not as transparent as hydrogen. Consequently it would become more difficult for the nuclear energy generated from the heart of the Sun to penetrate the opaque helium than it previously did through the more transparent hydrogen.

This halfway stage is almost upon us. The duration of the downgrade period as the helium increases and the hydrogen supply diminishes could be anywhere between ten years and a million, but the Sun's nuclear energy will have an increasingly difficult time fighting its way from the core to the photosphere.

At this point the crucial balance between energy generated and energy radiated will have been tilted the other way; more energy will be generated than the Sun can safely release. According to Dr. Gamow, these conditions will raise the interior pressure of the Sun to astounding proportions. Moreover, the nature of the nuclear reactions at the solar core will undergo drastic changes.

These reactions also depend on the temperature that triggers the Sun's atomic fusion. The pressure of this new kind of atomic reaction will generate even more energy, and the outer layers—no longer heavy enough to keep the solar core in place—will expand because the photosphere won't be big enough to radiate the colossal amounts of energy pushing upward from the super-*super*-hot core! As the Sun's hydrogen passes the critical stage of equilibrium where helium becomes the predominant element, the temperature increase will make the photosphere expand.

According to calculations by Dr. Iosif S. Shklovskiy of the Shternberg State Astronomical Institute in Moscow, when the Sun's supply of hydrogen drops to 49 percent and helium increases to 51 percent, it *will* expand and heat up to more than a hundred times its present temperature before the last atoms of hydrogen are consumed. There is some disagreement about the time this will require. Some scientists believe this catastrophe won't happen until 90 percent of the Sun's hydrogen is gone.

At a mean distance of 93 million miles, how could

such events affect our planet and all its life? Physicists say that Earth temperatures will gradually increase as the Sun becomes brighter and hotter. When it gets to be two or three times as bright as it is now, the atmosphere and oceans will become intolerably hot. If the Earth doesn't undergo some powerful geomagnetic reversal or change the inclination of its axis, many millions of survivors will migrate toward the Arctic and Antarctic, where the temperature will become hotter than that of today's equatorial regions.

However long this lasts, the social consequences of such vast overcrowding would be disastrous to millions of people as the glaciers and icebergs melt. For a brief period the polar regions will become tropical paradises.

Lush vegetation will proliferate in places where a few short years previously only mountains of blue and white snow reflected the cool midnight Sun. But the new tropical Arctic (and/or Antarctic) won't last, either. As the Sun continues to grow brighter and hotter, even those who survive will probably starve to death as the hot wastelands of the polar regions are reduced to scorched deserts and the boiling oceans of the equator spread toward the last polar outposts of the human race.

When temperatures reach the point where the complex protein molecules break down, the last heat-resistant microbes will have perished. No living thing will witness the Sun's terrible expansion. Its apparent equilibrium during man's brief period of scientific awareness may be illusory. Judging by the amount of hydrogen still held by the Sun, however (unless stellar physics is in error), this expansion hasn't happened. If it had, then we could expect the Sun to cool and shrink. Temperatures everywhere on the planet would then drop. This time the polar regions would begin to spread toward the equator and the oceans would freeze until all molecular activity would cease and the entire planet would become exactly like today's polar regions.

If life *had* somehow managed to re-evolve (or re-re-evolve, depending on the actual cycle of solar expansion and contraction) as the shrinking Sun reached a more normal size, such life would only perish again as the

Earth became a dead, frozen ball. The atmosphere would become a solid blanket lying on the dark planet's inhospitably cold surface. The Sun would shrink to white dwarf dimensions, eventually appearing as a bright point of light before it became a neutron star and winked out forever (plunging its retinue of dead planets into eternal darkness) before it collapsed into itself and became a black hole.

It need not happen this way, however. The Sun's strange activity might mean something else.

The Indian-American astronomer and mathematician Chandrasekhara Venkata Raman studied the way a star reaches the point of supernova explosiveness. Any star with a mass less than one and a half times that of our Sun (called "Chandrasekhara's limit") is believed to be incapable of exploding. Instead, it is supposed to die slowly as the star evolves from blue babyhood to white dwarf senility. The shrinking process supposedly maintains the energy equilibrium.

When the energy cannot be radiated into space fast enough, pressure rapidly builds up in the core. Stars with greater mass and volume therefore, are *unable* to maintain their pressure balance by shrinking. The result is an explosion of such terrible violence that in addition to destroying all of its planets, the total volume of the star stuff may expand as far as the next-nearest star.

Our Sun is the most enigmatic object of our scheme of existence. Since the modern astronomical symbol for the Sun (as well as the chemical symbol for hydrogen, its most abundant element) is a circle with a point in the center, it seems a rather odd "coincidence" that two disciplines which developed independently should arrive at the same symbol for the major element within the Sun (as well as for the Sun itself).

Until the discovery of the neutrino, no one knew that an accurate representation of the Sun and its neutrino core was a dot surrounded by a circle. This raises the interesting question of how ancient astronomers (circa 4000–2400 B.C.) with no admitted knowledge of chemistry, let alone atomic-particle physics, spectroheliograms or radio astronomy, arrived at the most perfect, all-inclusive solar symbol imaginable.

This evidence suggests prehistoric solar disturbances that may have caused radical changes throughout the entire planetary system. Such disturbances may have been responsible for terrestrial cataclysms of unimaginable violence and could have resulted in exactly the kind of Earthly and solar disturbances cited by Immanuel Velikovsky and as the geologic and fossil record indicates. If so, then civilizations as advanced as our own (or more so) may have been destroyed, and astrometeorology, which could have been the keystone of a mighty, ancient scientific system, may have reached us through the ages as astrology.

2

THE SCIENCES OF ANTIQUITY

WERE THERE EVER civilizations equal—or *superior*—to our own?

Pythagoras, Greek philosopher and scientist, circa 570 B.C., is generally credited for the discovery that the Earth is a sphere like the Sun and the Moon, that the stars are spherical and like our own Sun, and that all cosmic bodies radiate an invisible force or power that affects geophysical events. Another Greek, Anaximander, built the first gnomon for astronomical observations in Lacedaemon. With it, he was able to predict in detail the earthquakes that ultimately destroyed that city.

In 1704, Isaac Newton, who specialized in the study of ancient sciences, announced that in February 1750, when the Moon would be in perigee during a solar eclipse, and the great planet Jupiter also closest to the Earth, the Aurora Borealis would appear, followed by terrible storms and earthquakes that would batter England and devastate London.

Twenty-three years after his death the Northern Lights flickered on schedule; then came death-dealing storms with 100-mile-per-hour winds followed by a roaring series of earthquakes that buried screaming Londoners alive in their homes and beds.

Newton's astrometeorological abilities were derived from ancient sources. Kepler later expanded and added considerably to the work of Aristotle, Ptolemy, Galileo and others; in fact his initial fame was derived not through astronomy, but through his remarkably accurate long-range planetary weather forecasting.

Still, the Western scholars of the 10th through the 16th century did not conceive of industrial development; they were convinced that civilization was more advanced than it had ever been or was ever likely to become. They didn't know they were living in what would be called the "Dark Ages."

We're equally guilty of the same sort of "time chauvinism." We consider the present age as the most enlightened and superior in all history, and Atlantis a myth. The evidence, however, indicates that we're neither the greatest nor the most advanced culture. The possibility that history may have been interrupted by terrible disasters is not taken seriously by scientists or historians. We simply don't think in terms of great technological advancement during remote ancient times. We also balk at the notion that ancient structures could have been compared to modern skyscrapers. *Yet many were.* Available records indicate that some were taller. It's equally inconceivable to us that a great university with a hospital, a surgical theater, library and comfortable living quarters for 14,000 students was thriving around the time of the Biblical Deluge. Yet the Library of Alexandria had all this and more.

The historians of antiquity told of global catastrophes that erased mysterious golden ages of civilization and science. They also spoke of advanced societies far preceding their own times. According to Plato, the true pinnacle of greatness of the *ancient* ancient Greeks was about 12,000 years ago. So total was the reported disaster (or series of disasters) that the ancient Greeks themselves had no memory or tradition of the magnificence of their own antediluvian civilization.

Modern historians reject the idea that ancient man

possessed wide or accurate geographical knowledge. In the *Phaedo,* however, Plato proved that men once knew the size of the Earth. The people of the Mediterannean area, he said, occupied only "a small portion of the planet," and told of the existence of other continents.

Archimedes of Syracuse, one of the most prodigious mathematical geniuses of his time, was also credited with calculating nearly exactly the circumference of the Earth. But since he was at the time librarian of the Alexandrian School (a great center of scholarship founded by Alexander the Great), some scholars speculate that Archimedes gleaned his information from the manuscripts of a much older culture.

Meton, Thales, Pythagoras, Aristotle and Aristarchus of Samos traveled and studied in Egypt. Aristotle, Plato, Socrates and Archimedes owed an enormous debt to those remnants of a once mighty system of ancient knowledge possessed by the Egyptians. The keystone of this system was a scientific version of what we call astrology. Aristotle, Theophrastus and others were expert astrometeorologists.

By their own judgment, several of the Egyptians who passed on some of this knowledge to their eager pupils from Greece implied that Egypt itself was merely an offshoot of a much more advanced civilization—one that was destroyed in a terrible paroxysm of nature. The reported worldwide spate of volcanic eruptions, earthquakes, and tidal waves was so awesome and of such magnitude that the Deluge spoken of in the Bible was merely its aftermath.

The Biblical Deluge seems to have affected every known culture of Earth. Many of the ancient legends were revitalized when a team of British archeologists headed by Sir Charles L. Woolley began the excavation of the ruins of a site along the Baghdad Railway called *Tell al Muqayyar*. This site had lain undisturbed for thousands of years: it had been one of the surviving centers of knowledge following the destruction of the Library of Alexandria.

It took six years of intensive digging at *Tell al Muqayyar* to unearth some of these magnificent Sumerian temples. When the work was expanded, discoveries included ancient warehouses, workshops, courts of law and villas that actually compared favorably with some of the finest modern structures. They found evidence of the clock-maker's and lensmaker's art, a good indication that the Sumerians had mastered a sophisticated system of optics and may have had astronomical telescopes.

Completely intact vessels "of a marvelous design" were dug up. Golden goblets, mother-of-pearl mosaic tile flooring, precious gems and lapis lazuli (said by famed psychic Edgar Cayce to enhance human ESP when worn in the center of the forehead) were discovered within those gold, silver, bronze and ebony handcraft-laden ruins. Not even the fabulous tombs of Tutankhamen or Nefertiti in Egypt held such splendor and riches.

As the layers of tombs deepened and the archeological treasures kept appearing (the finds becoming richer and more complex as the scientists dug into the past), the Anglo-American team wondered just how deep and how ancient the digs would be. Each time they chopped through another structure to reach a new vault or room with a paved floor they expected it to be the final level.

But as they penetrated each floor, more and more ancient artifacts and treasures appeared in the baskets being hoisted out of the deepening pit. During the final summer months of this work, Sir Charles Woolley's party came to the end of its sixth season of digging. They had now penetrated into a strata of the Earth's mantle that had taken them backward from the twentieth century to the year 2800 B.C.

Still unsatisfied, Woolley continued the excavations; his party broke into and removed the foundations of this latest tomb. A few dozen thrusts of the spade revealed older and older layers of artifacts from still *more* previous civilizations, each of which, for some unknown reason, had chosen the same place to build its culture, even when it was obvious that it was the site of periodic cataclysms that altered the geography and changed the courses of rivers.

The archeologists dropped shafts at what was apparently the lowest level of ancient habitation, but still more artifacts came up. Beneath the floor of a king's tomb under a layer of wood ash, Woolley found numerous astrological tablets in an older and stranger language than anything previously known. They were now at a depth that corresponded to approximately 3000 B.C. They were becoming immune to surprise when they found under all this, still *older* strata; different kinds of tools, furnishings and strange artifacts kept appearing. How far could this continue? The great, ancient culture of Sumeria, he thought, must have reached an astonishing development at a very early age!

Finally, they reached bottom. The floor of this pit was smooth and flat; fragments of what seemed to be household utensils and tools of a strange design were found scattered around the base of the pit. The final few dozen thrusts of their spades revealed sand and clay—the kind that could have been deposited only by water. Woolley surmised that this was the accumulated silt of the ancient Euphrates River. Still—many questions remained unanswered.

So the excavators continued their work; thousands of baskets were lifted out of the slowly deepening shaft—sand, mud, more mud and sand—six feet . . . seven . . . nine . . . ten, 12 feet—

And then, abruptly, the sand strata ended.

The archeologist couldn't believe his eyes. Instead of virgin soil, the artifacts of still another highly advanced culture began coming up in the baskets! Strange, almost alien planetary tablets and ephemerides appeared, all undecipherable. With feverish excitement, Woolley's party probed deeper and deeper into the Earth. Then, in order to double-check their discovery, they sank other shafts hundreds of yards from the first one. The evidence remained consistent: they hadn't merely found the Flood—they had proved beyond all doubt that a complex civilization had existed long *before* the watery catastrophe.

About 16 feet below an ancient paved road which Woolley dated as almost 6,000 years old, the excavators stood among the ruins of the fabled city of Ur—one that had existed before the Universal Deluge.

The search still goes on, and each new discovery gives tantalizing evidence of even greater civilizations—some of them older than Ur of the Chaldees. Scholars of the nineteenth century didn't believe in the existence of this city (which was referred to in the Bible as Abraham's place of birth) because no one in those days regarded the Bible as a source of reliable historical information. But after Woolley's discovery of the city at the site of *Tell al Muqayyar* in Mesopotamia, this attitude started to change.

The result is that many legends and myths are now being reexamined and often interpreted as somewhat fanciful records—but of *actual* events. A short century ago no one took Homer's *Odyssey* or *Iliad* seriously, let alone as bona fide history. But because Heinrich Schliemann did, he was able to discover the buried legendary city of Troy.

Scholars who study human population patterns have come up with some interesting figures for the period between 6000 B.C. and today. They estimate that 2,000 years ago there were about 250,000,000 people on Earth—not very many considering that intelligent human beings have been around for nearly five million years! In 4800 B.C. the global population, they say, was 20,000,000. In 5000 B.C., we are told, there were only ten million people living on all the continents of the world. A thousand years before this—in 6000 B.C.—the experts claim that there were only *half* that many people on Earth. Based on these figures, the total world population for the year 10,000 B.C. was less than the population of Phoenix, Arizona, or Columbus, Ohio, today.

So in less than 12,000 years the population of the world is supposed to have increased 4,000 times! Most anthropologists believe it took about 8,000 to 10,000 years for humanity to emerge from the so-called Stone Age. No consideration is given to possible (if not probable) civilizations during the *previous* 50 to 100,000 years (a small fraction of the presently estimated 4½ million years of human existence).

Most of man's antediluvian works seem to have been destroyed during the cataclysmic furies of the terrestrial elements. In *Atlantis: The Antediluvian World,* Ignatius Donnelly claims:

> Science has but commenced in its work of reconstructing the past and rehabilitating the ancient peoples and surely there is no study which appeals more strongly to the imagination than that of this drowned nation, the true antediluvians. They were the founders of nearly all our arts and sciences; they were the parents of our fundamental beliefs; they were the first civilizers, the first navigators, the first merchants, and the first colonizers of the Earth; their civilization was old when Egypt was young and they passed away thousands of years before Babylon, Rome or London were dreamed of. These lost people were our ancestors, their blood flows in our veins; the words we use every day were heard, in their original form, in their cities, courts, homes and temples. Every line of race and thought, of blood and belief, leads back to them.

There are legends the world over about great beings "appearing out of nowhere" to educate the children of the survivors of a universal catastrophe in the basic arts and sciences—culture, writing, building, government and law. There's some evidence to support the theory that Egypt was a colony of a greater, more advanced civilization. Menes, the first king of Egypt, diverted the mighty Nile River and then constructed the city of Memphis on the cleared site. There is no archeological evidence whatever of any previous technological advancement before the mysterious appearance of King Menes where Memphis now stands.

He also created an artificial lake—a great reservoir—to irrigate thousands of square miles of farmland. The Moeris, as it was then known, "was 450 miles in circumference, 350 feet deep, with subterranean channels, flood gates, locks and dams," according to Ignatius Donnelly. It was a truly incredible feat.

The ruins speak for themselves; the Memphis constructed by Menes was greater by far than anything built on that location since. The entire valley and delta of the Nile, from the catacombs to the sea, teemed with hundreds of thousands of homes, temples, palaces, tombs, pyramids, huge obelisks, colossal statues and pillars. Every stone was covered with intricate bas-relief sculpture and inscriptions. The ruins of the Labyrinth astounded even Herodotus when he saw them; there were 3,000 spacious chambers, half above ground and half below. The square sides of the Temple of Karnak must have surpassed anything built in the ancient or modern world (following the apparent catastrophe that destroyed Thera and/or Atlantis). In view of what we think the builders had to work with, its dimensions astound even the modern imagination.

It was 1,800 feet wide and 1,800 feet high—taller and wider than any structures on Earth today. Archeologists of the nineteenth century estimated that the joints of all Pyramid stones had originally been no thicker than the width of silver paper. The intricacy, magnificence and and prodigality of Egyptian workmanship borders on the incredible. *Inside* the sanctuary at Karnak were lakes and mountains! Everything was completely enclosed by huge walls of intricately carved stone.

The Egyptians under Menes quarried on a colossal scale. They possessed knowledge of a very advanced order (astrophysicist Morris K. Jessup claimed that they had received the secrets of alchemy and levitation from a much older, even than extinct, civilization). They also had limitless organizational ability and astounding wealth. And yet, since its earliest dynasties, Egypt seems to have *degenerated.* This reverse chronology suggests the implantation of the whole Egyptian civilization by a much more advanced and sophisticated outside source.

By tracing these records from Africa to Asia you'll find that the Chinese also have a legend that the Earth undergoes periodic destruction by fire, hurricane, earthquake and tidal wave. After the last disaster had wiped out prehistorical Chinese civilization, a mysterious teacher named Tai-Ko-Fokee descended from the mountains and began teaching the survivors all about printing, ink, gunpowder, agriculture, mathematics, the manufacture of paper, astrology, and many other arts and sciences—all of which the diligent Chinese quickly absorbed.

Who *was* Tai-Ko-Fokee? And who were the other teachers—the blue-eyed Aztec king-god Quetzalcóatl and other bearded Caucasians recorded in the annals of the Amerindian cultures? Could they have been survivors of the worldwide disaster, or were they exotic "missionaries" assigned to prevent civilization from regressing to the level of splintered nomadic hunting groups?

Almost immediately following the cataclysmic separation of the world ages, the Chinese teacher descended from the Mountains of Chin. Starving bands of dazed and ragged survivors quickly learned to call him "The Stranger King." Although Tai-Ko eventually assumed rulership of all of China, he was *not* an Oriental. Old Chinese tapestry records depict him as a bearded Caucasian—actually a *Moseslike* figure with two small symbolic horns protruding from his head. Tai-Ko taught writing, agriculture and law. He recalculated the disaster-altered calendar and introduced a new system of chronology to divide time into years, months, days and hours. All this is supposed to have happened thousands of years ago. But to the surprise of modern scholars, the picture writing introduced by Tai-Ko-Fokee was found to be reflected in records of the Central American Indians in the sixteenth century when the Spaniards conquered the Americas.

These historical reports dovetail almost exactly with the geological evidence of disaster cited by Immanuel Velikovsky in his *Worlds in Collision* and other books. The great societies of the ancient past, he claims, "were utterly destroyed." Marine geologists once believed that they'd find on the floors of the oceans of the world only fine sediment that had drifted down to join the accumulated silt since the dawn of creation. They were astounded to find great stretches of granular sand in many areas of the abysmally cold, silent and virtually lifeless marine world. There's little movement in that awful stillness, almost no tide, or change of temperature, current or erosion of the silent depths. They expected to find only the microscopic debris of the ages.

Instead, they discovered mountains, volcanoes, sharp-edged lava structures, some of which were formed in the air above—and sandy beaches that could *only* have been formed by the interaction of land, sea and air! This was conclusive proof that some of the deepest parts of today's oceans once were great land masses. Only recently, divers and bathyscaph explorers discovered finely wrought stone columns and other structures in the blue waters of the island of Bimini and beneath 6,000 feet of ocean off the Chilean coastline.

One of the relatively modern, albeit less violent, examples of the type of catastrophe that destroyed several ancient civilizations happened when Mount Bandai erupted in Japan in 1888. Billions of tons of the Earth's crust were ripped out of just *one* of its four peaks and blasted with incredible fury straight into the uppermost reaches of the stratosphere. But even mighty eruptions like the explosion of Krakatoa in the Sunda Strait of Java, however, are mere firecrackers compared to the stupendous natural forces that raised the Atlas, the Rockies and the Andes mountains and spread mile-thick lava floes across a quarter-million square miles of India. Underneath the spongy subsoil a bed of lava covers almost all of South Africa, the Columbian Plateau in North America and most of the floor of the Pacific Ocean. Iceland has thousands of volcanic craters—plus well over a hundred volcanoes of recent origin. This island is actually the northern ridge of the subterranean Atlantic mountain spine. Many of the world's greatest glaciers in this area are not yet 4,000 years old. During the comparatively recent period there were four glacial and three interglacial periods.

Prior to what seems to have been a great series of worldwide disasters, human accomplishment may have reached heights that modern man finds hard to believe. No one knows, for example, how bronze and copper mines were excavated so high in the Alps or when they were abandoned. Tools of advanced design have been discovered in and around the passes of these mines along with artifacts from what seems to have been an industrial technology during the Stone Age.

The most compelling supportive evidence of the ubiquitous catastrophe are the oldest, tallest and most magnificent of all things still living on our planet. The annular rings of the gigantic redwoods of California accurately reflect several important changes in the Earth's electrical current, atmospheric upheavals and in magnetic storms on the Sun during the years 747 B.C., 702 B.C. and 687 B.C. Recent studies of anomalous solar activity may indicate a similar long-range cycle of radical changes on the Sun.

The period historians refer to as the Middle Bronze Age enjoyed a surprising amount of prosperity. During this time industry, art and trade flourished on an international scale much as they do today. But this civilization then reached an abrupt and catastrophic halt. Additional evidence includes ancient Oriental cities recently discovered along the Alaskan coastline. Deep trenches were gouged out of the Earth by glacial ice and frozen muck. Some of these cuts or scorings are hundreds of feet deep; many are miles in length. Any of the foregoing examples, if taken out of context, studied and examined as an isolated event, can be explained away as just another anomaly of nature. But when it's all arranged properly and seen in its true perspective, the evidence strongly suggests that science itself has a distorted view of its own history and evolution.

The time required by nature to change the shape of whole mountain ranges represents only a microinstant of an Earthtide forever in motion. We're somewhat like an alien from a dry world seeing a picture of the ocean—the crashing surf would seem motionless, hard and clear as glass. It's sheer chauvinism for twentieth-century man to insist that this point in time is the most advanced—that no prior accomplishment could possibly have been as great, or that today's fleeting styles and fads are superior to those of all previous epochs.

The lifespan of the entire human race, though it may continue to exist for scores of millions of years, is (relatively speaking) a microinstant when contrasted to all of geological time—and geological time is just hours and minutes of cosmic time, which in turn is a mere day of eternity. Man's "slow, steady progress from the Stone Age" is just a comfortable myth—an illusion that serves to safeguard the belief that there is only more and more progress—with no possibility of a catastrophic reversal for modern civilization.

That most ancient periods of Egypt's history were more advanced than all her subsequent dynasties implies that the culture was an implantation by a superior ancient civilization that disappeared after what might have been the worst disaster of all time.

That civilization, according to Plato, was Atlantis. Its kings controlled and ruled many colonies over large areas of what he referred to as "the great opposite continent." (If there were no Atlantis, how did Plato learn about the American continent?)

The antediluvians apparently enjoyed worldwide travel, which brings up another mystery: navigational instruments are not supposed to have been invented until the late fifteenth century. Without compasses, sextants and maps it would have been impossible to travel back and forth around the world.

But somebody was doing it—*regularly*.

The evidence makes it increasingly likely that the grandeur of ancient Egypt was but a reflection of the vanished Atlantean empire. The ruins of the magnificent temples at Karnak manage to convey a rough idea of the most impressive architectural feats of ancient *or* modern times. The Colossi of Amenophis I and Thutmose I were constructed in front of great pylons or massive gateways. These, and the statues in the "Halls of Annals," were precision-carved from granite, which was then quarried and transported by some as yet unknown means over long distances.

The ruins of Egypt reveal once great temples at Luxor, huge palaces at Amarna, royal tombs, private dwellings, monuments, roadways, chapels, government buildings, and colossus after colossus to stagger the eye and the imagination. The stupendous national Temple of Karnak actually enclosed a great natural lake. There's nothing like it in the world today. The halls of Karnak were so massive they could have contained a whole *series* of buildings as big as the Cathedral of Notre Dame—none of which would have touched its walls or ceiling!

The same prodigality of workmanship can be found in

South America. The ancient Peruvians constructed a stone aqueduct 450 miles long which extended across rivers and mountains. A structure like this, if built along the Eastern seaboard of the United States, would stretch all the way from North Carolina to New York City. That's a pretty fair piece of engineering for a bunch of "naked savages."

Gran Chimu, the capital of the Chimu nation in northern Peru, was sacked and destroyed by a series of wars. Its ruins still stand, however—20 square miles of palaces, tombs, villas, shops, private homes, great temples and huge pyramids, some of them a half-mile in circumference. There were municipal buildings, great halls, prisons, iron foundries and many more large and impressive structures. The famous Temple of the Sun is a pyramid 150 feet high, 470 feet wide and 810 feet long.

Just about everything of value in Central and South America was looted by the Spaniards. They shipped hundreds of tons of gold and silver (estimated at about 70 to 80 billion dollars even at today's rates) from Peru to Europe. These riches found their way into the vast treasuries of the Church, into the coffers of a whole line of kings, and actually financed the colonization of the New World. The ancient Peruvians built tremendous suspension bridges to cross mountains and rivers—centuries before they were dreamed of anywhere in Europe!

The sophisticated network of Peruvian roads surpassed anything built by the Romans in Italy, in the south of France, or in Spain. The roads of Peru were *macadamized,* i.e., made of pulverized stone mixed with lime and bituminous cement and walled in by strong abutments over six feet thick. These roads rolled through the mountains from Quito to Chile, from Cuzco along the coast to below the equator, and were about 25 feet wide.

The Incas themselves admit that all this was built long before their own time—*by bearded Caucasians.* In Cuelap, northern Peru, you can still see a solid wall of finely wrought stones 3,600 feet long, 1,500 feet high and 560 feet wide. Built atop this mass is another 600 feet long, 150 feet high and 500 feet wide. Inside the last 150-

foot-high structure there are numerous rooms and cells. Its original purpose is anybody's guess.

One of the most bizarre theories about this discrepancy between recorded history and mankind's real age is that the Earth suffers purposeful *periodical* devastations by a mysterious, irresistible force. Supposedly, after each catastrophic division of the World Ages, remnants of the human species slowly begin the long, laborious process of repopulating the world. After several generations of survivors have scratched out a bare existence, all memory of the catastrophic events sink to the level of mythology and legend that will persist for the next few thousand years.

"A couple of years ago," said astronaut L. Gordon Cooper, Jr., "I was on an expedition in South America which encountered the remains of a civilization 5,000 years old. The artifacts we found indicated that the civilization was extremely advanced. . . .

"It's members used the same symbols, signs and carvings as their contemporaries in ancient Egypt. From these discoveries in South America we know that ancient civilizations like Egypt *had* to know of the American continent. Even in those days people were somehow traveling back and forth around the world. How do we know that our civilization wasn't a very advanced one *millions and millions of years ago,* and then for some reason disappeared?"

During the period we call the Renaissance, the entire world seems to have completely forgotten the glory and knowledge once possessed by those ancient cultures. Presumably educated people before and during the time of Columbus believed that the Earth was flat, that it was stationary, the center of the universe—and that the Sun, planets and stars revolved around it. And yet it was common knowledge to the Greeks of classic antiquity that the Earth was a sphere that traveled in a generally easterly direction around the Sun, that the planets were worlds like our own, and that the stars were suns with their own retinues of planets and comets.

Pythagoras, the Greek philosopher-astrologer who was born in 572 B.C., was generally credited with discovering that the Earth is a sphere like the Sun and the stars. He entertained the idea that "Everything that is in space has a sound." We know now that every cosmic body radiates, otherwise there would be nothing for radio telescopes to detect.

Could the Taoists and Pythagoreans have been telling us what they knew about radiation? Was this what Pythagoras referred to as the Music of the Spheres? If so, how could he possibly have made such an astounding guess without the help of sophisticated instruments?

He introduced the musical scale, and after measuring the length of chords and listening to the sounds of the strings, he developed a mathematical correlation of these sounds. Pythagoras learned and taught that the planets of the solar system moved in orderly, preordained orbits *around the Sun.* A thousand years later Galileo was brought before the Holy Inquisition for teaching the same thing.

Pythagoras knew that planetary orbits are arranged in mathematical order. In 1772, John Ehlert Bode *rediscovered* this law, which we name in his honor. According to Bode, if the number 4 is added to 3, 6, 12, 24 or 48, etcetera, and then divided by 10, we get the approximate distances of the planets from the sun.

Judging by what the Library of Alexandria had managed to salvage from those forgotten antediluvian scientists, they seem to have known a great deal that modern science only now is beginning to rediscover.

How ancient was their astronomical knowledge? The Chaldeans and Sumerians had either witnessed or learned about many 3,600-year saros cycles from their more scientifically advanced predecessors. The great institutions of Alexandria reflected the glory of that dimly remote past, clearly indicating a single grand source of all their knowledge which was suddenly terminated. Democritus, Plato and Eudoxus also gathered remnants of wisdom from that mysterious civilization of a remote era.

Even by modern standards, the immense size and grandeur of the Library of Alexandria is awesome. Founded in 332 B.C. in honor of Alexander the Great, Alexandria was the capital of the Ptolemies for 300 years. The largest city in the West, Alexandria serenely boasted two celebrated royal libraries containing about 700,000 rare books or copies of books which preserved what was left of the knowledge of those remote ancient civilizations—after global devastations forced surviving scholars to attempt the restructuring of the knowledge possessed by the antediluvians. Their extraordinary achievement was obliterated in A.D. 391, when Theodosius I finally destroyed the great crypts of knowledge.

The destruction and burning of cultural records during what we choose to call "antiquity" nearly completed the erasure of advanced "prehistorical" civilizations. (Immanuel Velikovsky claims mankind is suffering from "collective amnesia.") Evolutionists filled in the gaps with fanciful half-human, half-ape creatures that supposedly lived and roamed Europe, Asia, Africa and America on an almost animallike level of existence between 30,000 to 60,000 years ago. But when Dr. Louis B. Leakey discovered a more human-appearing series of fossils which were over two million years old, he shattered much of our faith in the theories of orthodoxy anthropology. Even more astounding was the discovery of the existence of toolmaking and agricultural humanoids with a sophisticated method of communication—established by the younger Leakey—*4½ million years ago!* (Thomas Taylor, in his *Notes on Julius Firmicus Maternus* states: "Epigenes, Berosus and Critodemes set the duration of astronomical observations by the Babylonians at from 490,000 to 720,000 years.")

In the sixth century B.C. the fabulous collection of Psistratus in Athens was ravaged; all that survived were the poems of Homer. The books in the library of the Temple of Ptah in Memphis were utterly destroyed. In Asia Minor the library of Pergamus, which contained 200,000 volumes of medical, scientific and philosophical wisdom (salvaged, apparently, from previous natural catastrophes), was also totally destroyed. Carthage had a magnificent library which had accumulated over half a million volumes. But in 146 B.C., during a 17-day-long fire, Roman legions burned the entire city to the ground, including every book in the Carthaginian library.

The great libraries represented man's attempts to salvage everything possible of what had been known during the days preceding the cataclysms. It is ironic that the worst blow against the spread of mathematical and scientific knowledge was launched by one of history's towering figures—none other than Julius Caesar himself. During his Egyptian campaign, Caesar (possibly because of his bizarre jealousy of Alexander) burned the great Library of Alexandria to the ground. The *Serapeum* lost 300,000 volumes of ancient wisdom; the *Bruchion's* 400,000 volumes also went up in flames. They are gone forever. The loss is incalculable. No one will ever really know its complete extent, but it has been estimated that the carefully documented human wisdom of thousands of years was destroyed—an act of barbarism that could have set civilization back as much as 5,000 to 10,000 years!

We can begin to appreciate this only by trying to imagine where the modern world would be if the steam engine and electricity (to say nothing of atomic power and spaceships) *had* been developed several thousands of years ago. To salvage 700,000 volumes of wisdom from a preceding World Age, the keepers of the Library of Alexandria had to have had a plethora of material from which to copy. It must have taken them centuries of archeological probing to gather even that much from the previous epoch.

The Alexandria Library was also a research institute and a university that had full faculties teaching mathematics, science, literature, philosophy and medicine. There was an astronomical observatory, a chemical laboratory, a botanical and zoological garden and a 500-bed hospital with a huge surgical theater for operations and dissection!

Fourteen thousand students attended this ancient university: they were charged with the responsibility for preserving knowledge that had survived the barbaric destruction of the Library. Caesar also destroyed thousands of volumes in the Bibractic Druid College in Gaul (now Autun, France). Countless books on medicine, philosophy, engineering, chemistry, alchemy and astronomy were destroyed.

A similar fate befell much of the accumulated ancient knowledge in China. Devoted scholars who tried to preserve the precious records of man's great antediluvian past were defeated by the archenemies of culture. Emperor Ch'in Shih Huang issued an edict in 213 B.C. to destroy countless thousands of books on the sciences. This "tradition" of erasing all traces of the history of the preceding World Age is deeply rooted in psychic fear. Even in the modern academic world there is a powerful resistance to the idea that advanced civilizations—vastly different and in some cases perhaps greater than our own—could have existed so long ago.

This attitude may be traced to a deep-seated fear of change—in this case, to changing everything we *think* we know about humanity's true origins.

Based on the somewhat distorted information they had received from antediluvian times, Greek, Chinese, Egyptian, Hindu and Babylonian scholars believed that each star possessed intelligence. The early Popes held this opinion, as did Origen, Saint Ambrose, Aristotle, Plato, Saint Augustine, Theophrastus, Cicero and Plotinus. In more recent times, Benjamin Franklin exhorted his followers to "pray only to the nearest local deity, the Sun."

This ancient "religion of the planets" has come down through the ages in diluted form; we can trace its origins in the name of the days of the week. Monday is the day of the Moon, Tuesday of Mars, Wednesday of Mercury, etcetera.

Greek thought was infinitely superior to the philosophy of the so-called Dark Ages. But science—*real* science—was born in the remotest periods of antiquity. It was eclipsed in medieval times, rediscovered and resurrected piecemeal by the Arabs, who managed to salvage only fragments of that knowledge from the destroyed Library of Alexandria. It came into vogue once more during the Renaissance and was developed further by the scientists of the nineteenth and twentieth centuries.

Conceivably, there could be a repetition of the catastrophic division of World Ages. No one knows the exact cause or times of the terrible destruction of previous civilizations.

3

SITUATION OF SOME GRAVITY

SOMEBODY ONCE ASKED the great Irish playwright George Bernard Shaw his opinion of Christianity. "I think it's a marvelous idea," Shaw replied. "Too bad nobody has ever tried it."

Like some clergymen, scientists often practice a double standard by saying one thing and doing another. If they practiced the scientific method instead of extolling it, great discoveries would never be suppressed and discoverers would never be persecuted.

Scientists, however, tend to deny that perfectly valid, proven discoveries are ever ignored or suppressed. Their seeming resistance to new ideas, they say, is simply their way of insuring proof of a new discovery by having disinterested (and therefore, presumably, objective) scientists duplicate it by crucial experiment. (How to equate "disinterest" with "objectivity," however, is something for Yossarian or the Queen of Hearts to ponder.)

The fact is that for decades—in some cases centuries—there has been abundant evidence in the scientific literature to support the fact that the Sun and the planets are interactive. Energies ranging from the infinitesimally small to the unimaginably great are constantly reverberating through the solar system. These energies profoundly influence events in and on each planet, including the Earth.

But this isn't all. That evidence is fully backed by verified, prepublished records of successful long-range prediction of floods, hurricanes, drought, deep freezes and earthquakes by scientists and engineers who used planetary positions and solar dynamics in their forecasts.

To reject the evidence of astrometeorology because it might condone belief in astrology is to ignore established evidence and known, corroborated facts. This failure to use already available material is scientifically inexcusable. To claim ignorance of its existence is probably worse; it indicates lack of interest.

Why is it that astronomers, seismologists and meteorologists claim to know nothing about the published literature on astrometeorology? In all fairness, scientists are no different from other people. Scientific objectivity is a myth; scientists are just as much creatures of emotion as the rest of us. They will refuse to investigate anything they "know" is false—and the physical sciences have "known" for decades that all forms of astrology are sheer nonsense. So sure, in fact, are they of this that in September 1975, 186 prominent scientists—18 of whom were Nobel Prize winners—headed by Bart J. Bok, emeritus professor of astronomy at the University of Tucson, signed a statement virtually declaring war on astrology and astrologers.

"The accumulated knowledge of astronomy," said one eminent astronomer, "contradicts astrology. The planets are obviously too far away to have any perceptible effect on the earth or any terrestrial phenomena."

This "knowledge," however, is just a le-e-etle bit out of date. It was based on the consideration of gravity alone—*and*—in the now almost ancient days when magnetohydrodynamics, the solar wind and solar "magnetic field bombs" with power equivalent to millions of megatons were unknown.

This also happened to be the period when astronomers "knew" that Mercury didn't rotate with respect to the Sun, and that Mars was covered with "canals." And the idea that Venus might rotate retrograde was—well—utterly preposterous.

Now, however, engineers, who must work with facts that work, not theories that fail to, have observed as a fact of the real universe that astrological weather and radio-transmission forecasts *do* work. Only gradually are the underlying causes beginning to appear—but against all but overwhelming scientific resistance.

Considering that Pythagoras of ancient Greece compared the solar system to a macrocosmic atom—an interdependent unit—this is a very curious attitude indeed. Today, orbiting solar observatories, space platforms and delicate sensors have proven the existence, power and influence of the interplanetary magnetic and gravitational fields. (The Pythagoreans and Taoists, *without* our instruments, knew of these fields, and postulated some kind of radiation.)

In 1974, Dr. John Gribbin, an astrophysicist and editor of the prestigious British science magazine *Nature,* postulated that disturbances of the field by the planets coincide with disastrous earthquakes. With co-author Stephen Plagemann, a Washington-based astronomer recently engaged in upper atmospheric studies for NASA, Dr. Gribbin predicted (in their book *The Jupiter Effect,* about which more later) a catastrophic Los Angeles quake between 1982 and 1984.

Contrary to old-fashioned ideas about the Sun's stability, the common center of gravity of the solar system seldom stays at the superhot, superdense neutrino core of our local star. This ever shifting "point" of gravity churns up from the Sun's center anywhere from 10,000 to 400,000 miles through the solar plasma. It also whipsaws across the photosphere, sending up incandescent gouts of fire that splash down half a million miles away, or it corkscrews vertically through the surface, and blasts out into space for millions of miles—often near the orbit of Mercury. These effects are reflected in the ionosphere and in the very mantle and core of the Earth. It affects the ion content of the lower atmosphere, which is a determining factor in the health and well-being of vast numbers of human beings. Why the center of gravity of the Sun-Earth-Moon system should be the determining factor in hemorrhaging is a medical mystery, but the ancient "myth" about the Full Moon was verified by two Florida medical doctors. Carl C. McLemore and Edson Andrews, surgical specialists in eye, ear, nose and throat complaints, decided to pool the graphs they'd made of excessive bleeders over a combined period of eight years. They reported in the *Journal of the Florida Medical Association* that hemorrhaging reached a peak each month as the Moon opposed the Sun (i.e., at Full Moon), and that bleeding dropped to a monthly low at the New Moon. Amazingly, only *half* as many patients were operated on for adenoid and tonsil removal during Full Moon periods as at other times!

Even without consideration of force field effects on living organisms, these eight points are eminently worthy of keeping in mind as you read this book:

1. The Earth is actually deep within the Sun's magnetohydrodynamic "atmosphere"; the highly ionized, powerfully magnetic solar winds blow far out beyond the Earth to Mars—and beyond.

2. The Sun is an immense mass of totally ionized plasma—a practically perfect electrical conductor.

3. It has immense magnetic field forces throughout its perfectly conducting mass.

4. The planets revolve in orbit about the center of gravity of the *system*—NOT the center of gravity of the Sun! The Sun itself, therefore, must also swing around that constantly shifting center of gravity.

5. Tidal effects in a colossal, perfectly conducting plasma saturated with magnetic fields have *never* been studied! Modern mathematics probably isn't anywhere near being capable of it. But one can guesstimate that a thermonuclear reactor of the magnitude of our Sun, being churned gravitationally, with perfectly conductive plasma masses hundreds of times greater than Jupiter being dragged through immense magnetic fields, would not be conducive to peaceful coexistence!

6. And while the planetary positions may not have appreciable direct gravitational influence on events on Earth, the indirect effect of the varying gravitational

angles of the planets most certainly *does* affect—massively! —phenomena in/on the Sun.

7. Astrology has always been a purely observational study of correlations, without much effort to explain the observed correlations—a rule-of-thumb engineering type of approach. Very early, men observed the correlation between the constellation Orion rising early in the evening with the onset of cooler weather in the northern hemisphere. A rather natural human tendency to say "Orion *caused* the lower temperatures," is inevitable: the old, false logical proposition "Since B always follows A, A is the cause of B." *Post hoc, ergo propter hoc.* It is invalid with respect to the alphabet—however true the observation!—and with respect to anything else.

But the observation remains true.

As far as we know, the ancient Britons who built Stonehenge as an astrological observatory had no valid cosmological theories—unless they were survivors of a destroyed civilization—but they were damned keen observers; Stonehenge accurately predicted eclipses. That was a simple, accurate observation of a time/event correlation. *Why,* they probably did not know; but *that* they knew—and very accurately.

8. The observation, detailed in this chapter, of the correlation between the angular position of the Great Dipper and Earth's barometric pressure, currently has the status of "observational datum; explanation unknown."

But since we know that solar wind and interrelated magnetic field effects are a powerful influence on the Earth's weather, it's perfectly possible that the known to exist galactic magnetic field is involved in that observed small barometric cycle—i.e., that the Earth's ionosphere and troposphere are linked into the directional vectors of the galactic magnetic field—and that the remote stars, for all their remoteness, do relate to phenomena affecting Earth.

The facts reported here are, in and of themselves, highly interesting at least, astounding at best. It's doubtful, however, that they will be fully understood and correctly explained until scientists take the kind of information found in this book, dissect it, rip it apart again and give it a few dozen acid tests.

Part of the law of gravity states that the gravitational force of any body diminishes as to the square of the distance from that body. This may help explain the recent discovery that tiny Mercury's gravitational influence on the Sun is often greater than that of the largest solarian planet, Jupiter, whose mass virtually exceeds that of all the others.

It naturally follows, then, that there are numerous regions throughout interplanetary, interstellar and intergalactic space where null or zero gravity exists. In such places the total effect of all gravitational forces would be temporarily in perfect balance. Any physical body in such an area would be in a situation exactly the opposition of conditions inside a black hole (where a huge star has collapsed into its own field of gravity—a field so powerful that nothing, not even light, can escape from it). Such a body would be completely uninfluenced—in a sort of limbo insofar as currently known field forces are concerned.

In our local system, the Earth and all other bodies—not excluding the Sun—are forever being yanked in different directions by the combined and ever-shifting gravitational force of each member of the local cosmic organism.

During the astronomical renaissance started by Galileo's telescope, the popular misconception arose that all known planets orbited the Sun.

The fact is, they don't. The only proper definition is that the Sun and its retinue of planets orbit their common center of gravity. Since our star is composed of practically all the matter in the system, the center of gravity is almost always closer to the star than even to Mercury, the nearest planet. The center of gravity can also be halfway to the surface—a couple of hundred thousand miles from the center of the star. It might be just beneath the surface —or *on* the surface; it could be a few hundred miles above the surface, or . . . as far as hundreds of thousands of miles out in space. Considering, however, that Mercury,

Venus, the Earth and possibly Mars lie within the Sun's atmosphere, this is not a significant displacement of the solar system's center of gravity.

If these few facts are accepted and studied, a dynamic scientific advance, every bit as important and far-reaching as Copernicus' heliocentric theory, Newton's laws of gravity and perhaps Einstein's quantum theory—of which it is a part—combined, will become as familiar as today's use of lasers and computers.

It centers around the fact that our local star contains 99.86 percent—999/1,000—of the system's total mass. And yet the center of gravity of the Sun-Jupiter pair *alone* lies at the solar core! This places the mean Sun-Jupiter center of gravity some 30,000 to 50,000 miles *above* the Sun's surface. Clearly, Jupiter exerts an enormous gravitational drag on its parent star which is 865,-000 miles in diameter.

During the first couple of months of 1962, the center of gravity of the solar system was drawn out to an unprecedentedly remote region of space from the solar surface —in fact, to a goodly fraction of Mercury's perihelion distance—when Mercury, Venus, Mars, Jupiter and Saturn were in almost perfect alignment on one side of the Sun. Yet these disturbances in the symmetry of the solar magnetic field were often regarded with complete bafflement by old-line astronomers. Although the solar field has a marked effect on the whole electromagnetic spectrum, it is easiest to detect by the bending of light when it passes by the Sun, a star, or any body of great mass. A clear relationship exists between mass and electromagnetic deflection.

It's accepted that gravity bends light and undoubtedly other segments of the spectrum as well, yet little is actually known about the effect of the rest of the electromagnetic spectrum. Knowledge of the extremely long and short ends of the EM spectrum, in the words of one physicist, "simply oozes off into ignorance." In spite of this, evidence is accumulating that gravitational effects between the Sun and planets is not only dynamic but reciprocal.

On a practical engineering basis, magnetic storms and

solar flares are at least 93 percent predictable. John H. Nelson, by calculating the positions of the planets, predicted radio weather for the world's largest long-distance communications network—RCA, Inc.—with unwavering accuracy for 25 years.

"Mercury," he says, "when at perihelion, has 2.4 times as much effect on the Sun as the Earth itself. At perihelion, Mercury is even more powerful than Jupiter.

Nelson was—and is—mainly concerned with the quality of shortwave radio signals, which, before the widespread use of satellites, were transmitted by beaming them from Earth to the ionosphere, where they bounced back to a pickup station beyond the planet's curvature. Sunspots and solar flares cause great storms in the highest part of the atmosphere. When this happens, teletype machines transmit gibberish, radio and TV signals fizzle out and the communications industry loses money—or did, until Nelson startled the scientific world by discovering the cause, as well as a way to predict clear broadcasting weather.

John H. Freeman, a scientist with the National Engineering Science Company, found that the entire atmosphere interacts through its various layers. Astro-weathermen have long recognized this and used it in their forecasts. Ionospheric and tropospheric winds perform in the same manner and are triggered by sunspots, the solar wind, and the flares on the Sun caused by the gravity vector fields of the planets.

As Freeman puts it, "The ionospheric wind pattern is impressed on the tropospheric (lower) wind pattern, and the latter is closely linked to the geomagnetic field."

Nelson doesn't include gravity vector field calculations when he predicts solar flares and magnetic storms. For a couple of centuries the planets have been suspected of being responsible for solar activity. This intriguing fact is gaining wider recognition and use among NASA scientists. Dr. Richard Head, the National Aeronautics and Space Administration's top electronics research expert at Huntsville, Alabama, uses the same "tools"—the planets—to predict magnetic storms, and those awesome gouts of incandescent plasma that arc across the photosphere, as does RCA's Nelson.

The major difference between their techniques is that Nelson, instead of calculating gravitational effects, says, "I need a series of harmonics, or harmonic angles—multiples of fifteen and eighteen degrees, heliocentrically, among the planets—in order to render useful forecasts."

Why isn't his record of accuracy perfect instead of 93 percent? "The trouble is," he said, "that sunspots don't always affect radio distribution. We still don't know why. Even though you can predict when sunspots will occur, you're bound to be off about 7 percent of the time in predicting the destruction of radio signals."

When Johannes Kepler was a bright, dedicated young astronomer, he first achieved fame by predicting large, destructive—and therefore memorable—storms, according to the certain old rules of astronomy he learned from the Danish astronomer Tycho Brahe. Kepler went on to refine these ancient rules and aphorisms and discovered new minor "harmonics"—angles among the planets—that coincided with various kinds of terrestrial weather. This was before the laws of gravity were formulated. Obviously, then, much of Kepler's astrological work *anticipated* knowledge of gravitation.

The gravitation of the six inner planets, Mercury, Venus, Earth, Mars, Jupiter and Saturn, cause very rapid gravity vector collapses. These quick changes result in solar magnetic storms of varying intensities. The gravity vector fields were computer-checked by Dr. Head's group at NASA; not only did they match the sunspot cycle perfectly; they also synchronized with solar flares at 15-year intervals.

When he was editor of *Analog* (Science Fiction-Science Fact) magazine, John W. Campbell suggested a "put up or shut up" department called "Crucial Experiment" to prove by prediction, if possible, whether nationwide weather *could* be determined on a long-range basis for six consecutive months.

These predictions, based on George J. McCormack's updated synopsis, "The Theory and Practice of Astronomic Weather Forecasting," were published along with the

United States Weather Bureau's "Long-Range Weather Outlook"—plus a purely random or chance series of predictions derived by spinning a pointer in the "wheel-of-fortune" method. Interestingly, the system by which planetary forces were considered was consistently rated 94 percent accurate. The random forecast achieved 17 percent higher accuracy than the Weather Bureau's "Long-Range Weather Outlook." The Weather Bureau, incidentally, has at its disposal highly sophisticated telemetary systems, large computer installations, meteorological balloons, aircraft, rockets, weather-eye satellites, thousands of ground observers and in excess of $250 million a year *especially earmarked for finding a reliable system of long-range weather prediction.* After nearly 50 years of such lavish subsidies, Weather Bureau scientists are still no closer to such a system. It should be noted, however, that the method of the United States Weather Bureau is to observe what the weather is doing in one area of the globe, then try to guess what direction and development it will take next.

It seems that the discovery and study of planetary influence by men of all ages in advanced cultures is inexorably interwined with knowledge of gravity. The utter simplicity of the idea is probably its chief drawback; the nature of gravitation remains incompletely understood at best. By currently accepted—and somewhat nebulous definition: "Gravity is the acceleration of a body toward a central point; gravitation is the power of a body to attract any other body." This tells us what it *does,* not what it *is.*

The Sun attracts the planets, and vice versa. The difference is that Jupiter and Saturn, say, are capable of acting as huge but nearly ineffectual tractor beams. All the planets together, whether operating in concert or at cross-purposes, exert their coupling force on the Sun. They also affect each other gravitationally—in a very real but seemingly mystical way—modified by their angular distances.

Theoretically, everything in the universe affects everything else; that is particularly observable at relatively close distances, as with the planets as compared to distant constellations, which also have some effect on terrestrial life—a fact discovered almost 40 years ago when the United States Naval Observatory found that stars light-years distant had an effect on barometric changes. Pressures as high as 1/30th of that accompanied by severe thunderstorms repeatedly corresponded with the position of the pointer stars in the Big Dipper. Stars at these enormous distances cause great power changes in our atmosphere. Mercury, although tinier by far than some of Jupiter's moons, is so close to the Sun that its influence is stronger. The Moon influences the Earth—and vice versa—in different ways than do Jupiter, Saturn, or any other planet, depending on its geocentric right ascension, declination and angular distance from the Earth. But because these forces are also acted upon and modified by scores of other constantly-changing factors, the picture becomes so enormously complicated that only the use of sophisticated computers will be able to unravel the complex chain.

It would take the diameters of 108 Earths, placed side by side, to stretch across the diameter of the Sun. Interestingly, the Sun and Moon are each 108 times their *own* diameters from the Earth! The Sun is 400 times the diameter of the Moon and 400 times as far away from the Earth as the Moon. Nowhere else in the solar system does a planetary satellite have the same apparent diameter (as the Moon does when viewed from Earth) as the Sun. Among solarian planets, the Earth is unique in this respect as well as in the length of its shadow, which is cast into space and away from the Sun. This shadow is a mean 865,000 miles long—exactly the same as the diameter of the Sun. The Earth, plowing through the solar wind, creates a disturbance or "tunnel" more than ten times this distance. If you calculate the common center of gravity of the Earth-Sun system, the influence of the Earth by itself is so slight that this center of mass lies deep inside the Sun—close to the center of the star's incredibly hot, unbelievably dense core. Yet the Earth's influence is indeed "felt" by the Sun.

In the same year that the United States Naval Observatory announced its findings about barometric pressure fluctuating in phase with the position of distant stars, K. G. Meldahl published a book titled *Tidal Forces in the Sun's Corona Due to the Planets.* And Dr. Harry B. Marvis, a Naval Observatory astronomer, told the American Institute of Physics: "In accurate weather forecasting of the future, the contributions of the stars to barometric changes will have to be considered."

The results of Soviet space probes were published in four lengthy scientific reports and in a book titled *Science and Revolution,* which ties in the influence of the planets to mass human behavior. The Sun, a body of intensely hot plasma, flows in whirling gravitational and magnetic vortices—tugged about by its retinue of planets. It also reciprocates in various ways—some of them still unknown. This star presents mysteries unsuspected among other suns many parsecs off in space. At its ephemeral surface, for example, the solar temperature is 10,000° F. More than eight times the distance from the Earth to the Moon, the corona—at well over a million miles from the surface of the Sun—heats up to more than a *million* degrees F. Why?

The planets are responsible for solar activity which pulses and radiates outward in electrical and magnetic activity by fluctuations in the perpetually blasting solar "wind" and sudden gravitational changes, thus causing great storms to tear up the highest reaches of the Earth's atmosphere. Inasmuch as the gravity vector solar flare prediction technique *is* correct, then weather on the Earth's surface *must* be related, however indirectly, to the positions of the planets.

The condition of the high ionosphere is impressed magnetically and electrically on the lower troposphere with something akin to the relationship the print on this page has to the type that impressed it—i.e., almost a mirror image—or the electrostatic adhesive charge of a photocopying machine.

Profound changes in the Earth's magnetic field occur during solar and lunar eclipses. Electro-Weather, a tornado-forecasting service in Kansas City, once charted eclipses, planetary conjunctions and oppositions to predict when radical changes would take place in the geoelectrical current. The most radical of these Earth current changes always precede killer tornadoes that traditionally plague the Midwest.

The United States Geological Survey at Menlo Park, California, regularly reports anomalistic disturbances in the Earth's magnetic field—often many hours before destructive quakes occur. This is also an operational factor at the Earth and Planetary Sciences Division of the Naval Ordnance Depot at China Lake, California—the difference being that at China Lake, researchers have traced electro-geomagnetic anomalies directly to eclipses and planetary "harmonics" identical to those used by RCA's weather engineers and scores of independent discoverers dating back to Kepler.

In Isaac Newton's studies covering mathematics, astronomy, gravitation and ancient prophesy, he used astrology to predict the smashing storms, Aurora Borealis and series of devastating earthquakes that in the year 1750 buried thousands of Londoners alive.

Of all the planets, fast-moving Mercury is responsible for the most unusual kinds of weather. It helps to whipsaw solar plasma by exerting its influence on a regular rhythm of 88-day intervals. The Moon has been suspected of being the final triggering force for 'focusing" certain kinds of radiation from the Sun. Because of this, medieval astrologers referred to our satellite as "the lens."

Depending on the value of various celestial harmonics, it is likely that the prediction of earthquakes will be made hours—or days—in advance. Disturbances in the magnetic field of the Earth always occur at the site of an imminent earthquake. Fourteen hours before the Anchorage, Alaska, quake of March 27, 1964, for example, electrical earth-current readings from Kansas indicated both the disturbance and its general location. If a few hundred inexpensive earth-current recorders were strategically placed and monitored, the seismograph could well take a back seat in earthquake research.

The most direct approach would be to correlate every quake with electromagnetic disturbances and eclipses or major conjunctions immediately preceding them. Solar and lunar eclipses and opposition of Sun and Moon (at Full

Moon periods) have profound and diverse effects on human beings, too. An exhaustive three-year study in Philadelphia co-sponsored by the University of Pennsylvania, the American Institute of Medical Climatology, a group of hospitals, mental institutions, the fire and police departments and several large industrial corporations resulted in the conclusion that these celestial occurrences are directly related to changes in the ion count in the atmosphere, the barometric pressure, the amount of moisture, electromagnetic imbalances and ultimately important changes in the way people feel, think and behave.

This is connected to the partial or total cutoff of the solar wind during eclipses and radical changes in electrical earth current, as well as to the ever-varying location of the solar system's center of mass or gravity.

Medical researchers at Syracuse University, New York's Upstate Medical Center and the Syracuse Veterans Administration Hospital have spearheaded what may well be the timely nucleus of a whole new era of space medicine. Orthopedic surgeon Dr. Robert O. Becker and his colleagues mapped out the biomagnetic field generated by humans and other animals and discovered that both physical and mental diseases corresponded to and were regulated by biomagnetic changes. But what was the underlying factor?

Several years of study revealed that rapid changes in the Earth's electrical current and magnetic field were responsible for an overwhelming majority of their cases. They made the not too surprising discovery that these geomagnetic changes corresponded to periods of the greatest sunspot activity and to solar flares. Becker critically tested his theory by successfully predicting the times of the greatest number of admissions to six New York mental hospitals.

"Every organism, including the human organism," he said afterward, "demonstrates cycles of biological and mental-emotional activity closely linked to geomagnetic force-field patterns and more complex force-field interrelations, both planetary and solar-terrestrial in scope. Human behavior is influenced through the direct current control system of the brain by the terrestrial magnetic field, solar and planetary conditions, and both high and low energy cosmic radiation."

The connection, therefore, is obvious. Planets, orbiting their common center of gravity with the Sun, violently yank this point around inside the star—often at blinding speed. It can rip into the spinning solar sphere from photosphere to corona, tearing up fiery geysers that soar for hundreds of thousands of miles, and stirring up such awesome storms that many Earth-sized planets could easily be swallowed by them. These electromagnetic disturbances reach the Earth, 93 million miles away, eight minutes later, as tongues of charred particles, and affect the terrestrial environment—and all its inhabitants.

And on a greater time scale, changes in temperature and in the Earth's (variable) gravitational field has had profound political as well as military consequences:

Ever since prehistoric Sumeria was conquered by the Babylonians—and Babylon defeated by Egypt, then Egypt by Assyria and Assyria by Persia, the pattern of an intriguing natural law was observed. Almost never in history has any nation, any state or people from a southernmost latitude emerged victorious in a showdown with a northern foe. In those rare instances where the rule seemed to have been broken, there was a fast comeback victory by the north—and it stuck.

While civilization has been moving *westward,* the pattern of world dominance since the last Ice Age has been creeping ever northward. Historically, even in conflict within national boundaries, the southern part of the country is considered the "rebel." Since the north is usually victorious in these conflicts, northerners are prone to regard the southerners as "rebellious." The classic case in point of course, is the American Civil War. Another instance is Northern Protestant (British-dominated) Ireland's continual supremacy over the southern Catholic Irish Republicans.

Both France (Paris is 48° north latitude) and Germany (Berlin 52° north latitude—under Napoleon and Hitler, respectively—met defeat at the hands of the Russians when they attempted to invade Moscow (55° north latitude). Without the moral, financial and military support of both the United States and Great Britain, France has never been able to stand up to Germany.

It makes no difference if the southernmost nation has more wealth, a mightier army and greater population; either directly or through complex alliances, the north invariably triumphs. (The pattern in the southern hemisphere is reversed, which would seem to indicate that climate and temperature are the deciding factors—until the critical element of gravity is weighed in the balance.)

The United States dominates all South American countries above the equator. It's no mere coincidence that nations in the southern hemisphere have never developed an independent, native civilization. The lower part of the globe has never produced anything to equal the greatness of ancient China, India, Japan, the Valley of the Nile, or the Tigris and Euphrates valleys—*not even a written alphabet!*

The dominant, dynamic half of the Earth is the northern half. All transplanted European civilizations in South America, Africa and Australia are experiencing the same pattern—but in reverse order. Here, the *southernmost* latitudes are dominant. This gives the nation of South Africa the dominant position on the continent—at least until other African nations closer to the equator form working alliances with countries in the northern hemisphere whose capitals are closer to the North Pole than Pretoria is to the Antarctic.

The United States, once victorious against Mexico, to the south, has never gotten the diplomatic edge in its encounters with Canada. Our great northern neighbor has a population only slightly larger than that of New York City, but if Canada ever went to war with Mexico—or even the United States . . .!

Whichever way one chooses to look at it, the combined armed might of the United States (supported by United Nations forces) *lost* the Korean war when we undertook the defense of South Korea. To believe anything less of America's tragic siding with South Vietnam against the North Vietnamese is sheer delusion. We were beaten. This relatively simple lesson of geographic history has never been lost on the leaders of the communist world, who seem to use it to their advantage.

Historically, New Delhi (28° north) has lost India's every encounter with Peking (39° north). Again, it becomes increasingly evident that both Russia and China are thoroughly familiar with these climatological-latitudinal factors and use them in their calculations to further their cause. Both China and Russia know that the People's Republic of Mongolia (whose capital, Ulan Bator, is 47° north latitude) has nothing to fear from Peking, a full eight degrees to the south, but is yet ideologically dominated by Russia (Moscow, 55° north).

The People's Republic of China once tried everything short of open conflict to outdo the Russians in Mongolia and elsewhere. But against all logic, the result was that Caucasoid Russian, not Oriental Chinese, "technicians" occupied the country. Because of the wide (16°) latitudinal gap between Moscow and Peking, even a military force consisting of a billion Chinese armed with modern nuclear weaponry realizes it will never prevail over Russia. Propaganda notwithstanding, the wiser Chinese leaders seem to be painfully aware of this and abide by it.

But with our belief in the power of material abundance, we Americans learned virtually nothing from the twin catastrophes of Vietnam and Korea. If we had, we'd never have wasted nearly 30 years supporting Chiang Kai-shek's regime in exile on Formosa (24° north latitude) in opposition to Peking (39° north).

Although Peking's latitudinal distance is a mere 44 minutes arc (less than one degree) north of Washington, D.C., America felt the weight of that slight advantage in Korea, and again when we backed South Vietnam (Saigon, 10° north) against Hanoi (21° north.)

Again, the practical Chinese leaders took full advantage of the situation by pledging open-ended support to Ho Chi Minh when the tough leader of the Viet Minh guerrillas, after defeating the French army in an eight-year war, signed a "never say die" agreement with China in 1955 to hold out *indefinitely* against the armed might of the world's most powerful nation. The United States was deluded into sacrificing thousands of American lives and billions of dollars into the bottomless pit of the ultimately hopeless war against Hanoi, fully backed by Peking, which lies a dominant 18° north of North Vietnam. With only minor, temporary exceptions, invasions or attacks from the south of anywhere against the north are doomed to failure. In any such north-south conflict, no self-respecting gambler would—if he knew something of the history of geodetic equivalency—accept even million-to-one odds on the south.

As long as America's military and its leaders and policymakers continue to reject the obvious simply because the correlation carries no scientific approval or understanding, we will continue to blunder ever deeper toward eventual collapse of the United States of America as a world power. This process has been going on for some years.

Paradoxically, America's early success and progress dwindled with relative precision with the *southward* drift of its political power center and revolutionary activity. These centers were: Boston, 42° north; New York, 40° north; Philadelphia, 39° north; Washington, 38° north latitude.

Still . . . given time to reconsider and possibly accept the rather exotic possibilities, we can yet reverse the trend toward America's ultimate fade-out on the world scene. To prevent the northward flow of power and prestige from passing us by, it may be feasible to move the Capital farther northward. But where? By a curious geographical coincidence, the names of America's northernmost, southernmost, easternmost and westernmost states provide a remarkable clue to the solution of the dilemma. Just for fun, put the book down for a minute and try to remember which states belong in each category before checking the footnote.*

A closer look shows that Fairbanks, Alaska, is the ideal location for a new American capital. By transferring the seat of government to 65° north latitude, America stands

* Oddly enough, the last two states admitted to the Union answer all four cardinal requirements: Alaska is both westernmost *and* northernmost, while Hawaii is both southernmost and (surprisingly) *easternmost*! Hawaii is located on the *other* side of the International Date Line—farther east, in fact, than Maine.

to regain much of the clout, luster and morale enjoyed during Teddy Roosevelt's heyday. This transfer could mean a national rebirth. Although Brazil moved its capital in the wrong direction, it did create the new city of Brasilia and transferred the entire center of government there from Rio de Janiero—so it's not an impossible feat.

And if Russia (who would still oppose us ideologically even if we supported a successful Soviet drive to "liberate" China from its present leadership) ever countered with a similar northern move of its capital, the United States could transport "New Washington" even farther northward—*into the Arctic Circle,* if need be—and *still* be on American territory! (The Eskimos, who never had anything resembling a nation or even a capital, also have no language equivalent for "war.")

The correlation between political dominance and proximity to the polar regions is, apparently, not just superstition or coincidence. The explanation may be a combination of temperature, altitude and subtle variations in the local gravitational field at different latitudes.

Long before Isaac Newton formulated his now famous laws of universal gravitation, someone must have recognized that terrestrial gravity varied in different places—and that *the two extremes centered on the equator and at the poles.* If gravitation proves to be the explanation for political and military dominance, professional futurists will be interested to know that in 50 years or so, when all the inner planets are colonized, none of the Earth colonies will ever be able to support a declaration (or war) of independence. Mother Earth's gravitational strings are considerably stronger than those of her planetary neighbors!

4

WEATHER WARFARE

EACH YEAR ORTHODOX weather experts gratuitously offer scores of predictions about atmospheric patterns for the next dozen or so months. "Watch out for January," quoth Hurd C. Willett, Professor of Meteorology, Emeritus, MIT's estimable long-range weather forecaster, late in 1975. He forecasted an abnormally cold 1976 winter for most of the nation east of the continental divide.

Not so, contradicted the prestigious National Weather Service in Washington. "Temperatures along most of the Northeast Eastern [*sic*] Seaboard and all the southeastern states will have above normal temperatures in the winter of 1976." The NWS extended this optimism to the Pacific Northwest, parts of Nevada, Utah and Arizona.

But according to Anthony Tancreto, chief meteorologist for the National Weather Service in Boston, trying to predict exact temperatures and the amount of snow or rain that will fall "is completely beyond the realm of forecasting."

The American Meteorological Society and the United States Weather Bureau (later the National Weather Service) therefore know little or nothing about how the terrestrial weather machine operates and even less about how to predict what it will do next.

In spite of this demonstrated inability, these experts and their foreign counterparts have long been trying to control the weather—with a "Let's-try-this-and-see-what-happens" attitude. Manmade weather, crude and devastating though it is, has already made its debut. One way or another we've all experienced its effects. In recent years there has been a rash of record-shattering weather extremes—anomalies that give a mere hint of what the future may bring when the great powers gain enough sophistication in the art of meteorological manipulation to deliberately change the climate.

And you can bet that if it can be done, somebody is almost certain to try it.

The usual human arrogance is behind such tampering: these scientists refuse to recognize that for all its mighty untapped energy, the ecosphere is a rather delicately balanced solar-powered mechanism—a machine that just might be tilted in some irreversible direction by the wrong kind of prodding.

Weather warfare unfortunately is no longer in the realm of fantasy or science fiction. It's beyond the planning state, and has long been a reality. Oh, not the all-out kind of thing it could (and may) become in the near future; but man has been tampering with the weather for some years without the faintest idea of where the hell it's leading us. As with biological engineering, nuclear research or anything else, weather control and warfare can only be expected to escalate.

As long ago as 1966 the National Science Foundation warned: "The Soviet Union's weather modification program is by far the world's largest, exceeding that of the United States by several orders of magnitude. . . ."

It may be of little consequence or consolation that the scales could have been tipped the other way since then. When a disaster strikes, who cares who pushed the button or pulled the lever? India has been going full steam ahead with what they euphemistically call "weather modification projects." Ditto Israel, Mexico, Colombia, Japan, China and Australia.

Rainmaking by seeding clouds with silver iodide pellets was first accomplished on a large scale by a brilliant American business-weatherman, Dr. Irving P. Krick. But for centuries men have tried to extract water from the reluctant skies by prayer, dancing, sprinkling the blood of animals on the dusty ground—even by human sacrifice.

When silver iodide is scattered from aircraft, moisture forms on the crystals, condense and becomes heavy enough to fall as rain. Early in the game, rainmakers (always denounced as charlatans by orthodox weathermen) blasted or pumped silver iodide mixed with propane and acetone into the sky, often with remarkable success. Not until a Nobel Prize winner named Irving Langmuir duplicated the silver iodide vaporizing of clouds, however, did orthodox weathermen admit there could be something to it. By 1959, according to D. C. Halacy, Jr., in *The Weather Changers,* there were 36 official weather-modification projects in the United States.

Now the experts have dreamed up methods by which the levels of the oceans can be made to rise so high that the world's great coastal cities could be drowned. This would include London, New York, San Francisco, Tokyo, Rio, and scores of others. Moreover, there are now hundreds of scientific laboratories trying to learn all they can about lightning—*so they can deactivate it!* This sheer *chutzpah* boggles the mind because (as we'll see in the next chapter) lightning is very likely the fire of creation that originally sparked the beginning of life and keeps the atmosphere properly charged, i.e., it keeps us all alive.

So far, the most effective weapons in our attempts to enforce certain views on each other have been poison gas, nuclear bombs and missiles. Now it's weather warfare, which, next to biological combat, is probably the most savage and vicious form of mass destruction ever devised.

With no real understanding of the laws governing the Earth's living atmosphere, weather scientists are nevertheless at work trying their damnedest to manipulate it.

As long ago as 1956, maverick weatherman Dr. Irving P. Krick, whose forecasting company was then based in Denver, warned that unless America took the initiative, weather control by an enemy nation would be a reality in less than 20 years. In 1974, during closed hearings of the Senate Foreign Relations Committee, it was revealed that from 1969 to 1972 the United States itself waged weather warfare against the North Vietnamese. In Project Stormfury, military weather controllers are reported to have hurled killer hurricanes at other nations. A group of thirteen U.S. Senators headed by Senator Claiborne Pell (D.–R.I.) had been trying to have weather warfare outlawed. They were still trying when, at high noon on April 13, 1973, the United States was suddenly assaulted by "the worst outbreak of tornadoes ever recorded—*anywhere.*"

Within 18 hours an incredible 148 cyclones had ripped through 13 states, killed 315 people, injured 5,500 more and caused half a billion dollars' worth of damage.

"Nature simply doesn't behave that way normally," said one shocked Weather Bureau official in Washington. "The twisters were freakish . . . *almost as though they were artificially generated.*"

Nearly 50 years earlier, on March 18, 1925, a single killer tornado ripped through Missouri, Illinois and Indiana, leaving a staggering death toll of 689 lives lost. Nobody dreamed of blaming weather modification in those days. Things are different now.

Nations have made many agreements that certain methods of war and certain weapons must be outlawed. Sometimes it was for humanitarian reasons, such as the Geneva Conference rules on the treatment of prisoners of war. Everybody today, for example, knows that sooner or later bacteriological weapons, if used, will infect large segments of all terrestrial organisms; eventually this poisoned chain of life is sure to return to the nation that launched it in the first place.

Because of this boomerang effect, American legislators have been trying to add weather and climate modification to the list of inhumane weapons. Meteorologists long ago found ways to change the weather—accidentally and deliberately both. As just described, silver iodide, dry ice (or other particulate matter), when dropped into the right kinds of clouds, can either make rain or intensify already existing rainfall. These methods, first used by Dr. Krick, have been used to alleviate severe droughts in Texas, California and Florida. Project Skywater in Colorado does a good job of increasing the water supply (and farm production) of the Southwest. It is also used in other ways.

According to weathermen at the National Oceanic and Atmospheric Administration's Project Stormfury, they can now seed hurricanes with dry ice and other materials to disperse the fury of storms over wide areas or else completely neutralize them. In yet another experiment, cloud seeding has been used to reduce the size of large destructive hailstones.

Still—anything that can be employed beneficially can also be used destructively. In 1968 a geophysicist named Gordon J. F. MacDonald elaborated on the military applications of weather modification. Severe rainfall and cloudbursts, he said, should be used to camouflage American ground operations or to cripple those of an enemy. Also, by seeding clouds so that they exhaust their supply of moisture, drought can be created in lands downwind. Moreover, it will soon be possible to steer destructive hurricanes toward enemy shores—if, indeed, this hasn't already been done.

How much can we tamper with the atmosphere and get away with it? Even such mundane mass activities as driving our cars and using fluorocarbons under pressure for hairsprays, insecticides and deodorants add carbon dioxide and dangerous aerosols to the Earth's mantle of air. These chemicals screen and inhibit solar radiation. And since climate is essentially determined by the delicate balance between incoming and outgoing radiation, they do cause a greenhouse effect by preventing heat from being radiated from the planet's surface into space.

According to MacDonald, any nation might decide that global heating or cooling of the atmosphere would be to its own special advantage. That nation could then alter the aerosol levels of the ozone in the upper reaches of the atmosphere. He also suggested that huge holes could be blown by aerosol bombs in the ozone layer over any enemy nation. This would eliminate its screening effect and allow deadly ultraviolet radiation from the Sun to enter and stream unshielded to the surface where it would affect all living things. Two of the most immediate results would be to increase skin cancer in human beings and to kill off a large percentage of vegetation on which all other life forms are dependent for oxygen, thus triggering a chain effect of global death and devastation. Are these nations or radical groups insane enough to make such attempts? The answer to that is in the question, as we will see at the end of this chapter.

Increasing ultraviolet and infrared radiation would alter polar areas, melt the ice caps and drown all coastal cities on Earth. A new Ice Age would follow. Soviet scientists, the American Department of Defense, and several private corporations have been actively engaged in such weather modification for a long time. General Electric, for example, cooperated with the Department of Defense in Project Cirrus, which went a long way toward perfecting the basic technology of cloud seeding. The Advanced Research Projects Agency of the Defense Department, co-sponsor of Project Stormfury, released figures indicating that nearly $3 million was allocated to scores of scientists (employing the powerful Iliac IV computer) for a climate-modification project called Nile Blue. These scientists have since developed almost perfect computer models of the terrestrial climate. In 1969, at the request of the Philippine government, project Nile Blue produced more than 12 million acre-feet of rainfall in the islands.

During the decade-long war in Southeast Asia, the United States put its weather warfare ability to practical, if short-lived, use. American aircraft seeded clouds over the Ho Chi Minh Trail to such a degree that the increased rainfall did more than just hamper infiltrating Viet Cong troops.

In 1945, natural monsoon floods in North Vietnam killed more than a million people, but in 1972, thanks to weather modification by American experts, monsoon rains deluged the land; the resultant floods destroyed the entire rice crop and caused even bigger casualties. This would have been the first year that North Vietenam was going to be independent of China and Russia for its supply of rice.

The chairman of the University of Michigan department of meteorology, however, refuses to believe that American tampering was responsible for the Vietnamese floods. Still, Edward S. Epstein thinks that some sort of modification of weather is possible, even probable: "Fog and cloud dispersal methods have been studied to increase aircraft safety and now are utilized regularly and successfully. Obviously, these methods also have offensive potential; if you can clear clouds to land, you can probably clear clouds to bomb."

Senator Pell once demanded that Rady Johnson, then assistant Secretary of Defense, explain the purposes of a Defense project code-named "Intermediary—Compatriot"—*an offensive weather-modification project.* Johnson insisted that the Department's interest consisted chiefly in suppression of hail and lightning "to reduce damage to military equipment, dissipation of fog at airfields and harbors, and understanding of what capabilities our potential enemies may possess in the area of weather modification operations."

None of this answered Pell's questions about "Intermediary—Compatriot." So when the Senator went directly to then Secretary of Defense Melvin Laird, John S. Foster, Jr., Director of Defense Research and Engineering, curtly retorted, "Our work in this area is classified."

During budget hearings on Nile Blue, Atmospheric Research Projects Administration (ARPA) director S. J. Lukasik said, "Major world powers now have the ability to create modifications of climate that might be seriously detrimental to the security of this country." He denied, however, that Nile Blue was engaged in such activities. "Nile Blue is strictly a computer modeling study and no field experiments have been conducted."

That was in 1971. As usual in such confrontations, the picture changes as new facts emerge. "Weather modification as a weapon of war," says Pell, "can only lead to the development of vastly more dangerous environmental techniques whose consequences may be unknown and may cause irreparable damage to our global environment."

•

Pell's Subcommittee on Oceans and International Environment held fruitless hearings on the subject, idealistically insisting that it was "imperative that restraint be exercised early in the developmental stages before irretrievable precedents are set."

. . . or irreversible trends are launched. Such, apparently, has already been the case—both deliberately and accidentally—with changes caused by far more sophisticated tampering: i.e., with atmospheric electricity and the electrical currents in the Earth itself. This seems to have had a runaway adverse effect on much of the wildlife of our planet, which will be covered in detail in a later chapter.

The "irretrievable precedents" cited by Senator Pell seem to have resulted in mysterious new atmospheric phenomena called "supernovas" by the huge, multinational weather study known as the Global Atmospheric Research Program (GARP) and the Global Atlantic Tropical Experiment (GATE). These great storms appear "from nowhere" in the middle of the night. They are huge tropical disturbances (thunderstorms) that reach full-blown fury, often in less than two hours. They churn up the tropical Atlantic with explosive rage and then disappear about as quickly as they came into being. The National Oceanic and Atmospheric Administration calls them "supernovas" because their life cycle is about as violent and rapid as the sudden brilliant flareup of a great star before it disperses or collapses in death. No one knows where these storms come from or how they are formed, but they were first discovered by GATE—thanks to the Synchronous Meteorological Satellite, SMS-1—in the summer of 1974. The satellite's infrared cameras photographed the churning clouds as they developed through their own heat—even during the darkest, moonless nights.

GATE is an extremely appropriate acronym. The tropics are the "opening" through which more than half the solar energy reaching the Earth enters to fuel the vast heat engine that drives the world's weather. The "push" for the winds and other atmospheric circulation systems starts around the equatorial belt.

A team headed by Helmut K. Weickmann of the Atmospheric Physics and Chemistry Laboratory in Boulder, Colorado is trying to discover just how the supernova storms fit into the overall global weather pattern. In March 1975, according to Weickmann, they were striving to learn whether the storms were causes—i.e., significant contributors to tropical weather dynamics—"Or are they mere symptoms, visible signs of some much larger and even more mysterious process? At this state of our research," he said, "all bets are open."

You bet they are!

One atmospheric physicist suggested that a major power was secretly manipulating or at least tampering with atmospheric electricity on a truly colossal scale. Investigators had expected powerful convection currents (along the Intertropical Convergence Zone). "In fact we had expected this to be one of the strongest phenomena in the area," said Weickmann, "yet the clouds they found during GATE hardly reached a height of 40,000 feet and the air was so dry that their aircraft left almost no vapor trail at that altitude."

So where is the missing violence in the system? Something—or somebody—seems to be providing the extra impetus—the force none of the scientists admit being able to find. During their brief lifetimes, supernova storms swell into areas covering thousands of square miles, yet they are still only storms—atmospheric disturbances of a much smaller scale than the massive Intertropical Convergence Zone.

"It is not unreasonable, therefore," said Ray Hoxit, "that *there may be something else making up the difference; something, perhaps, of which the storms are just a visible manifestation.*" (Hoxit was then working with Weickmann on the problem.)

What might that "something" be? Deliberate manipulation of the normal atmospheric processes that enhance and intensify existing potentials? A vast new experiment by Americans or the Soviets? Manipulation of an advanced electrical nature—something done from great distances—has been suggested by the researchers.

"The supernova storms are the kind of system we

see in large Colorado hailstorms," said Hoxit. "They must come out of a strong atmospheric instability *God only knows where*—and we think nocturnal radiation process may play a role in their formation!"

Paradoxically however, dry land soaks up far more heat during daylight hours than do large bodies of water, and it radiates it much faster when the Sun "goes down." This provides a virtual "hot plate" that seems to motivate potential storms. "What we can't explain at all," says Hoxit, "is why and how these supernova storms form *over the oceans and at night!*" So they assembled and organized the data from many ships on station (at night) in the areas where the supernovas developed. Unfortunately, most of the aircraft data came from flights made only during daylight hours. Still . . . the planes did manage to discover large counts of ice nuclei (small particles on which airborne water freezes), but very low counts of condensation nuclei, on which water vapor condenses to form clouds. This suggested that the clouds became "rained out" before the water reached the atmosphere's freezing level, a condition that ominously suggests electrical manipulation of atmospheric forces.

Fast-growing supernovas may be an entirely new, completely unnatural phenomenon, but Hoxit doesn't think so. They're still trying to understand it in terms of cooling by radiation of the Sun's heat, when the atmosphere releases its stored solar heat and generates winds that bring in more cooler or warmer air, thus creating a "pre-storm environment."

In any event, the problems posed by these supernovas could be crucial—(if indeed they are natural phenomena) —in trying to understand the tropical birthplace of the world's weather. If not, it could be a whole new (and terrifying) ball game.

There's no longer any doubt that man's activities are altering the climate of the Earth. Whether this is due to deliberate design by forces beyond human comprehension or by sheer chance (cause-effect) is a moot point. *We're changing the weather of our planet*. The subtropical deserts are expanding at an alarming rate. When scientists from the University of California's Lawrence Livermore

Laboratory built a computer model (ZAM-2—Zonal Atmospheric Model) of global climate effects of large-scale destruction of tropical forests, they discovered a worldwide cooling of 0.2° C. Moreover, in tropical latitudes, this cooling dropped to more than 1° C.

In parts of South America, Central Africa and Asia—within ten degrees of the equator—the destruction of rain forests which are "merely" being chopped down for firewood has reached a staggering 34 percent! As a result of this immense deforestation there has been an increase in the reflection of solar heat, thus lower temperatures and less evaporation and rainfall near the equator. This *must* have serious implications for the rest of the world. There is less heat released when rain condenses from water vapor. This heat is the secondary mover that drives and circulates the massive currents of air between the tropics and the temperate zones. These currents carry both heat *and* moisture all over the world.

So—whether by diabolical design or incipient greed, humankind has already declared weather warfare against itself.

And, as usual, the makers of the policies we ignorantly, unwillingly support have devised an innocuous-sounding euphemism, "climate modification," for one of the worst horrors imaginable—global weather warfare. Although unpredictable, this Pandora's box of terror has already been opened. For several years Dr. Gordon J. MacDonald of Dartmouth College has been warning the Senate Foreign Relations and other committees that "a secret global weather war need never be declared or even known by the affected population."

Artificially induced floods, fogs, droughts, hurricanes, blizzards, tidal waves, tornadoes and even earthquakes can alter the climate of an entire nation. This kind of weather warfare would necessarily involve civilians, which is strictly prohibited by the internationally accepted "laws of war."

Dr. Pierre St. Amand, director of the Navy's weather-modification program, however, seems unperturbed by such violations. "Holes" can be created in the ozone layer of the atmosphere over any desired nation, allowing undiminished ultraviolet radiation to pour through. "At full force," says Dr. MacDonald, "it would be fatal to all life. . . ."

5

LIGHTNING AND OTHER STRANGE FORCES

WHEN IMMANUEL VELIKOVSKY, author of *Worlds in Collision,* asserted in 1950 that global catastrophes during historical times were associated with electrical and magnetic fields from interplanetary space, he was immediately attacked as a crackpot, a hoaxer and worse. The then current scientific fad was that only gravity and solar radiation (mostly light and heat) streamed through the vast abyss of "nothingness" between the distant stars and planets.

For some years now that "knowledge" is known to have been wrong, as has most of the "accepted" data with which they tried to vilify Velikovsky. None of his former detractors is known to have come forward to apologize, admit all the things he was right about, or to demand an open, formal reevaluation of his theories and all his then "incredible" predictions (which proved true).

Ironically, many scientists are still haranguing anybody who'll listen about how Dr. Velikovsky's now proven facts contradict "accepted" scientific dogma! It's all but impossible for these scientists to recognize that when they passionately believe in an idea or practice that happens to coincide with their own interests, that's the very time to question how fervently they'd still believe in it if it threatened their own interests.

The role of terrestrial and cosmic electromagnetism is slowly being recognized as a primal energy of the universe—possibly the key to the existence of life itself. Atmospheric electricity—lightning—is a *natural* form of the energy that man has harnessed to produce radios, television sets, powerful engines and even delicate sophisticated electronic brains. The complex symbiosis of the entire Earth organism is involved, and is a most subtle concept. For example, without plants to fix nitrogen, absorb carbon dioxide and emit life-giving oxygen, there'd be no life. Without cross-pollinating insects such as bees, few if any of the blossoming trees and plants would exist. Yet every living thing is permeated by, surrounded and influenced by a kind of electrodynamic "aura"—the composite radio "broadcast" of every cell, molecule, atom and organ of each organism. These subtle but powerful fields exist *before* the formation of every physical organism; they determine its size, shape and general condition. Moreover, they are measurable with sensitive voltmeters, which was proven repeatedly over a period of 40 years by Dr. Harold Saxon Burr and his colleagues at the Yale University School of Medicine.

According to Dr. Robert O. Becker, orthopedic physician and surgeon at New York's Upstate Medical Center, electromagnetism may be the very key to life itself. Dr. Becker uses weak electrical currents to speed up the healing of broken bones and torn flesh.

Negatively charged ions (electrons) were shown during a dramatic three-year city-wide scientific study in Philadelphia by the *American Institute of Medical Climatology* to influence almost 70 percent of the population *beneficially*. This led to the invention of negative ion generators which were initially used by men like Dr. Igho H. Kornblueh of the Frankford Hospital and the University of Pennsylvania Medical Center in the treatment of various accidents, illnesses and diseases. In one case, a young man suffering third degree burns over 90 percent of his body was placed in a controlled environment with two generators pouring a constant stream of negative ions over his body and, as he breathed, into his lungs. Result: he was taken off pain-killing drugs, and he not only recovered but did so six to seven times faster than anyone believed possible.

"The more we study and understand matter," says inventor T. Galen Hieronymus, of psionics fame, "the more it appears to be energy in a kind of 'frozen' state." That energy is, of course, a form of electricity, the existence of which was known—and to some degree used—by the ancient Egyptians. The Greeks of classic antiquity conceived of the smallest, indivisible unit of matter, the atom. Since then we've learned that the atom itself is an electrical entity—a state of energy—that contains both positively and negatively charged particles, each of which is inextricably "tied" or bound by an as yet unknown cohesive force into electromagnetic harmony.

Although it was a foolhardy experiment by one of America's most illustrious founding fathers which proved that lightning was a form of electricity, modern scientists have added little to the pioneering discovery of Benjamin Franklin. We still know very little about electricity, and even less about it in its most awesome manifestation—*lightning*. These ominous, capricious bolts from the roiling skies terrified people long before man began reckoning time.

Every second there are over 6,000 bursts of atmospheric electricity crackling somewhere on Earth, and they're *not* evenly distributed! Most of these bolts of lightning center on the equator (within 30° north or south latitude), with an amazing ten times as many thunderstorms raging over land as over the oceans.

Statistics based on mundane observations indicate that most thunderstorms, because of the Sun's heat, develop between two in the afternoon and eight in the evening (over land). Lightning's seemingly erratic bombardment kills about 150 Americans and incinerates more than 20 million dollars' worth of valuable property each year. This explosive lacing of electrical fire through the atmosphere ignites 10,000 forest fires and destroys more than 30 million dollars' worth of marketable timber each year.

Anyone who is ignorant or foolhardy enough to use a

telephone during a thunderstorm may join scores of those injured or killed by lightning in America every few years. Ardent golfers often join the growing throng of electricuted corpses who became human lightning rods during storms because the metal cleats on their shoes serve as electrical conductors to the ground.

But despite the fear triggered by its reputation as a killer, lightning has certain properties without which life on Earth would probably not be able to exist.

The Earth itself is analogous to a huge storage battery that is forever losing its negatively charged electrons to the more positively charged ionosphere which lies roughly about 40 miles above the surface of the planet. The Earth keeps in almost perfect electrical balance and avoids complete devastation because thousands of storms and millions of bolts of lightning each day keep pouring countless trillions of electrons back to the surface. This is because the flow of electrons always goes from negative (minus) to positive (plus). This seems always to have been a major characteristic of the terrestrial atmosphere—and, in the light of some recent scientific experiments and discoveries, it becomes especially interesting.

For example, there's a growing belief among some scientists who have actually experimented with controlled electricity that naturally occurring lightning may have been the catalyst to spark the beginnings of Earthly life sometime about four or 4½ billion years ago. Other scientists have put the figure at *350 billion years,* a "minor miscalculation, apparently, because the opinion of the majority of the world's leading thinkers about such things place the age of the universe itself at only 13 billion years.

It takes a certain kind of hubris to make "final" statements about Creation.

But British cosmologist Fred Hoyle, father of the Steady State theory of creation, has developed a new theory concerning blackbody radiation that extends the true age of the universe from 13 billion to more than 150 billion years. This kind of radiation, he says, is actually starlight coming from galaxies from the "other side" of a number of space time volumes which he calls "alternating layers of positive and negative electromagnetic forces. . . .

We may," he adds, "owe many aspects of our present-day world to remote ancestors on the other side of the barrier which has hitherto been thought to represent the origin of the Universe."

I have to admit that these mass-field equations of Hoyle (and Einstein) leave me more baffled than enlightened. I have a strong suspicion, though, based on years of (hopefully) logical and practical experience, that these "layers of positive and negative electromagnetic barriers" are as operative within the envelope of the terrestrial atmosphere as they are throughout the universe, which may be infinitely vaster than the electrochemical transducers in our skulls are able to conceive.

We know very little about electricity, especially in its most terrifying natural state—atmospheric lightning. At the world's foremost lightning research forum (Albany, New York's Atmospheric Sciences Research Center), scientists are trying valiantly to understand the almost mystical properties of legendary Thor's awesome bolts.

Lightning, one of the most common of all phenomena in nature, has generated fear since the earliest known times of history. One of the Albany scientists, Professor Richard Orville, figures that the number of thunderstorms hammering the Earth every day is about 44,000, and that almost nine *million* bolts of lightning accompany these storms! The entire atmospheric mantle, therefore, is kept in a constant state of electromagnetic turbulence.

Perhaps not so strangely, this atmospheric electrical activity is attributed to the very origins of life on our planet; under laboratory conditions lightning is known to split and convert ammonia, methane, water vapor and hydrogen into molecular components known as amino acids—the protein building blocks of life. These elements are believed to have been present in the atmosphere of the primordial Earth. Scientists of the stature of Carl Sagan (head of Cornell's Earth and Planetary Sciences Division at Ithaca, New York), for example, are firmly convinced, and with good cause, that we owe our very lives to lightning and electricity. Human cycles of well-being and activity are largely dependent on the negative and positive ion charge of the air we breathe. So much so, in fact, that negative-ion generators are coming into much wider use by scientists, doctors and other experimenters to increase the health and well-being of both patients and workers. Usually, the minutes spent breathing ionized air eliminate severe headaches and help restore a feeling of vitality and well-being.

Even the simple act of splashing water in a basin generates the ion charge that energizes you and makes you feel better. Your morning or evening shower isn't all that gives you the lift and exhilaration you experience; it's the negatively charged ions you breathe from the water splashing off the tiles and tub that does it. (An ion is simply a particle with a shortage or a surplus of electrons.)

Scientific studies of natural electricity have revealed that when large concentrations of positive and negative particles break through the insulating layers of the atmosphere, lightning flashes are likely to occur in one of several ways.

Most lightning—about two-thirds of it—either flashes inside one cloud or between a couple of adjacent clouds. These flashes almost never touch the ground and we see them, if at all, as a dimly illuminated streak, something like a flashlight glimpsed inside a tent at night on a forested hillside. But there are also brilliant blasts of lightning from Earth to the clouds and from the clouds through the atmosphere. Most of the lightning we see, which accounts for only about a third of the entire atmospheric electrical activity, is the stuff that strikes from cloud to Earth. Just about everything scientists know about lightning has been learned from these sky-to-Earth strokes of electricity. The Academy of Natural Sciences in Philadelphia displays a truly remarkable example of solidified lightning that struck a sand dune and left its fossilized "branches" embedded in the Earth from which it was later removed intact.

Most lightning is generated inside thunderheads called cumulonimbus clouds, which stand like colossal mushrooms, billowing five or six miles into the atmosphere. Many clouds, even taller, are often powerfully influenced by extraterrestrial forces—a fact about which most meteorologists seem unaware. Not only is terrestrial weather affected and influenced by certain planetary positions in relation to the Sun; even distant stars have a definite but predictable effect on the Earth's atmosphere. One study by the U.S. Naval Observatory, under Dr. Harry B. Marvis, in 1938 revealed that the pointer star of the Great Dipper repeatedly raised barometric pressure as much as 1/30 of that which occurs during great thunderstorms.

Our Sun, like all stars, radiates high-energy particles—cosmic rays that, as they strike the air molecules in the Earth's atmosphere, either add electrons to the molecules or knock them off, a process that creates the aforementioned ions. Although the energy from these cosmic rays is dissipated, the ionosphere is constantly being recreated and sustained. Without the protective shield of the ionosphere we would either be fried by ultraviolet radiation or genetically scrambled by cosmic rays that would be forever changing human (and other) genes and chromosomes. Something like this might cause the wildest throng of misshapen, undifferentiated and possibly helpless creatures in the known universe. So . . . the Earth's electrical current, atmospheric electricity and the ion content of the atmosphere contribute (in an exceedingly "well-engineered" interrelationship, by the way) to the beautifully balanced ecology we take so much for granted, but without which we'd either perish or never have come into existence at all.

The ionosphere is neutral, although electrically unstable. But the Earth itself measures 300,000 volts negative. Because our planet's surface *is* negative, and also because tiny particles of moisture are forever rising upward on strong currents of air, electrons are attracted to and attach themselves to these droplets of water and ride freely through the lower atmosphere into the high reaches of the ionosphere.

Author Herman Melville's immortal character Captain Ahab dramatically demonstrated an interesting scientific principle to the fear-stricken crewmen of the *Pequod* during a storm at sea by quenching the dreaded St. Elmo's fire with his bare hands. St. Elmo's "fire" (*corposant*) is the ball of light often seen around the masts, yardarms and other high points of sailing ships during storms. This is because so many of the superfluous electrons from the surface tend to congregate at high points on the planet's surface—everything from blades of grass, the tip of a sailship mast, the points of tall radio and television antennae and the spires of New York's Chrysler and Empire State buildings.

What happens is that these points discharge the electrons; they are released to join trillions of others streaming upward toward the ionosphere.

When those roundish, puffy white cumulus clouds stretch out and darken into gray, almost tornadolike cumulonimbus clouds, the electron-loaded particles (ions) hitching a ride on the water droplets are drawn with fantastic speed into a rarefied, and extremely cold altitude of about 25,000 feet. At that height it's about 40 below zero, and the water freezes into little crystals of ice and, thus transformed, starts falling earthward again. Almost paradoxically, inside the maelstrom of the thunderhead (as far as the best meteorologists are able to understand) the ice crystals are falling and the still-liquid water droplets, with ions clinging to them, are rising. Under these conditions you get rain, snow and lightning boiling madly around inside the elongated column of the mysterious thunderhead.

Here's another mystery: As you probably know by now, positive attracts negative and vice versa, and negative *repels* negative. The Earth, as we have seen, is negatively charged (300,000 volts' worth!), but so are the *bottom* parts of the clouds. Still, lightning strokes come from the bottoms of these clouds to blast the Earth. Actually, these ground and cloud charges should *repel* one another!

The tentative (still theoretical) explanation of this strange state of affairs *sounds* plausible enough, but for some strange reason, the earth directly beneath the supercharged cumulonimbus cloud suddenly becomes cleared of its negative charges, leaving the area completely positively charged.

This condition then allows the voltage inside the churning maelstrom of a cloud to build up such a powerful reservoir of electrical energy that it can no longer hold back the force. The electrons then blast out along the lines of least resistance at 186 miles a second, hotter than the surface of the Sun itself—to shatter the atmosphere with about *half a billion* horsepower! Cloud-to-ground lightning, according to Professor Richard Orville, "occurs in amazingly rapid 50-meter spurts, taking only 50 millionths of a second with hundreds of amperes striking at about one thousandth the speed of light."

Bolts of lightning can vary in thickness from the size of a thin man's wrist to the bellyband girth of a Japanese Sumi wrestler. These blasts of pure electrical power usually branch out to about a mile in length; some are as short as a few hundred to a thousand feet—but others can reach the staggering distance of a hundred miles or more in length!

You figure now that you have a pretty clear and straightforward understanding of the "mechanics" of lightning, huh? Wait. Before we even touch on the "impossibility" of barrel-sized red, blue or yellow ball lightning that strikes with devilish fury or simply floats through the air like a soap bubble, let's see what *really* happens in a stroke of lightning. What your eye sees at the flash *isn't* the downward cloud-to-Earth stroke at all; it's the brilliant *return* blast of electrons flashing back up through the channels that have already been ionized. It works like this: Anything sticking up high enough from the ground level, such as a tall pole, tree, antenna or spired building quickly builds up a powerful *opposite* charge from that of the downward bolt. This charge "leaps" anywhere from 300 to 600 feet into the air to meet its opposite number.

This causes an instantaneous short circuit from cloud to ground, and the cloud's electrons are sucked with indescribable fury out of the downstroke, leaving an empty channel, which is instantly filled when the return stroke, by some mysterious means, flashes up the channel to the thunderhead at speeds ten times faster than the downstroke—i.e., better than 60,000 miles a second—one third the speed of light!

What your eye records during this barest fraction of a second is actually trillions of particles of light energy, with ions flashing back and forth along the ionized stroke

—not just at mind-boggling velocities, but also at temperatures in excess of 30,000°, i.e., four to five times as hot as conditions on the surface of the Sun!

Then there's the thunderclap. Thunder is the noise of a shock wave caused when the air around the bolt of lightning first explodes from the violent changes in pressure and then rushes back in to fill what is essentially an electrically-caused vacuum. *Boom*! That clap of thunder speeds through the air at the relatively sluggish rate of five seconds to the mile, but because light travels at 186,200 miles per second, the flash arrives long before you hear the thunder. Except under very favorable conditions, you usually can't hear thunder if you're farther than eight miles away. If you happen to have a pretty good stopwatch or a very accurate electronic timepiece, it's easy to figure how far away the lightning is. Just check the seconds between the flash and the thunderclap. Ten seconds equals two miles away; two and a half seconds equals half a mile; five seconds equals one mile, etcetera.

Next to the (now understood) weird beauty of St. Elmo's fire, ball lightning is one of the most fearsome and mysterious of all natural experiences—unless you happen to be a character by the name of John W. Campbell, Jr., the big, brawny, outspoken edition of *Analog*, the aristocrat of all science fact and fiction magazines, who once told me of his own rather unique personal encounter with ball lightning.

"Shortly after I got my degree in physics, I was sitting on my front porch, and I saw a ball of lightning form in the field just across the road from me," he said. "I watched that ball bounce gently over the tops of the grasses, bounce off the side of a barn, go over and explode an eight-inch-in-diameter tree into oak toothpicks.

"The next time I was visiting back at MIT I went to see my physics professor.

"He assured me it was physically impossible for a ball of lightning to exist, that no competent observer had ever reported the phenomenon, and that there was mathematical proof of its impossibility! That's just fine! As far as I could make out, what constituted a reliable observer, a competent observer, was one who *didn't* report it. The fact of reporting it proved you were incompetent because they *knew* it was impossible!"

To this day, nobody knows what ball lightning is, and there are still many, many professional meteorologists who refuse to accept eyewitness reports because there is no theory in any of the textbooks to explain it. That's funny, because if there *were* such a theory in the books, but no concrete evidence of its existence, chances are that they'd surely "believe in" ball lightning. That's really funny.

Sure it is.

There are exceptions, however. Dr. Martin A. Uman, a brilliant professor of electrical engineering at the University of Florida in Gainesville, readily admits: "Ball lightning—which has puzzled scientists for centuries—is usually a by-product of lightning storms. But nobody knows what causes it . . . I'd say that 5 to 10 percent of the people in the United States have seen ball lightning. Sometimes observers say the sphere—usually red, orange or yellow—gives off heat and a strange, acrid odor."

Like UFO's—or some of the so-called "flying saucers" maybe?

Mrs. R. E. Carroll was naked in her tub, taking a bath at her home in Batesville, Arkansas, when a rumble of thunder preceded a terrifying sphere of fire:

"Suddenly a ball lightning came right through the bathroom window, hit the water in the tub, grounded on the chain of the tub stopper and exploded." (At this writing, Mrs. Carroll is living in Long Beach, California.) She added, perhaps not so surprisingly, "All the water in the tub splashed out—and I jumped out along with it, I was so frightened."

That jump could have been her salvation.

Another lady, now fully grown, recalled the terrifying experience she had as a child of seeing a ball of lightning dancing down the second floor of her cottage in Juniper Beach, Michigan. Mrs. B. F. Walker, who was being taken care of by her mother then, but who now lives in Harbor Bluffs, Florida, said, "It [the ball of fire] slowly revolved and floated down the hallway. I was petrified with fear; so was my mother."

Chemistry professor W. J. Frierson (now living at

Stone Mountain, Georgia) had an experience somewhat like that of John W. Campbell except that he was hit: "I stood on the front porch of my home in Hampden-Sydney, Virginia, holding a garden hoe as I waited out an April thunderstorm. Suddenly a ball of lightning about the size of a washtub hit the telephone wire about fifty yards from my home. It rolled down the wire to the house, then jumped toward me and hit the metal part of the hoe. I woke up two or three minutes later, flat on my back."

There are hundreds of eyewitness personal experiences with ball lightning, probably thousands, but these few are fairly common examples of those who saw and or felt the things and lived to tell about them. Thousands of others never survived it.

Mrs. Earl Reno of Nyack, New York, had a terrifying experience at four o'clock in the morning as she lay sleeping with her husband in her home: "Suddenly . . . this strange fiery blue-white ball came through a *closed* window (*without breaking or burning it*), skimmed across the room, across our bodies as we lay in bed, and disappeared through a solid wall! I was scared to death. . . ."

Small wonder.

What are these strange atmospheric phenomena that suddenly strike at the very core of our mundane existences? In recent years there has been increasing evidence of a kind of electromagnetic force that affects not only the way we humans think, feel and behave as individuals but also as national, religious and racial groups. This is, however, a sensitive question—so much so that it is best examined indirectly, i.e., through the correlation of some of our fellow creatures (or *beings*?) who are *also* affected by (in this case, manmade) electromagnetic forces.

6

ASTRO WEATHER FORECASTING IN THEORY AND PRACTICE

A CERTAIN CHAUVINISM exists among most scientists—as well as among the rest of us—which can be called "species specific."

It's a fairly simple matter to perceive nature's laws as governing all other living things while somehow overlooking Homo sapiens. Environmentalists can easily determine nature's operation, say, in a sudden explosion of the population of Norway rats, gray squirrels, lemmings, bluefish or crows. These numerical excesses are usually attributed to what appears to be a perfectly obvious component or agency of nature that happens to be disturbed. Result: the burgeoning numbers of animals are "stabilized."

But not us humans. Oh no. We're different. The attitude of science thus far has been that we're somehow divorced from the rest of nature. Of course, when it seems that the human population is about to decimate itself in a nuclear war, we're in control. We get together and call it the hell off. Still . . . more and more human beings are starving to death than ever before. And there come upon us worldwide epidemics of disease that wipe out whole populations.

But we humans are "in control," don't you see? We

develop vaccines that seem to stop the epidemics in their tracks. Not always, mind you. But enough to encourage total faith in the efficacy of our manmade science. Too often, though, the disease-carrying microbes mysteriously adapt, rendering our virulent vaccines as inert as water.

In all sincerity, the first responsibility of true science is to *understand* (not to control) nature—to recognize the beautiful, logical operation of universal design, intelligent principle and purpose throughout the tangible universe. These are clues. Clues to the *non*physical, invisible universe.

Materialistic science, with rather typical hubris, rejects astrometeorology because it can't measure the forces and congeries of energies forever flashing throughout our solar system and reaching us from distant stars and galaxies. This kind of science also rejects the conclusions of thousands of years of evidence compiled by some of the greatest minds the human race is known to have produced.

But there is indirect evidence—clues that make the truth obvious—which I'll try to prove logically.

Every predictive science aims to get the highest coincidence between its forecast and the ensuing event. Unlike orthodox weather forecasting, astrometeorology has been shown to have the highest ratio of structurally related coincidence between celestial phenomena and earthly weather.

The American Institute of Physics once announced the discovery (by Dr. Harry B. Marvis, a Naval Observatory scientist) that the stars exercise a *daily* influence on the weather. Dr. Marvis said, in the New York *Journal-American* of October 1, 1938, "Scientists had not even suspected that the stars of the Milky Way, from their tremendous distances, had any significant effect on the daily fluctuations of atmospheric pressure.

"In the language of astronomy, 'sidereal air pressure,' the rise and fall of the barometer in relation to the positions of the stars, is real and important.

"The Sun and Moon are recognized as the cause of air-pressure changes. By their positions they raise and lower the tides not only on land and sea, but also in the layers of the atmosphere."

Dr. Marvis discovered that the amount of atmospheric pressure due to the stars is sometimes, as high as one-thirtieth of that which occurs in common storms.

"In accurate weather forecasting, the contributions of the stars to barometric changes will have to be considered," Dr. Marvis contended.

An intensive computer study was made of a 50-year record of rainfall by Dr. Max A. Woodbury's research group at New York University in 1962. This study proved statistically that some of the most ancient ideas about lunar influence on rainfall were right on the money. When the results were checked against the findings of a control group in New Zealand, Dr. Woodbury proved that the *peaks* in rainfall graphs occurred regularly at the time of the *New* Moon and *troughs* occurred at the Full Moon. (This explains my personal observation over many years that the Moon is almost always visible at its full period.)

The Full and New Moon give us the two lunar aspects—conjunction and opposition to the Sun (i.e., zero and 180° respectively). The influence of the Moon also produces tides in the upper atmosphere; and the lunar component or effect on the daily temperature has been detected all over the world. The problem is that orthodox meteorologists just won't put all this exotic (albeit proven) data together into a comprehensive picture, which is what astrometeorology has been doing since prehistory.

Just before he died in 1962, Dr. Andrew E. Douglass, astronomer and director emeritus of the laboratory of tree-ring research at the University of Arizona, managed to finish *Dendrochronology*, a major work on his theories of the astronomical forces at work—the motion of the planets and behavior of the Sun and Moon—which he felt were responsible for the kind of weather we have. It's interesting to note that while Dr. Douglass, originator of the science of dendrochronology, spent his life proving the influence of the planets, his successor (an equally fine gentleman, by the way), Dr. Bart J. Bok, has been a lifelong and extremely powerful foe of astrology.

In the chapter on the sciences of antiquity, we covered

some of the seemingly incredible knowledge once possessed by ancient mankind. The first known work on weather and the atmosphere was *The Meteorologica*, by Aristotle, about 400 B.C. Although much of this material came from older sources, his treatise was expanded by his pupil Theophrastus sometime between 373 and 286 B.C. Those two volumes were *On Winds*, and *On the Signs of Rain, Winds, Storms and Fair Weather*.

These were the sole authorities on meteorology until the beginning of scientific investigations in the seventeenth century, when many astronomers were trying to throw off the "yoke" of astrology.

But by 1686, Dr. J. Goad's *Astrometeorologica*, based on 40 years of his own astro-weather observations and correlations, was published in London. This became the leading textbook and authority on the subject until the end of the nineteenth century. It had an invaluable transcript of Kepler's own diary of astro-weather observations from June 28, 1618, to August 9, 1629. Kepler expounded his theories on planetary phenomena in relation to atmospheric changes. It is a matter of historical record that long before he conceived his laws of planetary motion, Kepler's initial recognition was the result of his remarkably accurate long-range astro-weather forecasting.

In Real Universe terms, 50 years of critically-tested astro-weather forecasts made on a worldwide basis, more than a year in advance, by George J. McCormack, of Fair Lawn, New Jersey, duplicated and fully supported Kepler's theories.

After about 20 years of exhaustive, independent study and research, he discovered that the angles of 30°, 45°, 135° and 150° between celestial bodies synchronized perfectly with atmospheric reactions.

Commander R. J. Morrison of the Royal Navy, publisher more than a century ago of the world-famous *Almanac*, further refined the discoveries of his predecessors and added still more modern approaches to the work.

Morrison's successor, Dr. Alfred J. Pearce, continued the *Almanac*. He also published his *Weather Guide* in London in 1864, *The Science of the Stars* in 1881, and his magnum opus, the now rare and valuable *Textbook*, in

1889. In Volume II of this expanded work, Pearce added new discoveries, along with his own observations, and detailed instructions in the newer methods of weather forecasting. To support and dramatize the idea of astrometeorology as a science, he gave one case history after another and cited voluminous statistical data.

At the beginning of World War I, George J. McCormack meticulously duplicated, tested and proved Pearce's methods. By 1925 he had developed a new astronomical factor—*the key*—for timing atmospheric changes in eastward transit from any point of terrestrial origin to any other point of longitude. After experimenting with the key for 23 years and obtaining increasingly accurate forecasts, he used this key element with fantastic success for the late, unseasonably cold and snowy spring of 1947 in the Midwest.

Then, eight months before the Big Snow of December 26, 1947, which immobilized metropolitan New York, the now encouraged McCormack used his system again—with even more dazzling accuracy—when he predicted the exact date and extent of the storm and sent out 400 mimeographed copies of his prediction to every newspaper and radio station whose address he could locate.

On December 27, his local reputation became national and he was inundated with requests for more and more long-range forecasts during the next decade than any one man could possibly provide. As president and general factotum of the New Jersey Astrologian Society (also its chief librarian and teacher), McCormack began publishing his *Astrotech Weather Guide* and trying to teach his methods to others.

Unfortunately, few students had McCormack's dedication, persistence, scientific objectivity and intelligence. Every so often he'd find raw talent and do his best to inspire someone new to carry on, but he died with his dream of scientific acceptance only half realized.

"Gee-Jay" tried to teach his students (and the steady stream of newsmen and other curiosity-seekers who beat a path to his door) that the astrometeorological laws that govern weather are not at all limited to sunspot activity, the direction and speed of jet streams or the idea that the Sun alone controls the atmosphere. Based on the experimental research of his predecessors and fully supported by half a century of his own work, here's the theory McCormack developed and presented to a special seminar of the United States Weather Bureau in New York in 1963 and to the 44th annual meeting of the American Meteorological Society in 1964:

(1) The Sun controls the constitution of the atmosphere.

(2) Planets regulate *organic* changes in weather (a) by changing impressions when they are at certain points in their eccentric orbits, or by varying declinations north or south of the Earth's equator, thereby affecting both *electrical and chemical* changes in the Earth's atmosphere; (b) when in major stations—that is, either on the celestial equator, in maximum declination, in perigee (closest to Earth), in perihelion (closest to the Sun), or when apparently stationary in *geocentric* longitude; (c) by angular relationship with the Sun or between each other in longitude, and (d) by radical occupancy or eastward transit over any given terrestrial meridian or in angular relation to that meridian. These factors may be interpreted from *key charts calculated for the exact times the sun crosses the equinoctial or solstice points;* secondary charts prepared for the times of the New and Full Moons provide a more exact timing reference.

(3) The Moon is the *functional* element; it reflects barometric and atmospheric tidal changes that have already been indicated by solar and/or planetary phenomena.

(4) Seasonal *anomalies* of weather are determined as much by celestial bodies in *declination* (north or south of the celestial equator) as by longitude.

In 1961, when 70 to 80 percent of the celestial bodies were in *southern* declinations during winter months, McCormack accurately predicted a returning cycle of migratory severely cold winters in the northern hemisphere. At the same time, large segments of the southern hemisphere were hit by scorching heat and drought. Exactly one year later these same dominating patterns repeated the cold cycle experienced during 1934 over the eastern United States while the heat and drought were focused over South America—particularly Chile and Argentina.

Weather patterns migrate westwardly and repeat 87° apart each year because the sidereal (astronomical) year is five hours, 48 minutes and 45.51 seconds longer each 365 days; therefore the Earth rotates 87° *eastward* on its axis during this period.

This rotation of the Earth is one of the most important principles in determining just where major patterns of weather will be centered at any given time in the future. (It can be proved easily enough by setting up planetary charts for *past* weather patterns and then checking them against *known,* recorded conditions. This simple test is what convinced every astrometeorologist who ever lived.) The planets, always in motion, are always forming different patterns. The effect of one or more planets upon another is proved by the fact that astronomers have discovered new planets because of the orbital eccentricities of the *known* planets. These eccentricities are caused by the gravitational tugging of the unknown, unseen bodies. This simple gravitational observation also correlates to the Earth's atmosphere.

These continuously forming angles among the planets determine both the character and intensity of our ever changing weather. The same general types of weather patterns originate about 6,000 miles apart simultaneously, but with different degrees of intensity. Highs and lows therefore drift from west to east in the temperate zone. They change at various latitudes and even make complete reversals from north of the equator to south. These can be pinpointed astronomically and seen in satellite pictures, which prove the existence of the Coriolis force (water, for example, runs down the drain clockwise in the northern hemisphere and counterclockwise in the southern).

From seasonal solar and planetary charts in which he calculated the phase of the Moon, McCormack could predict the exact points in terrestrial longitude where anomalies or other atmospheric changes spawn—where disturbing types of weather reach any point of observation on a given date. It's important to know why, during certain parts of the month, these weather movements speed up and at other times slow down.

When any planet is either stationary, "on" the celestial equator, in maximum north or south declination, or in conjunction *or other major configuration* with the Sun, its character (in one degree of intensity or another) quite definitely impresses itself upon the Earth's atmosphere. It logically follows, therefore, that the Earth-Moon system in angular relation to, say, Mars-Jupiter has an equally profound effect on the atmosphere of Venus, and vice versa. McCormack calculated 1,008 such configurations for the Earth alone. The change usually reaches the meridian (your point of geographical observation) within three days. The hard-won "key" astronomical charts evolved by McCormack provide the specific timing and exact latitudinal coordinates.

All angles, or *aspects,* between the planets are based on multiples of 15°, as discovered by Kepler, who called them "magnetic." These are divided into two categories —positive and negative. The positive, or generally *fair,* weather aspects, though they do affect temperature changes, are 60°, 120°, 30° and 150°, with relative strength in that order.

The effects of planetary *conjunctions* are variable, and —*this is what blows the minds of astronomers*—depend on the *natures* or *characters* of the planets involved! Although orthodox scientists who are trained to deal strictly with materialistic concepts find this abhorrent, Aristotle, Kepler, Newton, Goad, Morrison, Pearce and McCormack all independently proved that different planets, orbiting in the same celestial longitude, synchronize with weather that blends the time-honored characteristics observed among planets of the solar family. These will be thoroughly described in the final chapters.

Negative or "discordant" angles between the planets (which tend to *lower* the barometric pressure) are 90°, 180°, 45° and 135°. A parallel of declination, i.e., when planets are exactly the same degree north or south of the celestial equator (at or near the time of a conjunction or opposition) usually operates with much greater intensity than the same aspect in longitude alone.

The basic impressions characteristic of the planets on the atmosphere can be confirmed by checking their transits over the Earth's equator—that is, when they are at *zero degrees of declination.* During these times they exert their most powerful magnetic, gravitational and other influences on the Earth's atmosphere, mantle, and all living things.

In the practical investigation of astronomic weather prediction, McCormack confirmed 64 different cycles, periodicities or rhythms in the atmosphere which he identified with *specific* astronomical phenomena. These periodicities range from 3.415 days to 248.43 years. They gave him the *why* and *when* of changing weather trends. From basic astronomical charts (horoscopes, essentially) set up for any place of observation during specific moments of time, the *where* and *how* are determined. In these celestial maps each of the 360 degrees in the circle of the ecliptic corresponds to a specific degree of terrestrial longitude.

In some ways these key astronomical charts resemble conventional weather maps. But more important, they give us the method to pinpoint the great *anomalies* of weather (and time them as they move eastward).

The foregoing are the basic tools developed, evolved and employed with such remarkable accuracy by George J. McCormack in his engineering approach to astronomic weather forecasting.

Now take a brief look at the other side of the picture. According to *Aeronautics and Space Report of the President,* published by NASA and signed by Gerald R. Ford in 1975:

> During 1974 . . . the United States in cooperation with other nations made substantial advances toward obtaining an understanding of the dynamics of global weather and in the development of satellite systems to gather and use this knowledge. In time [*get that,* "in time"] these can lead to accurate long range forecasts with potentially vast economic bene-

fits for agriculture, construction, transportation, recreation, and other industries.

From June 15 to September 23, the United States and 69 other nations monitored virtually every known meteorological factor along a 20 million-square-mile tropical area of land and sea stretching from the eastern Pacific Ocean across Latin America, the Atlantic, and Africa to the western Indian Ocean. Some 4,000 people using 41 ships, 40 buoys, 12 aircraft, and five United States satellites and one Soviet satellite probed from about a mile below the sea surface to the top of the atmosphere. Agencies of the U.S. participating included the Department of Commerce, the National Aeronautics and Space Administration, the Department of Transportation, the National Science Foundation, and the Department of State. [*Be it noted that the U. S. Weather Bureau is part of the Commerce Department.*]

The final paragraph of this part of the report:

The study, part of the Global Atmospheric Research Program (GARP) is called GATE for GARP Atlantic Tropic Experiment. The tropics are believed to be a key to Earth's weather. Supporting GATE was the initial task of NASA's Synchronous Meteorological Satellite (SMS-1), launched May 17. SMS-1 is the prototype of the forthcoming U.S. Department of Commerce Geostationary Operational Environmental Satellite (GOES) System. From geostationary orbit, SMS-1 maintains a 24-hour weather watch on most of the Western Hemisphere, transmitting data to produce a picture every 30 minutes. It can also acquire and provide information from hundreds of instruments mounted on balloons, stream gauges, ocean buoys, merchant ships, and fire, weather, agricultural, and seismic stations. It thus contributes to our growing capability to provide long range weather forecasts and predict climatic changes . . . which will alleviate the worst effects of severe storms.

Don't hold your breath waiting for this technological/scientific miracle to occur. Not so long as a generous Congress keeps lavishly appropriating funds to satisfy every whim of the weather bureaucrats. Both George McCormack and Irving Krick had nationwide and worldwide reputations for their abilities. Each could predict as accurately as Muhammad Ali could call the round in which his foolhardy opponents (with few exceptions) would fall.

The USWB has known about Krick's and McCormack's systems for over 30 years. And the libraries of the world contain bits and pieces of accurate, eminently useful planetary-weather data from the great practitioners of the past.

But they haven't done a damned thing about it.

Yet.

The final chapters of this book are devoted to specifically described and detailed characteristics of all the planets and their individual and collective influence on the terrestrial atmosphere.

7

THE COMING ICE AGE

METEOROLOGISTS ARE BEGINNING to warn that "A new Ice Age is coming. The world is in a cooling trend. Food will be so scarce that millions will starve."

"Not so," retorts California nuclear physicist and marine engineer Dr. Howard A. Wilcox. According to him, just the opposite is happening. He and his colleagues are so convinced of this that they've written a book called *Hothouse Earth* describing how the world's coastal cities will drown as the ice caps melt. He summarizes the conclusions of other weather experts who interpret and predict that industrial heat, pumped unceasingly into the atmosphere at ever-increasing rates, will raise the Earth's temperature to unprecedented degrees. This will eventually melt the polar ice caps and drown the most populated areas of the planet.

"Man is now generating heat into the atmosphere at about 1/10,000 of the rate at which the Sun is contributing heat to the Earth. The Sun is estimated to pour annually the equivalent of some 5,000 billion billion British thermal units (BTUs) of energy onto the Earth each year," says Wilcox. (One BTU is the amount of heat needed to raise the temperature of one pound of water at its maximum density 1°F.)

But nature has odd ways of confusing the most brilliant guesses of scientists. Take the odd quirk she has of causing summers to be hotter in odd-numbered years and cooler in even-numbered years. No one has been able to figure out why, but this gem was discovered in a statistical study by two University of Reading geophysicists; the Britishers Dr. A.H. Gordon and Dr. N.C. Wells did an intensive investigation of July temperatures over a period of 60 years from 1911 through 1970.

"The results," they reported, "show a highly significant two-year pulse in the July temperature. The main characteristic of the pulse during the past 60 years is the occurrence of warm Julys in odd years and cool Julys in even years."

They don't simply take it at face value, however. The scientists studied temperature records going back to those kept by Sir Isaac Newton himself in 1721. Apparently the geophysicists were unable to provide any kind of theory to explain why the hot-odd, cool-even pattern has so steadfastly held up for 250 years.

But columnist Sydney Harris echoed the fears of many of his readers when he wrote, "The more we learn about the weather, the more likely it seems that a new Ice Age may be upon us far sooner than geologists used to believe; contemplating what a mere four-inch snow does to the modern city, it would seem far more prudent for nations to spend billions on coping with global cold instead of intraspecies weapons for killing each other."

Of course, we mere mortals instinctively understand this, but its logic seems to escape the labyrinthian military mentalities of the tacticians at the Kremlin and in the Pentagon. Like most bureaucracies, their self-perpetuation is both terrible and inexorable. As the cost of supplies for troops, planes, tanks, ships and rockets inevitably goes up, special appropriations ("cost-of-living" increases) by Congress automatically take up the slack.

Be it duly noted, however, that neither are the economists truthfully explaining *why* the cost of foodstuff and other materials seem to be forever rising. Take coffee, for example. In 1976 you paid an extra three to five cents an ounce for your freeze-dried coffee. The big coffee distributors (led by General Foods) raised their prices across the board by about 25 cents a pound and all others followed suit.

Why? Well, the worst cold wave in 50 years destroyed nearly 80 percent of Brazil's 1976 coffee crop—nearly 1½ billion coffee trees. In the United States, wheat growers in Kansas and adjoining states were hit by a drought in the Great Plains that raised fears that another "dust bowl" effect, similar to that in the Depression-ridden 1930s, would soon hit the western cornbelt states. After decades of resisting the "idiotic notion" that weather was in any way connected with extraterrestrial forces, some of the experts are now beginning to concede that the droughts in Africa, Asia and the Americas may be related, somehow, to *sunspots,* of all things!

Imagine that!

An Iowa State University agronomist, Dr. Louis M. Thompson, who began charting weather patterns, sunspots, and their effect on grain crops when McCormack's "Crucial Experiment" was published in *Analog* in the early 1960s, noted that the level of sunspot activity began to decline in the autumn of 1975, and had continued to drop throughout the winter months of 1976, causing a shift in the jetstream, those high-altitude winds that directly impinge their patterns and influence on world weather. The ionosphere, magnetosphere and jetstreams are all subject to solar activity, particularly sunspots, which, in turn, are intimately associated with the angular positions of the planets and the solar system's center of gravity.

During what we consider to be "normal," i.e., good crop-producing, weather years, as the jetstream moves northward over the Great Plains of America and its cornbelt states, it drags in its wake heavy spring rains on which the soybean, corn and wheat crops thrive.

Dr. Thompson cautiously says: "The Great Plains region has had a record of droughts about every 20 years since 1800, and there's some correlation between these droughts and the 20- to 22-year sunspot cycle, but there's great reluctance by most climatologists to predict drought from sunspot data because no direct cause-and-effect relationship has ever been established."

(*There was also no direct cause-effect relationship in the correlation between high and low tides with the Moon until astrologer Johannes Kepler proved it. Even so, every "superstitious" fisherman and seaman believed in and used it successfully for several thousand years.*)

The former director of the High Altitude Observatory and the National Center for Atmospheric Research at Boulder, Colorado, laughed when I explained the basic theory of astrometeorology to him in New York in 1961. Dr. Walter Orr Roberts has sinced headed the National Science Foundation and is now back in Boulder as director of the program in science, technology and humanism at the Aspen Institute for Humanistic Studies.

Still, at the 1976 meeting of the American Association for the Advancement of Science, he expressed his fears, as a solar physicist, that the then-current drought over the western plains from South Dakota to New Mexico appeared to mark the start of the *ninth* recurrence of a series of droughts that have hit the plains at 22-year intervals. "This year the Sun is reaching the low point of its 11-year cycle of sunspot and geomagnetic activity," he told reporters, "and won't begin a significant rise in activity for another two or three years."

Like Dr. Thompson, he seems to maintain the scientific style against committing himself to a definite opinion. "There's no certainty that a drought is coming or that it will last a certain time," he said. (*Nevertheless, during the eight previous recurrences of the low point of the 22-year sunspot cycle there have been droughts that lasted anywhere from three to seven years.*)

"The subject is controversial because no one has shown any mechanical tie between solar cycles and drought cycles," Roberts said, then curiously reversed himself: "I have a very serious fear that the drought of the 1970s has begun. All the signs point to it. If so, the price repercussions and hunger repercussions will be felt by people throughout the world.

"I hope," he concluded lamely, "that I'm wrong."

Fifteen years before that statement, Dr. Andrew Douglass, astrometeorologist, astronomer, and world-famous originator of a new science called dendrochronology (determining ancient climatic changes by tree ring research), clearly predicted a 40-year drought and warned America (and the world) to conserve water for future use, learn new desalination techniques and how to recharge underground water when the drought would be at its peak.

Less than a year before his death Dr. Douglass was still hard at work on an invaluable manuscript on astrometeorology—in his words, "the astronomical forces at work—*the motions of the planets and behavior of the Sun which are responsible for the kind of weather we have. . . .*

"Studying the combination of tree-ring growth, sunspot cycle occurrences and planetary movements holds the key to the forecast of weather conditions over an extended period of time. . . ." *

According to reports, his astrometeorological book was requisitioned by the University of Arizona, ostensibly to be completed by his daughter and granddaughter from his voluminous notes. At this writing, nothing has materialized.

The late Charles Greeley Abbot was the oldest man ever to be granted an American patent. At the age of ninety-nine, Dr. Abbott contributed a solar-energy conversion unit to the world. He was head of the Smithsonian Institution in Washington, D.C., from 1928 to 1944. As an astrophysicist, he recognized the value of the works of the great names in the history of astrometeorology and undertook a private effort to discover the means other than gravitational by which planets influenced each other and produced sunspots and solar flares.

He was also a pioneer in his efforts to find ways of harnessing the Sun's almost boundless energy. "When our present supply of coal and oil is exhausted—and this will be sooner than anybody thinks—the daily ration of solar

* Author's italics.

energy will represent almost our entire means of livelihood," he warned in 1943.

Dr. Abbott died at the age of one hundred and one in Riverdale, Maryland, on December 17, 1973.

These three geniuses, George J. McCormack, Andrew Douglass and Charles Greeley Abbot, all independently warned of great natural disasters scheduled to begin in the late 1970s and early 1980s.

A meeting of experts in climatology, agricultural economics and political science was recently called by the International Federation of Institutes for Advanced Study (IFIAS) to discuss the prospects of imminent changes in world climate on the human population. "If national and international policies do not take deep freezes, droughts, floods and other anomalies into account," they said, "major crop failures will result in mass deaths by starvation and perhaps in anarchy and violence that could exact a still more terrible toll."

The climatologist who directed the Institute for Environmental Studies at the University of Wisconsin, Reid Bryson, referred to the first half of the twentieth century as "the most abnormally warm period in a thousand years. Our society has adapted to an unreal climatic 'norm' that is unlikely to prevail again any time in the foreseeable future. . . . The climate is now changing in ways that *must* have catastrophic impacts—like half a billion people starving to death. It has already begun. . . ."

Instead of selling huge quantities of wheat annually to the Soviet Union and China, advises Stephen Schneider, who now heads the climate project at the National Center for Atmospheric Research (NCAR) in Boulder, the physicist strongly urges that we should increase all agricultural food reserves and stock up in preparation for the coming unfavorable trends in world weather. "We can no longer afford to gamble," he said in 1976, "that we *won't* have another series of years like 1972 and 1974 when droughts, floods and early deep frosts cut drastically into crop yields."

Dr. Schneider advocates what he calls the "Genesis strategy," a food-reserve policy patterned after the Biblical story of Joseph, who advised Pharaoh to store grain during seven years of plenty so there would be ample food for the people during the ensuing seven years of famine.

Most climatologists are coming to believe that our weather is changing in ways that can only develop into a catastrophe of global proportions. The Arabs already know this; they've softened their position on oil only because they recognize that they need American and Canadian wheat, soybeans and corn far more than we need their petroleum. Ultimately, some sort of symbiotic global agreement will have to be worked out among contributing nations.

The one thing all climatologists agree on is the documented fact that for the past 25 or 30 years the northern hemisphere has been cooling off. The lengths of the growing seasons have been reduced proportionately, thus cutting down the supply of food and raising its costs. Scientists, who are more acutely aware of this trend than others, see more than just the direct effects of the cooling; they cite evidence that it is causing greater climatic unpredictability and variability—increasing numbers of droughts, floods, freezes and even earthquakes.

Their opponents don't interpret these facts as meaning a basic change in the terrestrial climate. They regard the unpredictable trends as mere fluctuations—like the warming and cooling trends of the last century—instead of drastic changes in climate.

At the University of Maryland, for example, Helmut Landsberg said reassuringly, "Atmospheric conditions as a whole, while mildly oscillating from year to year, have a fair amount of stability. They pendulate around averages that change only slowly."

But Dr. Walter Orr Roberts, who laughed in 1961 when I told him of G.J. McCormack's prediction of the biggest deep freeze in modern history in little more than twenty years, and now heads IFIAS, has since changed his tune. Early in 1976 he told reporters, "We feel that the downturn of temperatures since 1950—and rapidly in the '60s—probably represents a trend and isn't just a short-term chance fluctuation, with next year or the year after likely to return to the conditions of the 1940s. We feel that it's more likely that these colder average temperatures in the northern hemisphere will continue for 20 or 30 years [*this was Dr. Andrew Douglass' astrometeorological prediction on June 21, 1961*] and therefore we consider it a significant climate effect that the world will probably have to contend with for a long time."

Using Dr. Douglass' dendrochronology and other paleoclimatological evidence, scientists now estimate that over the last million years the climate of the Earth has been swinging back and forth between glacial and interglacial periods. The cold glacial periods or Ice Ages saw great sheets of ice creeping southward to cover most of North America and Europe. Forests in temperate zones froze, dried, cracked and were ground to sticks beneath the crush of billions of tons of advancing ice.

Most scientists feel certain that at least six of these extremely cold periods happened during the past half million years, but they also cite evidence that the pattern goes back at least several million years.

Here's their latest chronology: about 15,000 years ago, they believe, the glaciers began to retreat. By 3000 B.C. the climate in the temperate zones was only slightly warmer than it is right now. They have some fairly good evidence for the latter because Chinese records are available for a period covering 4,000 years—from 3000 B.C. to A.D. 1000. After that, sporadic records from the European inheritors of Arabic wisdom (mathematics, astronomy and astrometeorology) are available. Systematic planetary-weather record keeping probably began in earnest with the work of Johannes Kepler.

Scientists are now calling the cold period during the seventeenth and eighteenth centuries the "Little Ice Age," because during that time the oceanic ice grew tremendously off the coast of Iceland. Lush farms that the Vikings had planted and land they colonized in Greenland were abandoned to the elements. One French historian, Emmanuel Le Roy Ladurie, who had made a careful study of Alpine glaciers, noted that between A.D. 750 and 1200 they had melted considerably, shrinking to the north, but then they began to advance, and they grew, almost without interruption, between 1590 and

1850. All his evidence was meticulously documented. Then, in the late 1800s, the Alpine glaciers began their slow retreat again as a warming trend melted the ice—a condition that continued until the middle of World War II.

Those glaciers are now beginning another slow advance.

Such paleoclimatological evidence indicates to scientists that today's temperatures are much warmer than the average temperatures during the past few centuries, but that even those centuries were far warmer and free of ice than the average of the past million or so years. "It's only natural, then," said one climatologist, "that we may reasonably expect a return to much colder conditions, but it will be gradual; the most recent cooling trend, which began about 120,000 years ago, developed almost as rapidly as the warming trend that preceded it."

In the March 1976 issue of *Smithsonian* magazine, Henry Lansford covered the various conflicting theories of weather experts on the basic cause of the coming cold wave—theories that manage to avoid all mention of the planets as possible elements in terrestrial weather patterns. "Astronomical theories that attribute climate changes to shifts in the Earth's orbit or rotation on its axis; solar theories that propose that the Earth's climate varies in response to changes in the activity of the Sun (*Smithsonian*, September, 1975); and geophysical theories that link climatic changes to events and interactions within the land-ocean-atmosphere system."

He admitted that intense volcanic activity tends to cool the atmosphere. ". . . great quantities of ash and dust that are thrown high into the atmosphere by volcanoes can stay aloft for a long time, screening out some of the solar energy that otherwise would warm the Earth."

The aforementioned Dr. Howard A. Wilcox, who espouses the opposite, or "greenhouse effect," for the future, says a warming trend always coincides with an increase in carbon dioxide in the atmosphere. CO^2 is almost transparent to sunlight, shortwave solar radiation. But it's nearly opaque to *long*-wave radiation—the kind that land and sea give off when the Sun heats them.

According to Reid Bryson, the credit (or blame, depending on your viewpoint) for changes in temperature during the past century belongs solely to man's activities. "Carbon dioxide," he says, "which is produced by the increased burning of coal, oil and other fossil fuels since the late 1800s, caused the warming that continued through the 1940s. But at that point, smoke, dust, and other particulate matter from industrial smokestacks, slash-and-burn agriculture and other human activities reached such high levels in the atmosphere that their screening out of solar energy counterbalanced and then overrode the greenhouse effect, starting the temperature going back down. . . ."

Not everyone agrees with him, of course, but then hardly anybody agrees with anybody else in this complex weather puzzle.

Such a theory seems just too simplistic for most scientists; they don't believe there's any single mechanism causing major climatic changes. Mostly they're right. A mind-boggling array of complex processes involving interplanetary electromagnetic/gravitational and other forces acting on the Sun (and vice versa) are behind the intricate mechanisms of solar heat on the atmosphere, oceans, ice caps and land.

The human population on this planet is rapidly outstripping the production of food to feed it. No matter what the ivory-tower, long-term theories of orthodox scientists may be, the immediate prognosis is that we're facing extreme danger of possible catastrophe.

When the temperature drops an average of just 2° above the 40th parallel of North America, in all probability it will totally destroy the production of wheat and corn in the major farming districts of Canada. As the drought advances, the capacity of the land will be strained far beyond its production limitations by burgeoning numbers of people and cattle on the last remaining grasslands. The result: All vegetation destroyed by overgrazing, followed by mass starvation, malnutrition and pandemic disease.

The immediate threat of global famine is deadly serious; the catastrophic clash between swelling human population and dwindling food supplies is much nearer than anyone imagines. Even at this writing, the grain reserves of the entire world are down to less than a thirty-day supply—a fact the Soviet Union is keenly aware of.

The director general of the United Nations Food and Agricultural Organization, Addeke H. Boerma, said, "The chances of having enough food to feed millions of people depends on the whims of one year's weather."

Even now, up to eight thousand people die each and every week from starvation while hundreds of millions more suffer the debility of extreme malnutrition. And it's getting worse all the time.

As temperatures drop and food supplies diminish, floods, droughts, deep freezes and earthquakes coincide with the general cooling of global temperatures. There are, however, some interesting and useful clues—possibly solutions to help offset the coming combination of catastrophes—if a concerted, serious effort is made to understand the underlying laws governing weather.

For example, there are a few minor historical precedents connecting extremely cold cycles to the conjunctions and oppositions of the outer-gas giants—Jupiter, Saturn, Uranus and Neptune—because of their combined gravitational tug on the Sun and solar reaction to it. These great planets (or protostars, as in the case of Jupiter and Saturn) are orbiting toward a rendezvous on the opposite side of the Sun from the Earth in the 1980s. The consequent drop in global temperature is incompletely understood by most people, who simply shrug off as insignificant an average drop of 15°. "Hell," says Reid Bryson at the University of Wisconsin, "the Earth's average temperature during the Great Ice Ages of the past was only seven degrees lower than during its *warmest* periods. We've *already* descended about one-sixth of the way toward the Ice Age average!"

That was in 1975.

8

ECLIPSES, PLANETS, AND THE INCONSTANT SUN

ONE OF THE more baffling mysteries of solar astronomy is how the ancient Chinese (who are not supposed to have had telescopes) were able to record sunspots.

Whether ancient scientists used optical instruments or not (the evidence indicates that they probably did) is a moot point. More than 2,000 years of Oriental astrological records indicate that during certain periods there were *no sunspots at all.* This is supported by Carbon-14 studies of tree rings of the era.

Sunspots are commonplace today, indicating vast changes in our local star.

"A true and strange anomaly occurred in the early days of scientific observation," said astronomer John A. Eddy of Boulder, Colorado's, High Altitude Observatory. "For a period of 70 years—from 1645 to 1715—sunspots were almost totally absent on the surface of the Sun. Solar activity was at a near-zero level. This is totally unlike the modern behavior of the Sun, and the consequences for solar terrestrial physics seems to me profound.

"We now have to realize that the Sun's behavior has been better in the last 200 years than in the previous 1,000 years. . . . We've shattered the Principle of Uniformitarianism for the Sun," Eddy announced dramatically, adding that the Sun's behavior today is no longer considered a reliable guide to its activity during past ages.

Eddy and Dr. George B. Field, director of the Center for Astrophysics (of the Smithsonian Astrophysical Observatory in Cambridge), are increasingly intrigued by the "strange correlation between solar activity and long-range terrestrial weather patterns." The lack of sunspots between 1645 and 1715 coincides almost perfectly with the so-called Little Ice Age. "The climate curve looks a lot like the curve in solar activity," Dr. Eddy said.

If anything, Field was more impressive. "Maybe we've heard a turning point in the history of science," he announced during 1976's annual meeting of the American Association for the Advancement of Science.

In the new science of dendrochronology, when there's a prolonged period of inactivity on the Sun, the atmosphere, and all living things, absorb and retain greater amounts of the Carbon-14 isotope. Carbon-dating the trees that grew between 1640 and 1720 revealed a world-wide super-abundance of C-14 in the tree rings of that era. This fact surprised the scientific community and cast new doubt on the validity of the accepted 11-year and 80-year solar cycles.

"There should be no doubt about the reality of these coincidences," John Eddy said. "The evidence should encourage new attention to the possible causes of these long-term variations in the solar constant."

Although he made no reference to the planets, it seems almost inconceivable that John Eddy, George Field, *et al.*, had never heard of the planetary, astrometeorological work of Australia's Dr. E.K. Bigg, Dr. Andrew Douglass, John H. Nelson, or Dr. Charles Greeley Abbot.

Dr. Abbot was a gentle and kindly man with a droopy mustache, who saw into the future with such great accuracy that his intuition bordered on the psychic. His only apparent "vice" was a keen intolerance of anyone who deviated from the real scientific method—those who functioned on theory alone. He was a true discoverer, not a scientific mopper-up. He invented a host of devices that utilized pure solar energy. In 1925 he worked out and built a solar device to provide heat and energy for his California home. He was the first modern scientist to detect variations in the output of power from the Sun, and he worked unstintingly on solar-energy conversion units to help the world of the future to convert from coal and oil, which he uncannily foresaw as being dangerously depleted within his own lifespan.

In 1953 he reported *"an indisputable connection between solar variations, certain aspects of the planets and terrestrial weather."* His fascination with planetary-solar interaction lead him to forecast that it would someday be possible to make general weather predictions as far as 50 years ahead. Whether his discovery of variation in solar energy included unpublished knowledge of changes in the orbits of the planets themselves remains purely hypothetical. Still, if the planets do *not* deviate in their orbits, and astrometeorological forecasts for centuries—or even millennia—are possible, *why did he limit his predictions to 50 years?*

Dr. Abbot led a full, rich life and made valuable contributions to the general fund of human knowledge, but was never formally recognized for what might have been his greatest gift to modern science. Even though he was awarded the Draper Gold Medal of the National Academy of Arts and Sciences, most of his astrometeorological discoveries and experiments remain largely unknown and unsung. He died full of years and honors on December 17, 1973, confident that his vision of a turning point in the history of science was imminent.

Seven years before his death, he saw his theory partially vindicated when Dr. Richard Head, chief of NASA's Electronics Research Center, tentatively announced a rediscovery of the fact that the planets are the principal cause of changes in the gravitational field of the Sun. *Technology Week* magazine, in an article on May 15, 1967, bylined Rex Pay, reported, "If the gravity-vector solar flare prediction technique is correct, then weather on the Earth's surface is related to the positions of the planets."

The mechanism is fairly simple, according to a report by the National Engineering Science Company. "Since the orbiting planets cause solar gravitational and magnetic changes which cause variations in the Earth's ionosphere, then solar flare activity will be relayed through the ionosphere to the troposphere and will directly influence surface weather there."

The skeins of data are being woven into what amounts to a totally new picture of the universe. By 1930—only 65 years after the American Civil War—the major cities of the world were connected by shortwave radio, the cheapest and quickest form of communication possible. But the miracle of radio also had its drawbacks. Shortwave signals would fail for periods ranging anywhere between a few hours to almost a week.

Radio engineers soon discovered that the garbling and destruction of these signals were caused by magnetic storms, which in turn were associated with sunspots. By 1946, RCA, Inc., established an observatory in New York City to conduct intensive studies of sunspots. Because John H. Nelson was a radio ham and amateur astronomer, RCA outfitted him with a rooftop observatory, a six-inch telescope, a handsome salary, unlimited time, and told him to find some way of predicting *when* sunspots could be expected to ruin its radio transmissions.

According to Nelson, "It was apparent early in this research program that there was a chain reaction involving the planetary arrangement to the Sun and Sun to shortwave signals via the resulting magnetic storm." How he received that inspiration is puzzling because Nelson had no knowledge of or interest in astrology, and was completely ignorant of astrometeorology. Yet he independently rediscovered the same "magnetic" angles among the planets as the cause of sunspots that Johannes Kepler (who never saw a sunspot in his lifetime) used so successfully in making extremely long-range weather predictions.

Nelson spent five years studying radio-signal data which he compared on a daily basis with the arrangements of the planets. At first he used the heliocentric (sun-centered) system and found that storms most frequently coincided with planetary angles of 0°, 90° and 180°—the conjunction, quadrature (or square) and opposition aspects. *But not always.* Nelson was pretty discouraged by this until he conceived the idea of "multiple angular harmonics."

"Ultimately, I found the important harmonics by *dividing* the major angles into smaller components—*any even multiple of 15*. This is one-sixth of the square," he wrote in the August 1975 issue of the *Bulletin of the American Federation of Astrologers*. "The even multiples of 18°, one-fifth of the square, are also of value, but less so than the 15° series.

"Mercury is usually the trigger planet either as one of the planets making the *hard* angle or as an harmonic to two other planets that are themselves executing a *hard* angle. Because there are many harmonics, this system, simple as it sounds, can become quite complex. . . .

"Mercury and Pluto, which are both small planets, have a profound effect in relation to magnetic storms. What other mysteries do they hold?" he wondered.

Large corporations don't keep high-salaried executives on their payrolls for 25 years out of pure charity, so it isn't surprising that Nelson consistently produced long-range forecasts for RCA with an average accuracy of 93 percent.

Now retired, he is still an active scientific investigator. "I'm as enthusiastic as ever," he wrote in *Cosmic Patterns*. "This is a fascinating field of research. . . . No two sunspots are alike, no two combinations of planets are alike —consequently there are new things to learn almost every day."

He has evolved the system now known as Simultaneous Multiple Harmonic Relations involving several planets. "These relationships cannot repeat exactly in thousands and thousands of years when four, five, or six planets are involved," he wrote.

According to the modern astronomical interval known as a Great Sidereal Year, it takes about 25,000 years for all the planets to return to their original positions and relationships. The *Yugas* of the ancient Hindus are divided into 12 segments of 2,160 years each (the present one, the *Kali Yuga*, roughly coincided with the establishment of Christianity). Thus, 12 Yugas equal 25,920 years. The Chaldeans must have had very ancient knowledge of astronomy. They calculated the "Saros"—cycles of 3,600 years duration—seven of which equal 25,200 years. (Thirty-six hundred years is the exact time it takes for a "fixed star" to move through one degree of a 360° circle.) The intriguing thing about these repeating celestial events and their divisions is that most ancient people referred to them as World Ages—*each of which ended in a great disaster that engulfed entire civilizations.*

If these are mere myths and legends, there's no rational explanation for the fact that they persist among the remnants of every civilized society on the planet—including the Amerindians, Polynesians, Egyptians, Nordic and other peoples. The ancient Chinese encyclopedia, *Sing-li-tatsiuen-Chou,* for example, recorded cyclic destructions of mankind ending each World Age and casting its survivors into a Stone Age existence. The Hindu *Visuddhi-Magga* tells much the same story. Zoroaster (Zarathustra), the prophet of Mazdaism, the religion of ancient Persia, also referred to seven World Ages: "Many are the signs, wonders and perplexity . . . manifested in the world at the end of each millennium . . ."

Planetary calendar stones found in Mexico, Central and South America (particularly the Maya, Toltec and Aztec cultures) also counted seven earths and seven heavens separated from one another by four types of catastrophe—fire, hurricanes, floods and earthquakes. The Armenians and Arabs have almost identical traditions relating to the length of each World Age.

If ancient scholars could write matter-of-factly about stretches of time going back more than 700,000 years, during which modern-type human beings had built great civilizations, what are we to make of our relatively short historical epoch? Anthropologists now estimate that the genus Homo sapiens or something closely akin to him existed *over four million years ago.*

Are there cycles of World Ages? If so, is it possible that they end in catastrophes caused by some unknown periodic "beat" of the sun—possibly in response to specific unusual groupings of planets?

John Nelson says, "I have no solid theory to explain what I have observed, but the similarity between an electric generator with its carefully placed magnets and the Sun with its ever-changing planets is intriguing. In the generator, the magnets are fixed and produce a constant electrical current. If we consider the planets as magnets and the Sun as the armature, we have a considerable similarity to the generator. However, in this case, the "magnets" are *moving*. For this reason, the electromagnetic stability of the solar system varies widely."

Initially, Nelson used the heliocentric system and only six planets because he couldn't believe that Uranus, Neptune and Pluto, because of their great distance from the Sun, had any influence. "This decision," he said, "as I learned a few years later, was a grave mistake."

An amazing amount of precious scientific data is constantly being discovered and either forgotten or lost in blizzards of frivolous, often useless papers by "scientists" whose only function is to justify pet projects heavily financed by foundation or federal grants . . . *or just rejected because the new discovery doesn't jibe with the prevailing scientific opinion.*

Here are two examples: Astronomers were convinced for centuries that although Jupiter's Great Red Spot is a permanent feature of the giant planet, the usually brick-red oval area stretching some 30,000 miles parallel to the equator and believed to be 7,000 miles deep is simply part of the swirling masses of Jovian cloud belts. It had to be, they reasoned, because it constantly changes its position.

Then, in 1964, astronomer Alex G. Smith, of the University of Florida, who with a colleague had devoted eight years of intensive study to the planet, told the American Physical Society that Jupiter's rate of spin was constantly slowing down and speeding up. "Jupiter's sudden changes in its rate of rotation," he said, "are almost as surprising as if the city of Washington had begun to drift across the surface of the Earth at a rate of ten degrees of longitude per year." (A distance of 500 miles.)

Instead of being part of Jupiter's cloud cover, the Great Red Spot, he said, is probably attached to the surface. After studying powerful radio emissions from Jupiter for nearly a decade, Smith reported "significant changes in the rotational speed of the radio sources. We believe these sources originate on Jupiter's surface, which indicates that Jupiter is altering its spin rate."

He told the Society that changes in the rotation of the radio sources were almost exactly in phase with changes in the rotation of the Red Spot. "Coincidence may be involved," he said, "but we can't rule out the possibility that the Spot is a feature attached to the surface. If so, then great changes that have been observed in the Spot's motion over several centuries must be interpreted as dramatic alterations that have taken place in the rotation of the giant planet, a body that weighs as much as 318 Earths."

Data from the Pioneer 10 and 11 probes past Jupiter are still being studied. It was a surprise to the scientific world, however, when Mariner V measured great changes in the atmosphere of Venus in 1967, which seemed "attuned" to the 27-day cycle of the Sun's rotation. In 1974, the American astronomy satellite Copernicus repeated the experiment, this time in tandem with the Soviet Venera Venus probe and Atmospheric Explorer C and D satellites. Result: proof that the hydrogen in the atmosphere of Venus, Earth, Mars (and possibly Jupiter) was tied to the Sun's 27-day spin. A joint U.S.–French and Soviet announcement called it "a clear case of interplanetary synergy."

Another example of an important discovery either ignored or lost in a flood of computer data from Pioneer VI in 1966 are "rivers of radiation flowing outward from the Sun (in the plane of the ecliptic) like the arms of an octopus." This was announced to the 47th annual meeting of the American Geophysical Union by six scientists who based their discovery on 500 million bits of information beamed Earthward by Pioneer.

Physicist Kenneth McCracken told his colleagues that the streams of radiation emanated from one area of the Sun at one hour and from another area the next. "I just can't explain what causes it," he said. "These rivers of radiation are well defined and use the solar magnetic field as their highway, traveling along its lines of force at up to 1,340,000 miles per hour."

The radiation, *"some of it potentially hazardous,"* was known to be produced by solar flares and sunspots.

In a 1962 issue of *Science*, astronomer Donald Bradley of New York University's College of Engineering analyzed rainfall data for the U.S. over a 50-year period and reported that it usually rains a few days after the New and Full Moon periods. A Texas meteorologist rechecked the records of 40 years of heavy rainfall in San Salvador and confirmed Bradley's findings: "Flash floods in Texas are most likely to occur just after a Full Moon," he said.

Farmers had known this for centuries. (Bradley coyly feigned surprise. "We really just stumbled on the Moon correlation," said the man who wrote regularly for *American Astrology* magazine under the pseudonym of Garth Allen. "At first I couldn't believe it.")

Scientists, who still haven't accepted the data, use the excuse that "we don't know the explanation for this discovery." Actually, they're probably mad because an astrologer put one over on them.

In the more advanced areas of astrometeorology, the Moon is the final triggering element—in ancient times considered "the lens" that focused planetary and solar energies on specific geographical locations. The Moon is also a key in the timing of earthquake predictions, a fact that even orthodox scientists can appreciate because of its gravitational tug—*especially when combined with that of the Sun at New Moon and solar-eclipse periods.*

Like Bradley's correlation of lunar phase to rainfall, an equally reliable rule in astrometeorology is that "Major earthquakes always closely follow solar eclipses and often coincide with major planetary conjunctions."

Earthquakes have occasionally been timed almost to the minute of the first tremor. Kepler and Newton managed it by calculating the transit of the next planet *to the point in space where the eclipse took place.*

The Moon-Earth system is unique in the solar system, a fact that has intrigued astronomers since time immemorial. The odd fact is that when they are seen from the Earth, the Sun and Moon have precisely the same apparent diameter. The Sun is about 400 times the actual diameter of the Moon and 400 times its distance from the

Earth; yet the Moon's gravitational tug on the Earth is greater than the supercolossal grip of the Sun, *which holds both bodies in a complex, spiraling solar orbit.*

Nowhere else in the known solar system does this planet-satellite-Sun relationship exist. There are literally hundreds of similarly odd "coincidences"—perhaps thousands—but they are regarded by orthodoxy as scientifically inconsequential, therefore unworthy of serious consideration.

"I don't pay much attention to *isolated* planetary events," John Nelson told the Foundation for the Study of Cycles in Pittsburgh. "I find that to be effective there must be a *grouping* of planets, both heliocentric and geocentric, occurring in close time sequence . . . the Sun is activated by the angular relationship of the planets around it, which are tied to the Earth by *geocentric* (planetary) combinations as well. In other words, the tying of the planets to the Earth geocentrically at the time of powerful heliocentric combinations causes severe reactions among all terrestrial phenomena."

NASA physicist Dr. Stephen Plagemann and British astrophysicist Dr. John R. Gribbin (an editor of *Nature,* the internationally renowned scientific journal) announced their fearsome discovery in 1974: When all the planets orbit into one large group on the other side of the Sun by 1982, Los Angeles (and probably San Francisco) will be destroyed in one of history's most devastating earthquakes.

9

EARTH CHANGES OF THE 1980s— A NEW WORLD AGE?

EVER SINCE THE days of Edgar Cayce, the famed psychic from Virginia Beach who made such astoundingly accurate medical and other predictions, dire warnings of a worldwide spate of earthquakes and the possible end of civilization as we know it has been a favorite theme among individuals ranging from crackpots and charlatans to genuine prophets.

Generally, seisomologists tend to agree. They estimate that sometime within the next 50 years or so the San Andreas and/or Great White Wolf geological fault zones will slip, creating an earthquake of devastating proportions.

Since Cayce there has been an explosion of psychism and a plethora of self-promoting, publicity-seeking fakes and real psychics and seers, all prophesying the same thing. But when two respected scientists made an almost identical prediction in a book for a popular audience, it electrified scientists and layman alike and caused a controversy similar to that created by Immanuel Velikovsky's *Worlds in Collision* over a quarter-century ago.

In their book *The Jupiter Effect,* Drs. Gribbin and Plagemann presented a persuasive series of interrelated, virtually irrefutable facts that proved (as conclusively as it is humanly possible to prove anything without direct experimentation) that the complex, ever-shifting tidal-wave influence of the planets on the Sun (and vice versa) and on each other is real. Moreover, that sometime between 1977 and 1982, when all the planets align on the other side of the Sun, California will be all but torn asunder by one of the worst earthquakes in human memory.

Early in 1975, shortly after their book was published, I met John Gribbin at his home in Brighton, England, and was impressed by his genuine dedication to the pursuit of scientific truth. Both he and Dr. Stephen Plagemann realize they've put their professional reputations—even their careers—on the line. John Gribbin, a young married man with a small son, was, in 1975, totally different from the stuffed-shirt image of sciencedom. Consequently he has incurred the wrath of ultraconservative academia. "They didn't mind as long as we kept our opinions, data and theories confined to obscure scientific papers," the trim, athletic Gribbin said, grinning and stroking his sandy beard. "But they objected very strenuously when we put the whole thing before the public."

Not knowing if he was aware of my interests and writings, I asked, "Wouldn't it have been safer to *avoid* being branded as a supporter and defender of astrology?"

He gave this some thought. "It's becoming very clear that the Sun and Moon influence human emotions, and that the planets are involved," he said softly. "I'm trained in the physical sciences, so that's where I look for the answers. When we find such overwhelming evidence of this, what else can you call it but astrology?"

Meeting a real scientist is a pleasant experience. Of necessity he must be both intellectually honest as well as a man of courage and integrity.

"Of one thing we can be absolutely sure," he said. "The unusual planetary alignment will peak in 1982, and we can say with confidence that the Sun's activity will be unusual—*even for a time of solar maximum.* The reason, of course, is the rare and powerful series of alignments of all the planets as they approach the *super-conjunction* of 1982. Even Pluto plays a small part in affecting the Sun at such a time; the most important effects, however, are those of the tidal planets, especially massive Jupiter, with an extra thrust from massive Saturn, Neptune and Uranus.

"'When Jupiter aligns with Mars,' in the early months of 1982," he wrote in *The Jupiter Effect,* paraphrasing the song "The Age of Aquarius," "the Sun's activity will be at a peak; streams of charged particles will flow out past the planets, including the Earth, and there will be a pronounced effect on the overall circulation and on the weather patterns.

"Finally, the last link in the chain—movements of large masses of the atmosphere—will agitate regions of geologic instability into life. There will be many earthquakes, large and small, around susceptible regions of the globe. And one region where one of the greatest fault systems lies today under a great strain, long overdue for a giant leap forward and just awaiting the necessary kick, is California."

Prior to the 1906 quake in San Francisco, the great temblor of 1809 also corresponded with a similar planetary alignment. But Gribbin pointed out that no one could determine just how much stress was occurring along the San Andreas fault at the time.

"The key to the coming disaster is that this rare trigger should operate just when pressure along the fault is becoming intolerable.

"Most likely, it will be the Los Angeles section of the fault to move this time. Possibly it will be the San Francisco area which has a major quake. The prospect of both these sections of the fault moving at once hardly bears thinking about," said the scientist, who had once lived and studied in California. "In any case, a major earthquake will herald one of the greatest disasters of modern times."

That part of California isn't being evacuated for a complex series of reasons, the first being that the scientific establishment not only refuses to give its stamp of approval to the work of these two young scientists; it shows no inclination whatever to give any serious study to something they "know" to be unfounded, unproved, superstitious nonsense. The reason they "know" this is because every scientific textbook tells them so.

So far, there have been very few scientists of any generation honest, bold and curious enough to investigate the forbidden fringes of this "pseudoscience." Astrology was respectable in Aristotle's and Ptolemy's day, considerably less so when the New Cosmology was established by Copernicus, Tycho Brahe, Galileo, Kepler and Newton—*astrologers all*—but has been scientifically *verboten* ever since.

"Who's your worst critic?" I asked Dr. Gribbin.

"Oh," he laughed, "that'd be Jan Meeus from the unlikely-sounding town of Erps-Kwerps in Belgium. He's making the same kind of attacks on our work as the American scientists did when the entire community ganged up against Immanuel Velikovsky to have his books banned. Really irrational. We're getting a lot of criticism, but there are some people around who are trying to be more rational about it. Mostly they don't like our putting it in a popular book and saying what we have to say in a dramatic way. . . . We're not infallible, but this is important enough to be discussed and needs to be thrashed out logically, but I'm afraid in some ways it's too late already. It will be a nasty disaster. People will do the same things they did in 1906 in San Francisco. . . ."

I disagree with Dr. Gribbin in that I don't think it's too late even at this writing for tens of thousands, perhaps hundreds of thousands, of lives to be saved if a cool, rational, cooperative effort is made by families, groups and officialdom. There have been in existence for some time now detailed governmental plans for fast action in just such a catastrophe. In 1972, the Office of Emergency Preparedness commissioned the National Oceanic and Atmospheric Administration Environmental Research Laboratories *"to provide that Office and the State of California with a rational basis for planning earthquake disaster relief and recovery operations in the San Francisco Bay area."*

But what if, in spite of all preparations, a quake strikes prematurely? The literature reporting atmospheric and geophysical conditions with great earthquakes of the past few centuries has described a series of weird natural events coinciding with the disasters—anomalies even stranger than the odd behavior of lightning described in Chapter Five.

When these phenomena are considered in the light of the general theme of this book, they seem to be—in some as yet mysterious way—part and parcel of our complex star-interplanetary system, obeying the same laws as those to be outlined in the final chapters. These include thunder, strange atmospheric rumblings and explosions in the skies, hissing currents of wind in isolated areas, waves and strange commotions of the sea, meteors, auroras, electromagnetic disturbances, lightning, hail and rain when there's no accompanying storm, tornadoes and other whirlwinds. In addition, most animals and many people experience mental, emotional and psychic wrenches, sometimes hours or even days before the quake.

Charles Fort, the greatest deflater of scientific stuffed shirts in modern times, spent the major part of his life collecting data reported, recorded and witnessed by hundreds of thousands, perhaps millions, of people, many of them scientists, but rejected as preposterous, impossible, or downright hoaxes by scientific orthodoxy.

Comets, for example, are often associated with earthquakes and also with every conceivable sort of terrestrial catastrophe, including wars, epidemics, floods, even the fall of kings, emperors and other leaders.

In 1910, during the last appearance of Halley's Comet, Paris was flooded when the River Seine was swollen by unprecedented weeks of rainfall. The torrents in the city were so great that ten-story buildings were undermined and toppled into the swirling waters. Every bridge crossing the Seine was totally submerged. At the same time, similar floods occurred throughout France and in Germany and China.

Two years prior to the reappearance of Halley's Comet, another bright one—Morehouse's Comet—was interpreted by many astrologers in Italy as a dire warning of great earthquakes on the Italian peninsula. Messina was devastated by an earthquake shortly afterward. On March 17, 1906, an amateur astronomer named Ross reported his discovery of a new comet; it was being closely observed by the Lick Observatory as it neared its perihelion (closest to the Sun) passage a month later, April 17, 1906. When the killer quake struck San Francisco, the destruction of the city was completed by fires that burned everything to the ground. When Halley's Comet appeared in the skies in 1835 and 1836, New York City was virtually wiped out by uncontrollable fires that raged for several days and nights. A comet in 1755 coincided with a terrible earthquake in Lisbon that wiped out 40,000 lives. Meteors are also a fairly common occurrence during earthquakes. So are sudden, radical changes in the readings of magnetometers, gravimeters and devices that measure the EEC (electrical Earth current).

Early in the eighteenth century, a scientist named Von Hoff wrote a volume titled: *On the Influence of the Season of the Year and Time of Day upon Earthquakes.* Another book, now extremely rare, was published in 1729 by a professor at Lima, entitled *L'Horloge Astronomique des Tremblements de Terre.* He wrote of "the period of the tide and state of the Moon, as well as the Moon's place in the Zodiac; the critical time is confined to six hours and some minutes of the horary circle, within which the Moon is on the Meridian of the place." His results were confirmed by 143 observations in 1729 and by 70 in the following year, "which also proved correct."

Another writer of the era wrote that meteors "belong to the class of so-called globes of fire, and other extraordinary lights and illuminations (*Entzundungen*) in the regions of the air, which cannot be considered as belonging to the ordinary methods of electrical discharge."

Those strange "lights and illuminations" could be anything from auroras to UFOs. Whatever they may be, it seems certain that they belong to the same congeries of solar and interplanetary forces and energies as all other physical phenomena. As Philip Jose Farmer has one character say in his outrageous novel *Venus on the Half-Shell.* "Chance is merely ignorance on the part of the beholder."

"Meteors have been recorded to coincide with earthquakes directly over the stricken areas in 95 B.C., and

A.D. 893, 1001, 1325, 1640, 1674, 1683, 1703, 1737, 1752, 1756, 1810, 1820, 1821, 1824, 1828, 1829, 1831, 1833, and 1835. . . ." wrote Professor Von Hoff, who also observed, "There have been strange colourings of the heavens and unusual fogs noticed as occurring at the same time with earthquakes; such as the unusual colour of the sky at Lisbon on the 1st November, 1755, and the dry fog (Nebel), which was so thick as to produce total darkness, during the earthquake in Calabria in 1783."

The sources and scientific records of such phenomena are abundantly available, and Charles Fort collected them until his death in 1932. Initially, he accumulated 25,000 notes and stuffed them in pigeonholes that covered an entire wall of his home. They were not what he was trying to uncover, so he destroyed them and accumulated 40,000 more from the scientific journals of various nations during the past couple of centuries.

So powerful was his influence in unshackling the hidebound opinions of scientists that he eventually became a one-man institution, attracting freethinkers such as Oliver Wendell Holmes, Ben Hecht and R. Buckminster Fuller. The Fortean Society was founded by Tiffany Thayer to carry on his work. The last time I spoke with him, author-naturalist Ivan Sanderson and several assistants had inherited the job of decoding and classifying hundreds of shoeboxes full of Fort's notes—over 40 years after Fort's death. I don't know who is carrying on since Sanderson died. But Forteanism will always have its champions.

"Astronomers," he once observed, "are led by a cloud of rubbish by day and a pillar of bosh by night."

That was Fort—a strange, irreverent, brilliant, witty man. "I conceive of nothing, in religion, science or philosophy," he wrote, "that is more than the proper thing to wear, for a while." And "I do not know how to find out anything new without being offensive. . . . If our existence is an organism, in which all phenomena are continuous, dreams cannot be utterly different, in the view of continuity, from occurrences that are said to be real. . . . Witchcraft has always had a hard time, until it becomes established and changes its name. . . . There are persons who think they see clear advantages in a telephone—

then the telephone rings. . . . The unadulterated—whether of the food we eat, or the air we breathe, or of idealism, or of villainy—is unfindable. Even adultery is adulterated." And "I think we are property."

He accumulated countless records of events that were witnessed or measured or experienced, but rejected by science, and he put them into *The Book of the Damned.* "By 'damned,' I meant the excluded," he wrote. Three others followed: *New Lands, Wild Talents,* and *Lo!* He was mocked by *Time* magazine, which called him "a convinced prophet of footless negation." Fort laughed; he took nothing seriously, especially himself.

Fortean data include hundreds of examples of meteors streaking into areas being convulsed by earthquakes and weird weather accompanying or just preceding them:

> [From a *Report of the British Association:*] November 13, 1833: [after an earthquake in England] This thick fog . . . said to be precisely similar to the fog which accompanied the Lisbon earthquakes in 1807 and 1816 . . .
>
> July 26, 1804: Spoleto and as far as Nocera. Violent shocks, especially the first ones. . . . The air was full of thick fog, so that the Moon appeared a blood-red colour. [page 57]
>
> April 13, 1750: Lancaster to Wrexham, England . . . The heavens were obscured by a thick mist, in which red rays were observed converging towards a point near the zenith. The appearance lasted fifteen or twenty minutes. . . .
>
> April 15, 1752; Stavanger in Norway. Several violent shocks lasting several minutes. The weather was remarkably fine until 2 o'clock, when a small cloud rising extended itself over the heavens, and the whole evening there was a violent storm of wind, hail, and thunder and lightning; followed during the night by the appearance of a strange star of an octagonal shape, which seemed to throw forth balls of fire from its angles. [page 153]
>
> February 2, 1816; Lisbon. A severe shock . . . the people quitted their houses . . . heavy rain, and

> fog . . . A meteor appeared immediately after the first shock. Flocks of birds filled the air, uttering the most discordant cries. [page 106]

Charles Hoy Fort's original notes were made on anything at hand, scraps, envelopes, brown wrapping paper, etc. Many are almost illegible. During his tenure as secretary of the Fortean Society, Tiffany Thayer translated thousands of them. The best-known statement of Fort is, *"One measures a circle, beginning anywhere."*

This note is from the London *Times,* October 21, 1823 [page 2]

> 1823, Aug. 20. At Ragusa. Quake, phenomena black. On the 20th the air became (reverse) suddenly dark. A fiery meteor appeared over the city, and fell into the sea, followed by an earthquake that overthrew many houses. The sea retired nearly a mile from the shore.

The *Fortean Society Magazine* published the following items in its October, 1941 issue:

> 1819, June 16. Cutch, India/quake preceded by a violent wind and a noise like that of a large flight of birds (reverse) British Assoc. 1854/122.
>
> 1819, June 16. Quake of Cutch 1150 persons buried in the ruins of Bhooj. Said that from a hill was thrown (reverse) a ball of fire that then fell to the ground, scorching vegetation. Rain fell in torrents. Trans. Lit. Soc. Bombay. 3/90.

And from *English Mechanic,* 74:155:

> September 27, 1901: On the night of the Sept. 17 earthquake in Scotland, several remarkable meteoric appearances were seen an hour before the shock . . . areas of heavy fog . . . ribbon-like flashes of lightning seen through a dense mist, although no ordinary lightning was visible at the time . . .

From *Nature,* April 14, 1881:

> The destruction caused by the Chios earthquake has been even greater than estimated . . . the temperature on the 3rd was heavy and oppressive and the horizon was broken by broad flashes of light . . . seen through a heavy, descending mist. . . . In all this atmospheric disturbance however the inhabitants saw nothing extraordinary, and were far from being alarmed by what they fancied would result in a thunderstorm. At ten minutes to two in the afternoon a terrific shock was felt, bringing three-fourths of the houses in the town to the ground like so many packs of cards, and burying a thousand persons under the falling ruins.

From *Strange Phenomena,* compiled by William R. Corliss in 1974:

> In the south of Europe . . . numberless accounts of peculiar appearances before the earthquake, as red lurid skies, red and blue suns, and during the continuance of earthquakes of strange appearances and threatening portents [meteors] in the sky. . . .

Every conceivable atmospheric phenomena have been reported to accompany disastrous earthquakes throughout history:

> A calm sky, gray and cloudy, the atmosphere heated and heavy, occasional gusts of wind . . . Gentle showers of rain . . . The air clear, a gentle breeze blowing . . . The sun blotted out, the atmosphere black as night, lightning seen through shrouds of heavy mist . . . The sky red, great heat and stillness . . . Sudden drop in temperature, large hailstones . . . Showers of meteors seen rising from the south . . . Total darkness accompanied the first shock . . . A dense black cloud of vapor overshadowed the land . . . The atmosphere was filled with smoke or fog at Herculaneum so that a boat

> could not be seen 20 paces . . . Sulphurous or otherwise obnoxious odors and vapors were an attendant feature of the earthquake . . . The shock was accompanied ever and anon by flashes of electricity, rendered the darkness doubly terrible. At St. Louis gleams and flashes of light were frequently visible around the horizon in different directions, *generally ascending from the earth* [!] . . . Geese painfully aware of the approach of the earthquake at Calabria . . . The neighing of horses and braying of asses, the cackling of geese drove the people out of their homes in expectation of the shock . . . All birds appear sensible to the approach of the earthquake, but geese, swine, and dogs more remarkably than any other animals; the geese quit the waters before the earthquake and will not return to it . . . Globs of fire in the skies accompanied by great explosions and a fog that enveloped Euphemia [Sicily] before it was destroyed by the earthquake of 1638. . . ."

And so it goes—bolides, ball lightning, auroras, the radical behavior of gravity meters and magnetometers. Modern science is totally unable to deduce any connection among the extraordinarily diverse phenomena that coincide with the quakes of great intensity. Neither can I, except for the possible explanation that they are all related in some as yet unfathomable way. "One measures a circle beginning anywhere." It makes more sense than classifying, categorizing and compartmentalizing "unrelated" data into various scientific specialties (where specialists have no knowledge of or interest in what is being discovered in diverse fields). Discovering the system that ties everything together may be a gargantuan task, possibly one beyond our present capabilities—but I don't think so. Thanks to the efforts of Fort's successors, notably the *INFO* (International Fortean Organization) *Journal,* the Smithsonian Institution was finally prodded into moving closer toward recognition that such short-lived events, previously considered beyond the scope or capability of most scientists, should be studied—even nature's anomalies.

So, in 1968, the Smithsonian made a giant strike in the

right direction by establishing The Center for Short-Lived Phenomena. This has since become an international clearinghouse of interesting, unusual, even mysterious data on transient events. A global network of over 3,000 scientists, institutions, research laboratories and field stations feeds a continuous flow of information to the Center through its around-the-clock communications facilities. "The Center's immediate response capabilities and near-real-time reportage of often strange, sudden or unexpected short-lived phenomena" have made it, according to the Soviet Academy of Sciences, "the most valuable scientific organization ever conceived." The Russians appear to be among the most enthusiastic member-contributors of the Center. So far, however, the only types of events reported are Earth Sciences, Biological Sciences. Pollution Events, Astronomical Events, Urgent Archaeological and Urgent Anthropological Events. Its scope and its depth of reportage, however, are increasing rapidly.

But not fast enough to make predictions. Two scholars, Alfred L. Webre and Phillip H. Liss, in their book *The Age of Cataclysm* (published coincidentally in 1974 with *The Jupiter Effect* by Drs. Gribbin and Plagemann), also cite gathering signs of ominous portent for the immediate future of the world.

> Clear and incontrovertible evidence exists that large and densely populated areas of the globe face destruction from natural disaster: from earthquake, tidal wave, flood, and drought. There is evidence of a growing pattern in nature which is fundamentally hostile to man and which will persist through the next generation. While science does not yet know the exact intensity of these disasters, and their precise times of occurrence, it does know for a fair certainty that they are coming. While scientists still disagree on how widespread the pattern of natural hostility will be, it is known that at least a sixth of mankind, 500 million persons, will be affected by earthquake alone. Moreover, the coming disasters are in large measure likely to occur in areas of the globe which have no recent memory of natural catastrophe, and

where a modern civilization has grown up largely ignorant of and, in many cases, openly scoffing at nature.

America, the New Atlantis?

Despite its apparently sensational nature, Webre and Liss's book doesn't stop at presenting all the reasons for the coming earth changes. They also provide a detailed blueprint for its aftermath.

Under the subtitle "Survival and Regeneration," they outline the biophysical and psychosocial environment attendant to the expected disasters, and describe how a "Future World Society" can be built to continue—even to improve—the condition of the new global society, carrying over and adding vastly to the accumulated knowledge of the present world age.

My own estimate is that if this happens, a single new science will emerge—a mighty system of knowledge that will recognize the essential interrelatedness and unity of everything known and knowable.

Of necessity, part of that system will be a highly refined version of the fragments of data that have trickled through to the present era as astrometeorology—one of astrology's several facets.

As the Chinese scientist and philosopher Su-Shu Huang described it: "Although seemingly unpredictable, the progress of a science usually has three stages. First, some new means of experiment or observation is developed into a powerful tool. It provides a fresh look at Nature. In the second, the proliferation of data may cause frustration and bewilderment, since the new results may not be understandable on the basis of known scientific principles. In general this stage lasts longest. But sooner or later final clarification comes, for someone develops a new concept that explains the baffling results naturally and in a straightforward manner."

Let's try to do just that.

10

CYCLES–BASIC PRINCIPLES OF COSMIC WEATHER PREDICTION

SOME ELECTROMAGNETIC WAVES are so short that it takes hundreds of them to span the breath of a human hair. Others change in length from a few miles to as much as—for all we know—a thousand light years. There are cosmic cycles so long that they reach across measureless vistas of time—far beyond all known or suspected human history. Yet ancient peoples all over the world had broad knowledge of such cycles—cycles that often extended long before their own vast historical epochs.

. . . Chaldean and Metonic eclipse cycles, for example, and the Hindu *Yugas*. Following the *Maha* and other *Yugas*, the *Kali Yuga* cycle began at approximately the same time as establishment of Christianity as a religion about A.D. 321. Each Yuga is one twelfth of the anciently known Great year of 25,920 years—2,160 years long. The *Yugas* are based on the precession of the Equinoxes, the slight *backward* motion of the Sun during each succeeding spring and autumn equinox. It takes 72 years for the spring equinox to precede just one degree.

Capricorn, Aquarius and Pisces are the last three signs. From about November 22 to March 21 the Earth's orbit makes the Sun appear to move through these signs—in that order. On March 21 the Sun again enters the first sign, Aries, and repeats its 360° transit above and below (north and south of) the plane of the ecliptic.

Because the Sun appears just a little earlier each March 21 (when the celestial equator and the plane of the ecliptic coincide), this slight increment accumulates into 30°, or an entire zodiacal sign (*not constellation*), every 2,160 years. The Age of Pisces, therefore, began about A.D. 321, coinciding with the establishment of the Christian church. Prior to their emancipation by Constantine, early Christians used two fishes joined together as their symbol. The preceding Age, Aries the Ram, began around 1840 B.C., and the Age of Taurus the Bull in 4000 B.C. The symbols of both ages were *horned* animals.

Astronomically, the Age of Aquarius won't begin until 2480, so we're still in the Age of Pisces, current fads and songs notwithstanding. It's interesting that in each age the gods of the previous dominating religion become the enemies of the new one. The Christian concept of Satan is that of a *horned* creature. It's no mere coincidence then, that Baal, the Semitic deity of the Old Testament during the Ages of the Ram and the Bull, was also a horned creature. Baal, in all his manifestations, varied according to local custom. At Edron he was called Baalzebub; scores of cities bear variations of his name to this day—Baalbek, Baal-hamon, Baal-borith, Baal-peor, Baal-perazim. Baal-gad and Baal-zephon, to name a few. The horn of fertility correlation was carried into the later ages and nations, Pan, the Greek god of fertility, and those lesser deities, the satyrs, were all horned creatures with insatiable sexual appetites. The concept drifted into parts of Asia where even today there is a brisk, lucrative sale of powdered rhinoceros horn, which is considered an aphrodisiac.

Because the worship of Baal was characterized by fertility cults that engaged in mass orgies, conflict arose in places such as Baal-peor between worshipers of the God of Israel and the Hebrew Baal-worshipping apostasies, ostensibly because the latter were orgiastic. Initially the Hebrews used the name of Baal for their god without discrimination, but the growing clashes involved elements of nationalism, ethics and moralism, and the ensuing struggle for supremacy between monotheism and Caananite polytheism (Baal-worship) intensified. Eventually the name Baal was totally altered or discarded among monotheistic Hebrew names. Esh-baal became Ishbosheth, Jerubbaal was changed to Jerrubethesheth, and Meribbaal became Mephisosheth, and so on.

In the Old Testament (notably Hosea 2. 16, 17) Baali, in Hebrew meaning "my Baal," is abandoned, and over a period of time Baal-peor and its derivatives became symbolic of shameful apostasies. Public sexuality became generally taboo. By the time of the dawn of the Age of Pisces, it was well established in Judaism, Christianity and Islam that the horned creature was the principle of evil—oddly enough named "Satan" by all three of the monotheistic religions. His chief activity in the world, which he allegedly still roams, is the destruction of souls, his favorite method being temptation, particularly in carnal or sexual activities.

If religions are not abandoned within five centuries—at least the kinds that encourage one faith to regard all others as "wrong," thereby making man his own enemy—what will the dominating religion of the Age of Aquarius be like? Whatever humanistic cults may arise, maybe it's not completely facetious to expect that *their* devil will be some form of fish.

According to the kabalistic cycles, the last Age of Aquarius was about 26,420 years ago. Just as the Great Year of 25,920 years is divided into 12 segments of 2,160 years (one Zodiacal Age), these ages are divided into subcycles of 360 years and *sub*-subcycles of 36 years each.

In Sepharial's Hebrew astrology: *The World Horoscope,* and in the *Kali Yuga,* these 36-year cycles coincide in the most amazing way. In my own book *Astrology: The Space Age Science* (Signet, The New American Library) I published an interpretation of the *Kali Yuga* cycles covering almost a century; they were divided into *seven*-year segments, beginning in 1912 and ending with the year 2010.

These interpretations were given to me by George J.

McCormack in 1961 when he had just received them from his colleague, Nora Forrest, in Cleveland, an elderly and respected practitioner and scholar of astrology. "They were given to me by Raymond McDermott of Pittsburgh in 1945 and I was asked to watch their accuracy. He passed away four or five years ago," she wrote in 1961, "was blind and secured this from some of his Theosophical friends during the First World War."

That was either in 1914 or 1918, I'm not sure. Nora Forrest assured us that they were exactly as she received them at the end of World War II. I included them in my book in 1966 just as I had received them. Although I can personally vouch for their authenticity only since 1961, I have every confidence that they are also authentic since 1945 because I knew Nora Forrest to be objective, factual and ethical.

The 36-year Aquarian sub-subcycle of the World Horoscope began in 1945 and will end in 1981, coinciding closely with the period of expected cataclysms; it's interesting to note that world conditions characteristic of the astrological nature of the sign of Aquarius (freedom, equality and eccentric humanism) commenced with the end of World War II—a victory which brought two former adversaries, the United States and the Soviet Union, into a close alliance (the Soviet Union's horoscope, as well as that of the United States, the United Arab Republic, and to a lesser degree, that of Israel, have strong Aquarius aspects). America has the Moon in Aquarius, Russia has the Sun in Aquarius. All four nations, despite vast ideological, political and geographic differences, have played major roles in world events during the Aquarian cycle. This changes in 1981 when we enter the Pisces cycle. What will happen between 1982 and 2017, when the 36-year cycle of Aries begins?

Considering the dire and ominous prophesies, forecasts and predictions previously outlined, the following three seven-year segements of the *Kali Yuga* are an indication of human endurance and survival:

1961-1968 Ruler—Sun/positive. *There is an old prophesy that the greatest of the Popes is to arise in this century and this would seem to be the time for the "Flower of Flowers" as he is called. It is to be the last glory of the Catholic Church as changes in the church rules are indicated. This is the period in which the United States of America could have its first Catholic President. Racially, there is a decided coalition among the nations. Asia and Africa may be unfriendly to the United States.*

1968-1975 Ruler—Moon/positive. *Wide changes in ideas are instituted about property, and taxation will be more reduced than economists in 1945 thought possible so soon. Racially, the Arab peoples will be feeling the strength of unity and it will take statesmanship to keep the new power within bounds.*

1975-1982 Ruler Mars/negative. *Rumors of wars and dissatisfaction with restraints on nations are indicted. Possible war will threaten from Arabs and from Eastern Asia. Since this is a negative Mars cycle, the period of peace should not end entirely.* THIS IS THE PERIOD IN WHICH NATURAL CATACLYSMS COULD TAKE PLACE.

They continue in this vein, predicting travel into unknown worlds between 1982 and 1989. And by 1996, terrible calamaties that engulf the world, and a kind of superwar—an Armageddon-type conflict. One of Nostradamus' quatrains is interpreted as an invasion of Earth by alien beings. The conspicuous accuracy of past interpretations of the *Kali Yuga* inclines one to check them periodically and, if they continue so accurately, a talented astrologer should be able to decipher its cyclic system.

The interaction of cosmic with atmospheric and geologic events can be discerned more easily, however, without recourse to such arcane or occult systems. In astro-weather forecasting, the revolving Earth, the Sun, Moon and planets pinpoint the time and reveal the character of coming natural events.

The crucial periodicities are the orbits of the planets (Earth included) around the Sun and the Moon's 27⅓-day orbit of the Earth. The Earth's daily rotation on its axis is as important in timing astrological events as it is in computing the exact ebb and flow of the tides.

Geocentric (Earth-centered) instead of heliocentric (Sun-centered) calculations are used for the simple reason that we live on the Earth, not the Sun. Heliocentric charts are valuable in forecasting solar storms, sunspots, and the like, but the Moon's effect, relatively, is *billions* of times less on the Sun than it is on the Earth because the small lunar influence on solar activity is inseparable from that of the Earth, as was pointed out in Chapter Three. With good computers, an astrophysicist probably could determine the insignificant effect of Mars' two tiny moons on the Sun.

It is absolutely necessary, yet relatively easy, to master the technique of computing the exact positions of the planets, the Sun and the Moon as observed from any point on the globe and for any given moment in time. The circle in the center of the geocentric chart represents the Earth and is surrounded by 12 segments (areas or "channels") through which the planets move at varying velocities, depending on their mass and distance from the Sun. Our local star's position at each of the four seasons (and the aspects made to it by the planets) is the chief determining factor in long-range forecasting.

Positive and negative angles constantly forming and separating (not only among the planets but also to local geographic meridians) correlate to electromagnetic, gravitational and other subtle forces that shape atmospheric conditions. The exact calculation of the eastern horizon at any meridian, which *constantly changes according to the latitude,* is also very crucial.

The Earth turns on its axis, constantly altering the fine "tuning" of exogenous forces which are calculated according to planetary positions over various geographic locations. This is analogous to tuning in different radio stations or switching TV channels.

When conjunctions between major planets are divided into subcycles of one-eighth their orbits, they serve as the basis for other familiar periodicities. The 13.81-year *synodic* conjunction period of Jupiter and Uranus, for example, is an important and powerful generator of the 41-month economic cycle used so effectively by astroeconomists. *Synodical* pertains to the "conjunction of two heavenly bodies—of the revolution, or period of revolution, of a planet between two successive conjunctions with the Sun, or of a satellite between two successive conjunctions with (or occulations or eclipses by) its primary planet."

In a slightly more technical application of astro-weather interpretation, the astrometeorologist figures the influence of eclipses, the 18.6-year rotation of the lunar nodes,* the 11.88-year periods of Jupiter's perihelion (closest to the Sun), and the 15-year *major* perigee (closest possible approach to Earth) of Mars. The Red Planet also makes a series of *minor* perigee passages at approximate two-year intervals.

The angles formed, or configurations among, the planets are basic elements in astronomic weather forecasting. They indicate the times of major, intermediate and minor changes. The influences of the major planets often last out the entire season. The more fast-moving inner planets activate brief or sporadic changes in the weather by quick-forming aspects to the Sun and/or the Moon. Naturally, since the Moon is the fastest-moving celestial body (in the geocentric scheme), it makes more transitory aspects than any other. Configurations of fast-moving bodies—Moon, Mercury and Venus—provide very exact measures for *timing* changes in the weather.

Specific areas for such changes are determined as far in advance as desired from key maps of these planetary configurations. With a little practice, it becomes fairly easy to set up a chart, say, for Philadelphia or New York, and with simple calculations transpose it for Butte, Montana, or anywhere east or west of the original meridian.

Without realizing it, the United States Weather Bureau and all orthodox meteorologists have been using the Moon for over a century to time atmospheric conditions as they move eastward. In geocentric longitude the Moon's average daily motion is 13° 10′ (13 degrees, ten minutes). There are 360° of both geographic and celestial longitude *and* latitude; each degree is composed of 60 minutes (′)

* Nodes are those points in space where the Moon (or planet) crosses the plane of the ecliptic.

of arc and each minute contains 60 seconds (″) of arc. Very exact measurements of the surrounding celestial sphere are possible because there are 77,760,000 seconds of arc in the complete circle of 360°, i.e., 60″ × 60′ × 360° = 77,760,000.

Numerologists make much of the fact that whichever way you measure it, the number *always* add up to 9. There are 3,600 seconds in one minute of arc—3 + 6 + 0 + 0 = 9. And there are 216,000 seconds in one degree of arc: 2 + 1 + 6 + 0 + 0 + 0 = 9. Also, there are 21,600 minutes of arc in the circle, which adds up to 9, as does the complete 360° and its component 77,760,000 seconds.

The curious coincidence that the digits of cosmic figures so often reduce numerically to 9 is regarded by the occult-minded as profoundly meaningful. They cite the Bible (Revelations XIII:18): "Here is wisdom. Let him that hath understanding count the number of the beast; for it is the number of a man; and his number is six hundred three score and six." Six hundred and sixty six (666) adds to 18, the digits of which add up to 9. As noted earlier, the precession of the equinoxes occurs a fraction earlier each year. It takes 72 years for the Sun to precede just *one* degree of celestial arc. Seven plus 2 of course, are also 9.

The Grand Year known to ancient astrologers is the same as modern astronomy's Great Sidereal Year—25,-920 years—the time it takes for the Sun to precede through the entire 360° of the zodiac. The digits add to 18, which again adds up to 9.

Whether you add up the minutes of the day (1,440) or all the seconds (86,400) the digits always add to 9. Whether it's merely a mathematical peculiarity of multiples of 9 or has some deep occult significance, the fact remains that *any* number of degrees of equinoctial precession equate to 9. Two degrees take 144 years, three degrees 270 years, ten degrees 720 years, five degrees 360 years, and so on and on.

Interesting as they are, the foregoing facts might be dismissed lightly if it weren't for the fact that the average normal rate of human respiration is 18 times a minute and the mean normal heartbeat 72 times a minute. In one hour, therefore, the average heart beats 4,320 times, and the average number of respirations is 1,080. Your heart beats an average of 103,680 times each 24-hour day; in the same period you inhale and exhale an average of 25,920 times (remember the Great Sidereal Year?). There are so many "coincidences" that you're almost compelled to perceive an overall pattern of principle with the number 9 intimately involved with human existence. The human gestation period, for example, is about nine months or 270 days.

Is it also mere coincidence, therefore, that the major harmonious angles formed among the planets (30, 60°, 120°, and 150°) equate to 3 or 6, and that the adverse or major *discordant* aspects of 45°, 90°, 135°, and 180° each add to 9? Masters of the kabalastic system observed that the reduced sum of *all* digits is 9. Therefore, 1, 2, 3, 4, 5, 6, 7, 8, and 9 equal 45, which adds up to 9!

There does seem to be a close bond between numerology and astrology, but one we can't do justice to here.

The average daily motion of the Moon, 13° 10′ (about 33′ an hour) moving eastward, varies, being faster or slower at different times. Consequently, when the lunar motion of 33′ of celestial longitude is transposed to the Earth's surface, it corresponds to the average west-to-east movement of atmospheric conditions. Under new dominating seasonal patterns, transitions develop into eastward-moving weather changes.

The three fundamental rules in astrometerology are that (a) the Sun dominates the constitution of the atmosphere, (b) the planets correspond to organic changes, and (c) the Moon is *functional,* meaning that our satellite triggers (and times) the constitutional and organic modifications of weather patterns in eastward transit. The Moon is in no way fundamental; all its transits and configurations with other bodies are *secondary* or reflective.

The fact that orthodox meteorology places such great reliance on a seemingly endless supply of sophisticated computers, and other sensitive instruments, on balloons, aircraft, rockets, Weather Eye satellites, thousands of ground observers and a huge store of weather records going back a century or more, gives the field no ability at all to predict weather reliably 20 or 30 days in advance. As for accurate *seasonal* forecasts, George J. McCormack, an old man armed only with pencil and paper—in a published series of tests in 1963 and 1964—proved he could predict the dominating patterns of entire geographic areas two and even three seasons in advance with as much accuracy as, or more accuracy than, standard meteorology can predict for the next 48-hour period for just *one* specific location.

In such extremely long-range forecasting, however, the global picture must be taken into account. First you must know what you're looking for and where and how to find it. Scientists refuse to accept this, but there *are* definite (critically tested) weather cycles.

The *dominating* patterns of very abnormal weather migrate over great distances *westward* each year, and to different regions each season. *Minor* migratory weather patterns occur on a monthly basis.

When George McCormack formally presented his system to the Weather Bureau and the American Meteorological Society in 1963 and 1964, he made a *non*-weather prediction: "I will venture to say that by 1981 this system of astronomic long-range weather forecasting will be part of the standard curriculum in our universities."

They weren't buying it.

It took the combined efforts of Senators Jacob Javits and Kenneth Keating, and, over an extended period, Keating's successor, Robert F. Kennedy, to twist enough arms and bring enough political pressure to bear on the chief of the United States Weather Bureau to set up a special seminar in their New York offices so that McCormack could present the results of his life's work to the government. To say that the weather bureaucrats unwillingly complied with their orders, and in a cold, unfriendly manner, is an understatement. They were downright hostile. Even the enthusiastic support and presence of John H. Nelson, who was then making successful planetary weather forecasts for RCA, did nothing to neutralize the preconceived contempt in which the weathermen held the "outsider."

It was contagious. The science reporter sent over by *The New York Times* had already interviewed the local bureau chiefs when we arrived; they merely confirmed what he already "knew"—that anybody who believed in the influence of the planets on *anything* was nuts. He made no attempt to conceal his disdain.

McCormack was understandably nervous; here he was making the first formal presentation of the system that had made his name and image a household word among the editors of half a dozen New York and New Jersey papers, and was being mocked for his efforts. "Look at that," the local bureau chief stage-whispered to his assistant as the old man was reading his paper to them. "His fuckin' hand is shaking!"

Some scientists.

The thick dossier of newspaper stories, including many headlines of McCormack's bulls-eye long-range predictions notwithstanding, the report on the seminar sent to Senators Javits and Kennedy by the chief of the USWB in Washington (with copies relayed by them to us) merely confirmed our worst suspicions. It was a grab bag of negative opinions—statements like "There is no basis for further investigation . . . no valid theory exists . . . Everyone knows there's no appreciable effect on the weather by cosmic bodies beyond that of the Sun . . ." etcetera.

McCormack drew a detailed picture of the relationship between Saturn and influenza epidemics for the reluctant meteorologists, several of whom exchanged snickers when he told them of the connection between weather and health. "Saturn in Aquarius is the key to the next outbreak of influenza," he told them. "On February 19, 1964, it transits 15° 43′ Aquarius on the exact degree of the total solar eclipse of February 4, 1962, which fell on the sixth house over the United States. The deduction should be fairly obvious."

A deadly flu epidemic struck early in 1964. In June, *The New York Times* published a graph indicating the numbers of hospitalized flu victims over the previous 15-month period. *The highest peak of the graph was Febru-*

ary 19. In New York City alone, 250 people died of the disease.

No comment from the Weather Bureau.

Under planetary configurations involving Venus, the weather tends to be more moderate and gentler than that of any other planet. Rain or snow falls vertically with no wind. Even when Venus is aspecting unpredictable Uranus, the rain is a gentle drizzle. With Mars, Venus corresponds to a dashing rain, and with Saturn a deep low pressure, but not very powerful air flows when following normal patterns.

Every eight years Venus reaches the same longitude on approximately the same date of the year. In the following chapters, basic rules such as the fact that we get the wettest, sloppiest sort of weather when Venus is in Scorpio, will be presented in finer detail.

PART TWO

11

MAJOR STATIONS AND ASPECTS OF PLANETS

WALTER GORN OLD, an astrometeorologist of the past century, widely known under his pen name Sepharial, made this observation: "Watching for coincidences is a necessary process of scientific discovery; and coincidences between astronomic and atmospheric phenomena should be observed and noted. We know nothing of physical causes except by observing instances of what appear to be invariable and necessary sequences. After a certain amount of experience we assume the invariability and the necessity and we do so most readily when one set of experiences is backed up and supported by other sets of experiences. The observation of sufficient coincidences in number may justify the acceptance of an empirical law according to which we may, with approximate safety, predict that when one of the events happens, the other will accompany or follow. To get beyond a merely empirical law of this kind, we require the support of another series of inductions or as many more as we can obtain."

This is the practical engineering approach: If it works, use it; the hell with how or why—we'll learn that later. Because theoretical scientists insist on understanding *why* first, they've hindered the progress of science.

Watching for coincidences between astronomic and atmospheric phenomena means referring to cardinal solar ingress charts (the equinoxes and solstices), and eclipses, both of which are implemented by New and Full Moon charts as *timing* elements. From these maps of the planets at the exact times of the year when the Sun enters the four cardinal points—the moment each of the four seasons begins—you calculate where the planets are in any of the cosmically "active" lines or angles to specific locations on the Earth. When planets at these times are grouped together in the sixth segment of the chart, their influence on public health in that area should be carefully studied.

The cycles of conjunctions (0°), oppositions (180°), trines (120°) and quadratures (90°) among the planets are especially important when they occur among the massive, slow-orbiting outer planets—Jupiter, Saturn, Neptune and Uranus. Mars has a two-year minor perigee and a 15-year major perigee (i.e., closest approach to the Earth) period which coincides with and intensifies the potential for inflammatory-type epidemics (called "martial" ailments).

According to Ptolemy's 35th aphorism, "When the Sun arrives at the place of any planet, he *excites* the influence of that planet in the atmosphere." With a little practice, this can be verified by recording the dates when the Sun forms a conjunction with any planet in *geocentric* longitude. At the times of conjunction and opposition, planets (including the Sun and Moon) that are at the same degree above or below the ecliptic (which is the orbit of the Earth around the Sun because it is in this plane that eclipses occur) are said to be in *parallel declination.* In other words, if Jupiter, Mars and the Sun all happen to be 3° north of the ecliptic, they are parallel in declination, which reacts on the atmosphere exactly as would a conjunction and is interpreted this way. If, say, Jupiter and Saturn happen to be in conjunction (or opposition, square, trine or any other aspect) and at the same time *also* parallel in declination, it *intensifies the aspect.*

These interpretations, particularly when there are many factors to be considered, require considerable practice in the art of *synthesizing* all the elements. No computer in existence at this writing is capable of making such judgments. It is not, however, all that difficult to learn astrometeorology. What it requires is time, effort and the enthusiasm it takes to master anything worthwhile. But of one thing I am certain—as McCormack told the weather bureaucrats, astrometeorology will become a respected profession, and anyone who masters the fundamentals now will become one of the scientists who practice, teach and perfect it in the future.

Never, therefore, overlook parallels of declinations among or between celestial bodies that happen to be in any of the other angular relationships in celestial longitude. If Mars and Venus are both 15°, 12′ of Leo, and each happens to be, say, 18° north *latitude*, their conjunction influences the atmosphere with intensified strength. *Contra*-parallels of declination—the Sun 8° north latitude, and Uranus 8° south, for example—are also effective, but not so much as the parallel.

In tracing the historic epidemics of cholera and influenza, I learned that a Chinese astrologer named Ling traced 19 distinct plagues that occurred at 17-year intervals from A.D. 287 to A.D. 460—a period of 173 years. In 1918, astrometeorologist John Hazelrigg (G. J. McCormack's teacher) found that the adverse configurations of the major planets, notably Saturn and Neptune, coincided with epidemics in 1832, 1849, 1866, 1883 and 1910.

According to Pythagoras, the mathematician and astrologer of Greek antiquity, easterly winds that move in a direction contrary to the normal rotation of the Earth, which is from west to east, are under the dominion of Saturn and have been observed to prevail coincident with outbreaks of disease.

Every time a planet transits the point in celestial longitude where the last solar eclipse occurred, there's a terrestrial reaction corresponding to the nature of the planets involved, the aspects they make and the sign in which the eclipse took place. The aspects, incidentally, aside from the conjunction (0°) are multiples of 15 and 18, i.e., 30, 45, 60, 75, 90, 105, 120, 135, 150, 165 and 180 degrees, and 36, 72, (90), 108, 126, 144, 162 and (180), respectively. However, the conjunction, opposition, square, trine and sextile are the fundamental, most important aspects.

The basic celestial maps are essentially the same kind of horoscopes as those erected by a very painstaking astrologer. It's only fair to report that a very large percentage (the majority, in fact) of the charts I've seen calculated—often by those who practice astrology professionally—are slapdash approximations, mathematical near misses, and at times totally wrong. I once saw an astrologer charge a client $125 without bothering to erect a chart; he made his interpretations directly from the ephemeris (a book giving the geocentric positions of the Sun, the Moon and the planets day by day, sometimes for periods of five to ten years or more). All too often astrologers use rules that have no scientific or empirical basis whatever. With no practical experience in observation or testing, they have interpreted horoscopes in which mythical or imaginary "points in space" were used. Some of these, the Arabic Parts, for example, contain "the Part of Fortune, the Part of Death," etcetera, as though they were real planets. One such school of astrology is called "Uranian," and uses eight mythical planets that supposedly *lie beyond the orbit of Pluto!* One very successful writer and teacher (who, incidentally, influences the minds of thousands of students who attend his "school") even added six *additional* planets that he supposedly detected orbiting *beyond* the eight of the Uranian system. He teaches this system to gullible people (at very fat fees) who flock to his classes and conscientiously copy down the distances, orbital speeds, celestial longitude and declinations of fourteen nonexistent bodies, then use their "knowledge" to cast and interpret horoscopes—often professionally. Some of these charlatans actually issue "diplomas."

The different systems of *house division* are something I won't go into except to say that astrologers using them often give totally unrelated interpretations based on the same data. Small wonder, then, that in the September–October 1975 issue of *The Humanist* magazine (now defunct), an attack against astrological fraud and charlatanry was launched by astronomer Bart J. Bok and signed by 186 scientists. It's perfectly understandable (except that none of the scientists had ever taken the trouble to investigate or test astrology before condemning it).

A simple investigation of people born at the same time and place, however, should reveal whether or not planets influence people who have the same horoscopes. In such cases, "parallelism" should be evident in their lives. (I'm investigating one group—children born during the five-planet conjunction and total solar eclipse in Aquarius of February 4 and 5, 1962. If you know of such people, or are one, I would be very happy to hear from you.)

Although the calculation of planetary positions for a specific moment in time and geographic longitude and latitude must always be done with care and precision, anyone of average intelligence can learn to do it in an hour, more or less, as we'll demonstrate.

The charts used for seasonal forecasts, i.e., when the Sun enters the two solstices and the two equinoxes (or any *one* of them) are called *ingress maps*. Because the Sun is always south as seen from the northern hemisphere, the *upper* part of the chart (shown in figure 1) the Mid-heaven, is south. Planets at the four cardinal points, that is, the first, fourth, seventh or tenth sector (or "house"), counting *counterclockwise* from the Ascendant (the eastern horizon or extreme *left* of the wheel), are more important when they appear in these angles of the ingress maps.

To supplement each solar ingress, the lunation (New Moon) and Full Moon charts provide additional chronological refinement. These bimonthly charts will reveal solar and lunar eclipses because they occur only when the Moon's nodes are aligned in the same direction as the Sun. Eclipse charts are especially valuable, and should be studied for future planetary transits across the eclipse point or any of the aforementioned aspects that trigger the degree of the previous eclipse.

The *meridian* (the observer's geographic location or *any* chosen terrestrial latitude and longitude) is extremely important because the planetary aspects to that point (in astrometerology) operate the same as those aspects between and among the planets themselves.

The *cusps* (lines dividing one channel or "house" from another) are the same from pole to pole. At any longitude, the exact degree and minute of the ascendant varies according to the terrestrial *latitude*.

Weather patterns normally travel in the same direction as that of the Earth's axial rotation—from west to east. Whatever attractive force, mechanism or characteristic exists at the point of observation (the meridian of the chart), it is determined from the fourth sector (house or channel). Any planets in that "angle"—whether in a solar ingress chart or by transit—will have a strong impression on the atmosphere and should be given serious study and consideration.

Any basic astronomical textbook will provide necessary knowledge, or the "feel" of the solar system, purely the mechanics of its structure and function, the mass, volume, velocities and orbits of the planets, satellites and the Sun. A solar year, for example, is exactly 365 days, 5 hours, 48 minutes, 45.51 seconds long. The revolution of the moon —i.e., its *tropical* period—is 27 days, 7 hours, 43 minutes and 4.7 seconds. But the *synodic* period—from New Moon—is 29 days, 12 hours and 44.05 minutes. Its apogee (maximum distance from Earth) is 252,710 miles, and its perigee (closest Earth approach) 221,463 miles.

The plane of the lunar orbit is inclined at an angle of 5° 8′ to the plane of the ecliptic—the Earth's orbit. The lines at which these two planes intersect are called the north and south lunar nodes. These nodes "moved backward" 19° each year and take 18.6 years to retrograde through the 12 signs of the zodiac. There are two major eclipse cycles, the Metonic and the Chaldean. The Metonic is 18 years, 218 days, 21 hours, 22 minutes and 46 seconds. This was deduced by Meton, the Greek astronomer of Athens (circa 432 B.C.) and embraced 235 lunar months. The Moon's phases in every 19th year occur on the same date. The number of any year in the Metonic cycle is known as a golden number and is used to determine the date of Easter.

The Chaldean eclipse cycle is 18 years, 10 days, 7 hours,

42 minutes and 34 seconds; the discrepancy between this cycle and the Metonic cycle is explained by the difference between the *synodic* (Metonic) as compared to the tropical (Chaldean) periods.

It takes 27 days, 13 hours, 18 minutes and 3.31 seconds for the Moon to orbit from perigee to perigee (closest to Earth), and this is called the anomalistic lunar month. At perigee, lunar influence on the Earth is stronger. After nearly nine (actually 8.85) years, the lunar perigee returns to the same position.

Concentrations of the planets, the Sun and/or Moon in southern declinations—i.e., south of the plane of the ecliptic—intensifies the lower temperatures of the northern hemisphere and increases the heat in the *southern* hemisphere. When planets are bunched in northern declinations, the reverse is true.

According to their natures (combined with the characteristics of the sign they're in), the influence of major planets on the atmosphere when they're (a) on the celestial equator (0° latitude), (b) in perigee, (c) in perihelion or (d) at their solstitial colure, is more widespread and pronounced. Colure describes the situation when two great circles which intersect each other at right angles at the poles divide the equinoctial and the ecliptic into four equal parts. One passes through the equinoctial, the other through the solstitial points of the ecliptic.

Finally, when timing planetary aspects and all other phenomena, the 24-hour clock is the most practical, with midnight at 00:00. Noon is 12:00, 16:00 stands for 4 P.M., 20:00 for 8:00 P.M. and 11:30 P.M. becomes 23:30 P.M.

12

NATURE AND CHARACTERISTIC FORCES OF THE PLANETS

IN THE MYSTERIOUS and often mystical realm of particle physics, scientists are hot on the trail of the elusive "ultimate" particle. The atoms that make up molecules are themselves composed of electrons, protons, neutrons and positrons that seem to closely resemble tiny solar systems. Beyond the ongoing discovery of mesons, quarks and theoretical tachyons, however, physicists are finding energy particles with characteristics such as "strangeness" and even "charm." Some of these are ultra-heavy, astonishingly long-lived subatomic particles.

Nobody knows just how, where or when the even more intriguing natures and characteristics of the larger bodies, the planets, were discovered, but each planet has a character closely related to the area of the zodiac with which it is associated or said to "rule." Mars and Aries, the fire sign (0° to 30° of celestial longitude) have this affinity; so do Mercury and the air sign, Gemini (60°–90°), Saturn and the earth sign, Capricorn (270°–300°), and Neptune with the water sign, Pisces (330°–360°).

These are just examples of the four "elements," fire, earth, air and water, which are *symbols* of the kind of influence each planet has. Here, then, is a preliminary description of the positive and negative characters of each celestial body in relation to its effect on the Earth's atmosphere.

Mercury, the Sun's closest and fastest planet, has an observed electrical influence on our atmosphere (related to high barometer). Its effect is modified, however, by the nature of any planet it conjoins or with which it comes into any other aspect. By forming an angular contact with Mars, Mercury generates acute, often sharp and whipping winds. With Venus, gentle breezes, tending to southerlies. When Mercury is stationary, or in superior conjunction with the Sun, it produces a high barometer and strong winds, and during winter months, cold waves, high winds and often blizzard-breeding storms over the higher inlands. In parallel of declination or any of the following five aspects with Uranus—0°, 180°, 60°, 45° or 90°—Mercury correlates to erratic, gusty or gale winds downslope, with falling temperatures.

If Mercury happens to be in apparent retrograde motion, there will likely be storm emergencies for power and communications lines. In favorable aspects to Saturn, Mercury coincides with rising barometer, lower temperature and variable cloudiness. In the negative 90°, 180°, 45° or 135° aspect, the innermost planet causes the barometer to drop, increases cloudiness, spawns counterclockwise air flows, and dull weather and indicates coming atmospheric disturbances. With Jupiter, Mercury indicates northerlies and approaching fair weather, with a clear, fresh atmosphere and cumulus clouds.

When Mercury is conjunct with or in negative aspect to Neptune, the winds are southerly with sometimes dead calm and rising warm, moist air. In cities and industrial areas there are inversion and smog, with fog and low visibility near rivers and other waterways. Mercury-Neptune aspects during warm periods bring misty, hot, oppressive calms that often precede afternoon or evening scattered squalls. As for its configuration with Pluto, the effects of the innermost with the outermost (known) planet seem to resemble the same sort of abrupt changes as does Mercury with Mars.

Venus' influence on the atmosphere is always soft and

gentle, seldom generating winds. Under positive aspects: sunny, seasonable weather, southerly breezes and rising temperatures. When in conjunction or negative aspect with Mars, Venus produces heavy rainfall, especially when transiting through the water signs (Cancer, Scorpio or Pisces). Venus is sloppiest when transiting through 210° to 240° of celestial longitude (Scorpio). It is cold and at its iciest from 300° to 330° (Aquarius), but least likely to cause precipitation in this sign. In conjunction or negative aspect with the Sun, Venus is conducive to rainfall during any season. Positive aspects between the Sun and Venus, however, indicate beautiful, sunny weather. In conjunction with Jupiter, Venus normally indicates rising temperatures and generally fair weather. *Any* aspects with Saturn, however, either positive or negative, tend to cause varying cloudiness. Negative Venus-Saturn configurations indicate low pressure, counterclockwise air flows and a generally gloomy atmosphere. Saturn with Venus will stir up windblown rainfall. Venus and Uranus in negative aspects (including the conjunction) indicate deeply penetrating, chilly weather. Any rainfall is likely to be a cold drizzle.

The most brilliant atmosphere, with blue, cloudless skies and crisp, still air happens when Venus is in the "crystallizing" 60° angle with Uranus; visibility is usually excellent. When Venus is in conjunction (0°), square (90°), opposition (180°) or parallel in declination with Neptune, the heaviest downpours (in localized areas) happen almost without warning. Venus conjunct Neptune at from 210° to 240° (Scorpio) breeds flash floods or heavy early-winter snowfalls over high inland elevations.

Mars generally indicates westerly winds (Martian action is always intense and energetic). Although the Red Planet is in perigee almost every two years, its nearest *possible* approach to the Earth at average periods of 15 years is preceded by abnormally hot summers and severe droughts, as happened in 1892, 1909, 1924, 1939, 1956, 1971 and will again in 1986 and 2001. If Halley's comet reappears on schedule in 1986, the heat and drought will be cataclysmic. The evaporation, with or without the Martian perigee positions, is intensified when Mars occupies the celestial longitudes of 120° to 150° (the fire sign, Leo).

Jupiter, the most massive of all the planets, is normally a fair-weather planet. Its major stations and positive configurations with other bodies always coincide with clear skies and northerly air flows with fleecy, fine-weather clouds. When Jupiter's influence is strongest, skies are clear and there is above-normal sunshine. Jupiter's orbital period is 11.86 years. During each alternate 5.93-year period, it transits the northern declinations—i.e., north of the celestial equator. This adds to the sun's warmth during spring and summer in the northern hemisphere and softens the harshness of the fall and winter. This position in 1981–82 should help alleviate the deep freeze of that winter.

Atmospheric temperatures rises when the Sun forms a 60° (sextile) aspect to Jupiter. When Mars and Jupiter are in configuration, especially in conjunction at higher declinations, heat and evaporation intensify, particularly when Mars is at or near perigee. For some reason, atmospheric oxygen seems depressed by major aspects formed between Jupiter and Saturn. Because they are both slow-moving planets, the lows are deeper, more prolonged and widespread, and temperatures are generally below normal (as on May 23–31, 1977).

Jupiter's major angles to Uranus (every 41 months) have been related statistically to magnetic disturbances. Ninety-mile-per-hour winds have been clocked during these times. Finally, Jupiter in the 180° (opposition) aspect to Uranus on October 8, 1962, was pinpointed off the Oregon coast by G. J. McCormack on October 10, when the functional Moon transited Jupiter and opposed Uranus on the meridian at 129° west longitude. The terrifying storm struck on schedule.

In a seasonal chart, Jupiter on the lower meridian (beneath the Earth) generally indicates plenty of sunshine and pleasant weather. This nadir position of Jupiter presages an open winter; in spring or summer, fine growing weather for crops; and in the fall, good harvesting weather.

Saturn's revolutional period is 29.45 years and may be identified with the extremely cold winters of 1865, 1905, 1934, 1963 and 1992. It was safe to predict the bitterly cold winter of 1963 because both Saturn and Uranus made their winter solstitial colure during the winter of 1958, with Neptune nearby. The ensuing series of wintery deep freezes centered north one year, and the following year through the middle of the nation. The third year (1961) it happened in the deep south and the following year returned again to the north, but developed its maximum intensity the next year 10° to 15° eastward.

Saturn's influence is mostly correlated to low barometer and counterclockwise air flows. Under Saturn, atmospheric disturbances are more enduring, and overcast weather is more widespread. As Saturn impresses the atmosphere, winds change to northwest, the air clears and temperatures fall—slowly but decisively.

The conjunctions, oppositions and 90° aspects of the Sun (or any of the planets) with Saturn generate cloudiness and atmospheric disturbance. Basic seasonal charts determine the geographic location. The 60°, 120° and other positive aspects are conducive to generally fair weather, rising barometer and lower temperatures. Persistent cold occurs under combined Saturn-Uranus aspects, as, for example, during their conjunctions in 1981.

Saturn on the equator usually aggravates chronic cloudiness, low barometer and abnormal rainfall, as in March, 1967 and will again in February 1981.

In celestial maps set up for the solar ingress or, at the times of New and Full Moon, planets at the meridian (the overhead or mid-heaven position at your place of observation) are more important than at any other position. Next in order of importance are those in quadrature (90°) to the meridian.

The best evidence of astrometeorology's validity is in using these general guides in actual observation. For accurate interpretations and forecasts however, *precision charts are absolutely necessary.*

Strangely enough, *Uranus,* insofar as its electrical potential is concerned, is regarded in astrometeorology as the celestial "twin" of Mercury. The seventh planet, which rotates almost horizontally on its axis, is related to descending cold air and to the northwest wind. Uranus signals the approach of *highest* barometric pressure and seems to dominate the icy cold air in the highest reaches of the atmosphere. Long observation has led to the belief that the strongest influence of Uranus affects the movements and paths of the jet streams—those 35,000-to-40,000-feet-high rivers of bitterly cold air which are 25 miles wide, several thousand feet deep and forever zooming eastward at hundreds of miles per hour.

Ridges of descending cold, dry air with pressure of more than 1,024 millibars are typically Uranian. This is confirmed by northwest winds and 30° drops in temperature within several hours of a planetary aspect with Uranus. Mercury with Uranus increases high wind velocities and deepens cold temperatures.

Polar air doesn't always originate in Canada or other northern climates and latitudes, but from the upper atmosphere. The highest geographic latitudes all over the globe, naturally, feel the maximum intensity of cold waves. *This should be ample warning to the northeastern and northwestern and border states of the U.S. and to Canada in the winter of 1981–82.*

The anomaly happens when, in eastward transit, these major highs center over the Gulf states; they then develop into what we call "Bermuda Highs."

Neptune on the nadir (directly beneath the Earth at any point of observation) or in other negative angles to the nadir, conduces to abnormal wetness, dominating southerlies, or ascending air currents, excessive humidity, sporadic heavy rains, winter snow with alternating thaws, and flood hazards. This was particularly so during Neptune's recent 14-year transit of the area from 210° to 240° of celestial longitude (Scorpio) which ended in November 1970, when Neptune finally entered Sagittarius for another 14-year tenure. Its dominating pattern is usually decisive. Still . . . other than interpreting "variable extremes with 57 varieties of moisture," during spring and summer seasons, it's usually wiser to generalize Neptune's ephemeral changes. An outstanding peculiarity of Neptune is that lows tend to be of the semitropical type.

The kind of disturbances usually generated by Neptune are preceded by low hazes, fogs and smog that move in narrow paths and cover small areas at a time, drenching isolated locations with torrential downpours or heavy snowfall, depending on the season, while skipping over other areas. Because of rising air currents in mountain areas, Neptune causes brief winter thaws and snow slides. In summer, while crossing bodies of water, freakish changes under Neptune aspects are intensified. When Mars and Mercury add their influence to Neptune's, sudden brief turbulence—dangerous for small sailing craft—disrupt airline schedules, airport activities and important space launches.

Pluto wasn't discovered until 1930. Because of this relatively brief period of observation and correlation, plus its tremendous distance, small mass and slow orbital velocity, its effects are not well known. Practical observations during this period, however, indicate influences somewhat similar to those of Mars, perhaps more amplified. These tentative conclusions, it should be pointed out, are evolving by a laborious process of observation and elimination over many years of data exchange among the few practicing astrometeorologists left in the world.

It takes Pluto about 21 years to transit each 30° of the ecliptic—*one zodiacal sign*—circle. It is always wise to observe weather during periods when the outermost (known) planet is in apparently stationary position or when in conjunction with or receiving major aspects from the Sun, especially the 180° and 90° angles in geocentric longitude.

The Moon is not only *the final triggering element* for for any point of observation, but also governs the 3½-day 7-day and 14-day—or, to be more precise, 13.66-day—weather periods. By its declination the Moon contributes partially to determining the latitudinal paths of highs and lows. The lunar nodes are those points where our natural satellite's orbit crosses north to south or vice versa on the plane of the ecliptic. The Moon's north node recedes through the 360° of the ecliptic plane in 18.6 years. When the lunar node retrogrades to the point of the vernal equinox, or 0.00° of longitude, the Moon's *maximum declination* can be as far north as 28°44′. When the north node is at the opposite point of 180° celestial longitude, the maximum declination does not extend above 18° 10′ north.

These differences of roughly 10½° in declination of the lunar nodes at 9¼-year intervals seem to influence warm ocean currents from the tropics toward the Arctic and back, with parallel effects on the tides of the atmosphere in the coldest northern latitudes. The tide-rising power of the Moon relative to the Sun is 11 to 5.

Each of these elements should be tested with sharp scientific objectivity. Only after persistently investigating and critically testing his forecasts from 1925 to 1947 did G. J. McCormack become convinced of the Moon's influence in *timing* eastward progress of atmospheric changes. Every aspect of the Moon indicates barometric changes in some degree, *but not necessarily locally.*

An easily proven, long-established rule in astro-meteorology is that when the nature of Saturn is duplicated by the presence of Mercury or Venus between 300° and 330° of celestial longitude (Aquarius), the season becomes much colder. If, then, a conjunction or other configuration happens at the New or Full Moon, its effect will become stronger still. If the configuration of planets forms an *opposition* on the meridian of the *seasonal* chart, the aspect and the change in weather is intensified.

The following eight chapters are a detailed elucidation of the foregoing two—specially designed for those students seriously interested in the practical workings and interpretation of the solar/interplanetary medium and its energies on the terrestrial atmosphere, and, in some cases, the Earth's crustal movements.

13

THE INFLUENCE OF MERCURY

SURPRISING AS IT was, the discovery of craters on Mars (instead of the nonexistent "canals" astronomers had been observing since the days of Giovanni Virginio Schiaparelli) was small potatoes compared to the craters of Mercury. The Sun's innermost planet has a sidereal cycle of 87.97 days; its influence on our weather ranges from gentle breezes to high winds and is keynoted by cold temperatures and lusty gales, especially when in configuration with major planets. At its major stations, Mercury influences high barometric pressure and is associated with the color violet in the spectrum. Does that seem strange? Keep reading.

When positioned between 90° and 120° of solstice, equinox or lunation charts (i.e., the fourth sector from the ascendant), Mercury governs the direction and velocity of prevailing winds. Because of its closeness to our local star, this planet can never be more than 28° from the Sun (as seen from the Earth, of course). You can't see Mercury for more than an hour and a quarter after the Sun rises or sets. Like Venus, its orbit lies within that of the Earth, so Mercury is referred to as an "inferior" planet. But because of its speed, this fastest-moving of all the planets is an important "triggering" element in atmospheric changes. It forms "magnetic" angles faster than any other solarian body except the Moon.

Under Mercury, the centers of low-pressure areas attract the prevailing air flows. Mercury is an "electric" planet ranking second only to frigid Uranus. When, during a solar ingress or lunation, Mercury is at the lower meridian, you can safely predict intermittent strong winds and unseasonable coolness. In winter months, particularly when in parallel of declination with major planets (especially Uranus), Mercury generates wind-driven sleet or snow.

At superior conjunction or in equal declination with the Sun, Mercury stirs up and accelerates wind velocity. This is also true at its greatest elongation from the Sun, also when it reaches an apparently stationary position, and either at its maximum north declination or at zero (00°00′)—the celestial equator.

In solar ingress (solstice and equinoctial) and lunation charts, the maximum intensity of the foregoing atmospheric conditions originates and moves eastward whenever Mercury is found at the "angles," particularly the fourth (90° –120°) and tenth (270° –300°) channels, but also at the first (0° –30°) and seventh (180° –210°) channel (see figure 1). These four are the cardinal angles—east, north, west and south, going counterclockwise around the chart—or left, bottom, right and top (see figure 2). Wherever Mercury is so positioned, the meridian for which the chart is erected—that specific point in geographic longitude—is where the maximum intensity of atmospheric conditions will originate and then move eastward. When Mercury is conjunct the Sun, or in equal declination with it—especially when in apparent retrograde motion—there is usually a high barometer and powerful winds. All Mercury-Uranus aspects intensify coldness and spawn frigid blasts of air.

Mercury in aspect to Venus is conducive to gentle southerly zephyrs and rising temperatures. (Low-pressure regions usually stem from south to north.) Mercury in aspect to Mars tends to create westerly winds; the adverse aspects intensify these into gusts. In summer, Mars-Mercury aspects tend to create red-colored clouds and cause the season to be generally hot and dry. In winter, however, the same or similar aspects bring more seasonal temperatures.

The character or nature of the sign in which Mars is located has a profound effect on the atmosphere, and can cause sudden changes in the afternoon or evening. And if the Moon happens to be in perigee at or close to the same hour, the likelihood of thunderstorms is increased. Mercury either in parallel of declination or in conjunction with the Sun is usually a harbinger of high winds, and during winter months brings cold waves and breeds blizzards.

Mercury in aspect to Jupiter makes for long-lasting, mild and pleasant weather. It is not usually hot, but does tend toward dryness, with woolly clouds, moderate breezes, northerly winds, fresh invigorating air flows and generally fair, temperate weather. Mercury in Sagittarius: with Saturn, snow and frost; with Jupiter (usually after a time of snow or rain), pleasant, seasonal weather; with Mars, moderate to strong northerly winds; with Venus, increased rain and refreshingly clear breezes. Mercury in Capricorn: varieties of uncomfortable, distressingly miserable weather. In Aquarius: following periods of wetness—cold, dry, windy weather. In Pisces: cloudy and fogs with low visibility in the south and increased winds in northerly sections. In Aries: increased rainfall. If retrograde—windy, but with mild temperatures. In Taurus: cooler, with greater wind velocity.

Mercury in Gemini: with Saturn—in spring and summer seasons, increased gusts after rainfall or storms; in cold seasons, increased snowfall. With Jupiter—mild, southerly winds. With Mars—prolonged rain and wind in cold seasons and rain and thunderstorms in warmer periods. With Venus—misty drizzles to heavy showers. In Cancer: with Mars—thunderstorms and occasionally tornadoes (depending on other aspects). With Jupiter—dry, mild, pleasant weather for prolonged periods, and relatively cooler trends. In Leo: extremely warm, often hot, weather, particularly in warmer climates. In Virgo and Libra: possible tropical storms (under other strong aspects) but usually temperature with moderate rainfall. In

Scorpio: fast-moving high-and low-pressure areas cause rapid changes in temperature.

Mercury with Saturn: Lowers the barometric pressure, increases relative humidity, causes prevailing easterly winds. Sometimes overcast skies and variable cloudiness. Mercury with Uranus: predominating northwesterly gusty winds downslope, rising barometer and lower temperatures. The conjunction, square and opposition aspects during cold seasons (and when either planet is stationary or aspected by Venus, Saturn, Neptune or Mars) indicate major storms and possible blizzards. These are particularly troublesome periods for all forms of communication, power and transportation systems. In warmer seasons, the foregoing configurations indicate gusty, erratic winds and scattered thunderstorms downslope. These are breeders of tornadoes in the Midwest and Southwest, particularly if the aspects are *angular,* i.e., in the 30° angles at the Ascendant, Nadir, Descendant or Mid-heaven (see figures 2 and 3). Under all Mercury-Uranus aspects, temperatures tend to drop—sometimes drastically, depending on other aspecting planets.

Mercury with Neptune: Usually calm, humid and hazy, with occasional upslope air flows. At night, fog and smog in valleys and lowlands. Sudden changes, usually line squalls which are often scattered.

Mercury with Pluto seems to act pretty much the same as Mercury-Mars aspects, although more acutely. Such configurations are good for timing atmospheric changes. Ingress and lunation charts will give you the keys to *where.* Nevertheless, keep clearly in mind (at least for the time being—the key to timing atmospheric changes from any point of origin eastward to any other geographic meridian will be covered later) that the foregoing illustrations don't necessarily mean that the results of these planetary configurations will occur at your location on the exact date they occur. All this requires practice, experience—and patience.

In Mercury-Venus aspects, there can only be the conjunction, parallel, 30°, 45° and 60° aspects. These bring gentle breezes, rising temperatures, fair weather southward, and some humidity. In the north, increased cloudiness, often with predominating southerly winds.

Mercury-Mars: Here, you synthesize with the nature of the sign Mercury is transiting. Mercury-Mars generates sharp, energetic weather action; it is never gentle. The winds are usually prevailing westerlies, with sudden gusts when there's a parallel, conjunction, square or opposition aspect. During summer months these aspects generate scattered electrical disturbances, with thunderstorms and often hail. In cold months the wind is pronounced, but temperatures tend to be seasonal. Turbulence in the atmosphere usually reaches full gale force when Mercury is either negatively aspected to Uranus and/or forms a conjunction with the Sun. Mercury's influence is stronger in the higher elevations when in configuration with Jupiter or Uranus, and more potent in the lowlands when in aspect to Neptune, Saturn, Mars or Venus. When transiting from one configuration with a "warm" (in the sense that it influences the Earth's atmosphere this way) planet like Mars to a *negative* aspect to "cold" planets such as Uranus or Saturn, there are bound to be strong ensuing winds, and if Mercury happens to be in (apparent) retrograde motion at the time, always interpret the *negative* natures of the planets involved, even if the degree of the angle(s) formed is generally considered to be positive!

Mercury-Jupiter: Generally induces a rising barometer and moderately strong northerly air flows. Temperatures tend to rise when Jupiter is in northern declination. Mercury-Jupiter aspects are conducive to clear skies, fleecy clouds and a fresh, wholesome, healthy atmosphere. However, if either planet is retrograde, you can expect scattered cloudiness with variable winds; if Mars is also involved, light, quick rainfall and a low barometer, and in summer months, atmospheric electrical disturbances, high temperatures and sharp, quick winds.

Mercury-Saturn: Dull, gray skies and a tendency to east winds and/or counterclockwise air flows. All Mercury-Saturn configurations breed variable cloudiness and tend to lower temperatures. Positive aspects however, merely indicate partly cloudy skies and cooler temperatures. This is particularly so when the "crystallizing" 60° angle exists between Mercury and Saturn. With the negative (45°, 90° and 180°) angles, as well as the conjunction, the barometer will fall, cloudiness will increase and the winds will usually be easterly. The barometer is generally lower and the humidity higher in the lowlands. Fair, cooler weather, however, will dominate northern areas. Atmospheric changes under Saturnine aspects are invariably slow to develop and equally slow to disperse. Precipitation is usually followed by cooler temperatures as winds change to northwest and the skies clear. Cold waves and low-pressure areas are Saturnine in nature.

Mercury-Uranus: Erratic gusts of wind, cold dry air masses and high barometric pressure. Sudden drops in temperature, with northwest winds. In the foregoing, the 60° aspects are *extremely* powerful. In wintery months, stratus clouds and bleak, penetrating, blustery cold weather accompanies the conjunction, square, opposition, 45°, 135° and parallel of declination. All Mercury-Uranus aspects cause sudden, frequently spasmodic weather changes. Conjunctions, parallels and oppositions generate isolated high-velocity winds. In warmer months these aspects intensify turbulence above the 10,000-foot level and generate scattered severe thunderstorms and cold fronts—also isolated hail, particularly if cold dry descending air masses from the north meet rising, moist warm tropical air masses from the south. Higher elevations, naturally, receive the maximum impact of sharp drops in temperature.

When Mercury combines its effect with that of Uranus on the lower meridian at an ingress or lunation, therefore, it is safe to predict gusty winds, high barometric pressure and unseasonably cold temperature. When either planet is located between 60° and 90° (the third channel), weather changes originate to the northwest of your elected point of observation.

Mercury-Neptune influences weather somewhat like that of aspects between Mercury and Venus, but the influence is more extreme. With positive configurations, Mercury-Neptune generates a misty atmosphere, especially close to bodies of water, generally fair weather and air movements ranging from dead calms to gentle breezes. Configurations between these planets cause temperatures to rise and creates nebulous weather, with upslope flows of air, quick changes and variable winds. The conjunctions and parallels, like all negative configurations, generate high relative humidity, lower barometer, haze and air inversion layers over cities and industrial centers.

Mercury-Neptune aspects breed clouds, and during colder seasons cause fog and low cloud ceilings. When these aspects are triggered by the Moon, they bring mild showers and ominously dark, low clouds. During cold months, ice and snow melt. In the spring, probable tornadoes in the southern plains states. In summer, oppressively sticky atmospheric conditions (i.e., warm, humid and still), a quickly dropping barometer and sudden squalls scattered through lowland areas. Neptune seems to concentrate its influence over relatively small areas, but acts more intensively over water. Because of this, the negative Mercury-Neptune aspects generate narrow, localized squalls with absolutely unpredictable pathlines!

Mercury-Pluto: Although this is still problematical, Mercury with Pluto seems to act as it does with Mars, but more intensified. Whenever in doubt, or during critical times when you want to put your observations of a planet's nature to the acid test, check weather at any point(s) of observation when it it at 00° 00′ (the extended terrestrial equator). It will be several decades before Pluto crosses the celestial equator again. (Its revolution around the Sun takes 248.43 years.)

14

THE INFLUENCE OF VENUS

LYING UNDER THE turbulence and roar of the Venusian atmosphere are untold mysteries that belie our supposed knowledge about Earth's "sister" world. Venus is the only planet in the solar system, for example, that rotates on its axis in a retrograde motion. The length of its day is 243 times as long as that of an Earth day. According to legend, Venus was ejected as a comet from Jupiter about 3,500 years ago. The controversy still rages, but in astrology, Venus and Jupiter are generally regarded as *beneficial* planets, influencing Earth's atmosphere in positive and pleasant ways.

When Venus is in Scorpio there is usually above-normal rainfall—possibly snow. In Sagittarius—milder temperatures and/or gently falling snow. In Capricorn—especially in the northern sectors, an abundant snow; in the east, lower temperatures and moderate rainfall. In Aquarius—cooler, with precipitation about normal. In Pisces—slightly increased precipitation, temperatures normal. In Aries—showers and mild temperatures. In Taurus—moderate temperatures and generally pleasant weather, but when in apparent retrograde motion, moderate to heavy rainfall, depending on other aspecting planets. In Gemini—mild temperatures, lovely atmospheric conditions and fertile growing seasons. In Cancer—abundant rainfall and flooding in lowlands, particularly so if Uranus, Jupiter or Mars also form configurations. In Leo—frequent rainfall and thunderstorms. In Virgo—usually gentle showers. In Libra—beautiful weather, gentle breezes and light rainfall.

The tendency of Venus is generally to spawn atmospheric moisture. Traditionally, Venus represents copper and symbolizes the color yellow. Its revolutional cycle is 224.7 days. It is normally responsible for gentle winds—prevailing southerlies—with higher humidity, lower barometer and rising temperatures. Venus has an eight-year cycle, during which there is statistically higher average precipitation. Although its magnetic field is insignificant, astrologers for some unfathomable reason refer to Venus as "a celestial magnetic conductor."

Lowered barometric readings, misty, foggy weather, cloudiness and fertile, gentle rainfall with warmer, humid air are the rule when Venus is either stationary in longitude, at the celestial equator (zero degrees of declination) or at her greatest northern declination. When in southern signs (from Scorpio to Pisces) in solar ingress and/or lunation charts, Venus on the meridian induces calm weather and gentle showers. At or near the upper meridian, lower temperatures will dominate northernmost areas and storms will center southward. At or near the lower meridian it will cause the heaviest precipitation northward; when downslope, temperatures will rise. The third (60°–90°) channel or the ninth (240°–270°) channel should be regarded as the dominating geographic areas just west of your point of observation, therefore in eastward transit. Venus at or near the meridians during cold months indicates snowfall and/or freezing rain. More than most other celestial bodies except the Moon, Venus reflects the character of the sign it happens to be transiting, as well as other planets to which it forms configurations.

When adversely aspected by Neptune, Mars or Saturn, or on the celestial equator, for example, Venus triggers copious rainfall. In harmonious configurations, clear and sunny weather. It's related to the wettest periods when in the water signs, Cancer, Scorpio and Pisces; the sloppiest weather occurs when Venus transits either Scorpio or (frequently) Taurus. It is at its coldest when transiting Aquarius, causes the most dashing rains in aspects with Mars, and more long-lasting precipitation in aspect to Saturn. The two "benefics," Jupiter and Venus, are conducive to pleasant weather. In winter months, freezing rain or snow with cold, windy drizzles coincide with Venus-Uranus aspects.

It's important to remember that *all* rules are only approximations. It takes time and patience to grasp the significance of individual and collective combinations, and requires the art of fine synthesis to interpret all the elements of an astrometeorological chart. When they are not considered with all other planets, signs and aspects in solstice or lunation maps, none of the rules, in and of themselves, are absolute. For example, in adverse (conjunction, opposition or square) aspect to Neptune, Venus usually indicates torrential downpours, but if two 60° aspects are also operating between Jupiter and the Sun, the reaction is drastically altered.

Venus and the Sun: As seen from the Earth, Venus' greatest arc of elongation from the Sun can't be more than 48°. The most important configuration it can make with the Sun, therefore—aside from the conjunction and parallel of declination—is the 45° angle. Although it can also form the semisextile, or 30° aspect, which generally conforms to fair, mild weather, this is only of minor importance. If Venus happens to be in apparent retrograde motion (or just turning retrograde), particularly when in Taurus, Cancer, Scorpio or Pisces when it forms the 45° aspect (closest to the arc of its greatest elongation), this is a good indication of very heavy precipitation. Oddly enough, Venus conjunct the Sun is one of the "pluvial" harbingers, with high cirrus clouds that blanket or screen out the solar disc after an almost stillness of air movement and warmish temperatures, even during winter months, during which this conjunction usually piles up snowfall across inland areas and higher elevations. In parallel of declination with the Sun, Venus brings warmer temperatures, although it usually gets colder after Venusian-triggered precipitation.

Venus-Mars: Temperatures rise and fair weather is the general rule when positive aspects occur between Venus and the Red Planet (even more so at the 60° sextile and the 120° trine aspects). It's important to remember that inasmuch as the Venusian tendency is to increase atmospheric moisture, flexibility is the best advice when you're interpreting Venus-Mars aspects. However, in *all* configurations they indicate rising temperatures and higher relative humidity. Your interpretations should scrupulously regard the relative strength of all configurations that increase precipitation, i.e., the possible angular position to the *west* of your point of observation, their declinations and the signs tenanted by each planet, and whether they're on the celestial equator.

When Venus is in Aquarius or near the top, or South Tropic, on your map, it generally indicates cold rain and freezing drizzle or snowfall followed by a sharp drop in temperature. The effect of both bodies (Venus and Mars) is strongest along the coastlines, in lowlands and the lower stratas of the troposphere (closest to the Earth). Rain is usually triggered during warm seasons under configurations between these planets, and precipitation during cold seasons happens a little later than the actual time of the aspects. Their combined configurations are generated *in advance,* however, when the Moon moves into a conjunction or quadrature (90°) aspect as much as a day or two prior to the actual aspect! When considering all aspects among celestial bodies, always look upon the Moon as a functional "trigger" and the Sun as the organic force in generating terrestrial weather.

Venus-Jupiter: Venus making the square, semisquare (45°) or opposition angles to Jupiter will usually generate gentle south winds at the lower troposphere and north winds above 10,000 feet, which is conducive to cloudy weather. However, with these two "benefics," nearly all configurations correlate with beautiful atmospheric conditions, fresh, clean air and sunny weather—particularly the parallel, conjunction, sextile and/or trine angles. If the Sun also happens to aspect either planet, temperatures will rise, but if Mars gets into the act by any of the potent angular relationships, chances are that atmospheric disturbances will occur, especially during late spring and summer seasons.

Venus-Saturn: With Saturn, weather changes are slower to develop, and they last much longer. The most noticeable effect of Saturn in adverse aspects is humidity and cloudy dullness. Even with positive configurations, Saturn inclines toward concentrated cold weather. Cold fronts occur under the crystallizing effect of Saturn's 60° aspects to Venus, or when it also happens to be at one of its major stations. When there's precipitation under Venus-Saturn aspects, it is usually followed by lower temperatures which are more intense inland. Although some cloudiness may attenuate the Sun's light and heat, the sextile, trine and semisextile (30°) aspects of Venus-Saturn bring cooler but fair weather. Sextile configurations cause definitely falling temperatures, moderately high winds and a high barometer; in winter months, freezes and cold waves.

Saturn's characteristic dull, leaden skies and gradually increasing cloudiness are enhanced by the conjunction, square, semisquare or opposition with Venus, and indicate easterly winds and a lowering barometric pressure. Under these conditions, increased humidity and a damp, chilly atmosphere can be accompanied by heavy downfalls that go on interminably (or seemingly so). If Venus is southing during winter at the same time, rain will turn to sleet or snow. During warm seasons, heavy, prolonged rainfall. In spring and autumn, especially along the coastline and lowlands, fogs and poor visibility.

If Mercury and/or Uranus add their influence, temperatures will drop and a slow, cold rainfall with intermittent drizzle and winter snows will follow. If Venus and Saturn are at or near an opposition or conjunction and *also* in parallel declination, you can expect excessive downpours with oppressive, low-hanging dark clouds.

Venus-Uranus: Under the positive angles—i.e. the trine, semisextile, and especially the sextile, you can expect moderate winds with a slight drop in temperature. Generally, however, this indicates a high barometer and brilliant, sunny weather. Under these aspects during early fall or late spring, unexpected frosts develop overnight. During warmer months, rainfall usually happens *before* these aspects are fully formed!

The air is bitterly, penetratingly cold when Venus forms an adverse aspect with Uranus—especially a conjunction and parallel of declination at the same time—and even more so, if either planet is in apparent *retrograde* motion. This creates a cold, damp atmosphere and spasmodic drizzling rain. Similar damp, cold rainfall occurs under prevailing stratus clouds during the opposition, square, semisquare and 135° angles of Venus-Uranus. When Mercury joins its influence either in early spring, winter or late autumn, driving sleet and snowstorms raise hell with all forms of transportation, power and communications (including satellites). Venus in Aquarius makes cold weather colder; in Cancer, Pisces or Scorpio, she increases the moisture, and in Gemini, Aquarius, Libra, Virgo and Sagittarius, she tends to make the atmosphere much drier than usual.

Venus-Neptune: With all configurations, the atmosphere ranges from fog to mist and the barometer falls slowly, with southerly winds and rising temperatures. The air is usually still and the chief characteristic of Venus-Neptune is humidity. Calm, misty air and higher temperatures usually accompany the positive angles of 30°, 60°, 120° and 150°. In summer months, local cloudiness and light rainfall dominate the higher inlands, with sultry weather in late spring or summer and increased humidity along coastlines and lowlands. Heavy sleet and wet snow in December 1977, when Venus was conjunct Neptune, caused cloudiness to develop quickly. There was almost no wind—smoke rose vertically, causing widespread air inversions.

Under the negative 45°, 90°, 135° and 180° aspects, the heaviest downpours center over narrow regions, often causing semitropical cloudbursts during brief periods. You can safely predict floods when Neptune is on the meridian or in quadrature to it. And if Venus happens to be conjunct Neptune in Scorpio at the same time, cloudbursts and extremely heavy flooding are a virtual certainty—more so in low-lying areas, waterways and coastal regions.

Orthodox weathermen are always taken by surprise

when Venus-Neptune aspects operate jointly. Inundations develop almost without warning and are intensified by a cold front from the north. In your search for seasonal extremes of rain or snowfall (one inch of rain is equal to ten inches of snow), try to remember the location of Neptune on the meridian during the *preceding* solar equinox or solstice. The same rule applies to lunation charts. Inasmuch as there are twelve lunations and four solar ingresses each year, this means the careful calculations of 28 charts per year, each of which can be transposed to any point of geographic location in order to determine the prevailing seasonal and bimonthly weather patterns at your chosen point on the globe.

15

THE INFLUENCE OF MARS

THE UNQUESTIONABLY GREATEST space event of 1976 was the Viking mission: two American spacecraft landed on Mars while two parent craft monitored the Red Planet from high orbits. Scientific studies of the results were complex and extensive. The first tantalizing chemical processes detected, however, were not believed to be biological.

They were like nothing Earthbound scientists had ever seen—either in nature or their own laboratories.

NASA biologist Dr. Norman Horwitz announced in late August that the data received and the activity detected by the robot lander "increase the chance that it is a living biological process." But the leader of the biology team, Dr. Harold P. Klein, carefully said, "At this stage, it's either a biological explanation or some even fancier chemistry than we had recently talked about."

"Fancy chemistry" was quickly interpreted by the media as scientific jargon for life-as-we-do-not-know-it. Before the question could be settled, Mars swung around behind the Sun, effectively blocking out all communication. So the two orbiters were deactivated. The landers continued gathering scientific data during the solar conjunction, storing it for the time Viking mission officials would awaken the orbiters to transmit their findings.

In late December Mars and the Earth cleared Viking's radio path as they swung away from the colossal electromagnetic roar of the Sun. Five top NASA space experts unofficially admitted that three scientific experiments proved the existence of life on Mars. Maurice Parker, Viking project's public affairs manager, said, "We went to look for signs of life, and we found signs of life. Everything strongly indicates there are microscopic organisms eating, breathing and sleeping on Mars."

NASA's chief scientist, Dr. Gerald Soffen, added, "We now have plenty of evidence of life on Mars . . . something on the planet which both eats and breathes—and the only place in Nature where both eating and breathing goes on is in a living cell!"

The bewildered scientist explained. "I expected any signs of life to show up very slowly on our detection equipment, but I was wrong. The positive results in the life-searching equipment simply vomited out all at once. We were all shocked. We'd never expected it to happen like that. But there's something very strange going on up there—something we don't fully understand. We're totally baffled by the absence of any remains of once-living microscopic life."

The chief of the mission's molecular analysis team is Dr. Klaus Biemann, a professor of chemistry at Massachusetts Institute of Technology. He designed the test to detect organic wastes. Like "the majority of the 70-odd Viking scientists," he was astounded when the experiment continued in total darkness to reveal that the little creatures were eating and resting in a regular cycle identical to the Martian day and night. Not only did the strange life forms give off oxygen as they fed on a nutrient solution; they emitted 15 times *more* oxygen than the NASA team required for solid evidence of the existence of life!

Bizarre forms of life-as-we-don't-know-it straight out of science fiction? "Yes," said the formerly conservative Dr. Klein. "The reason we didn't find any organic debris could be that these little buggers are such effective scavengers that the colony wouldn't produce any waste. It would be eaten by the others."

Dr. Biemann agreed. "We've found no remains of dead bodies. This leads me to suggest that life there may be continually consuming its dead. Another explanation could be that they've developed colonies with shells or walls around them, which conceal evidence of dead microorganisms."

One experiment was to detect gases emitted when a living organism digests food. Radioactive nutrients were mixed with a sample of Martian soil. The results were startling. Within seconds, something in the soil started eating the liquid food and giving off radioactive gases. The astounded experts repeated the experiment three times—with identical results.

"Then," Dr. Klein said, "the activity in the experiment increased at a tremendous rate, and suddenly declined. It was as if some efficient microscopic scavengers had consumed the solution at a fast rate, then died off like they'd been poisoned by it."

According to Dr. Klein, they may be similar to the microorganisms that are believed to have begun our own evolution on Earth billions of years ago. "It's possible the Martian organisms are now beginning their own evolution . . . they may be primitive forms of life which have never been known on Earth."

Members of the Viking team, however, didn't openly discuss the possibility that Landers I and II may inadvertently have instantaneously triggered the evolution of life on Mars! Despite every precaution, *some* terrestrial organisms could easily have survived the long space voyage. This raises the staggering question of the origin of life on Earth. The same sort of thing may have happened here.

The surface of Mars is much harsher than the Earth's. Winds blow across the surface at more than 200 miles per hour. These gales often lift planet-wide clouds of dust that scour the landscape like steel wool. Deadly (to us) ultraviolet rays bombard the surface, and there is less water on most of Mars than in the driest places on Earth. In spite of this bleak and forbidding environment, at least one hardy life form can, according to the testimony, not only survive, but thrive, on the Red Planet.

The blinding dust storms that obscured man's first closeup views seem to coincide with several angular positions of Mars' three innermost neighbors, especially the Earth, with the Sun *and* Mars.

The axial rotational periods of Earth and Mars are about the same. Mars spins once every 24 hours, 37 minutes and 25 seconds. Its orbit around the Sun takes almost two Earth years (actually 1.88 years, or 687 days). For obvious esoteric reasons, Mars symbolizes the color red and "reflects" positive electricity. Under Mars, the winds are generally westerly with rising temperature, which causes evaporation. The Red Planet's influence is penetrating, sharp and strong. According to John Hazelrigg and G. J. McCormack in the *Yearbook of the American Academy of Astrologians* (Hermetic Publishing Co., New York, 1917):

> From remotest antiquity it has been observed that when planets are in conjunction, or at certain angles in longitude with the Sun, they produce atmospheric conditions peculiar to their nature and quality. The ancients attributed these atmospheric changes to the action of life, and contended that each color of the solar spectrum had certain qualities of its own. It was observed that the positive red ray corresponded with configurations of Mars, and that the negative blue ray predominated when Saturn was exerting his influence. Once this hypothesis was fully verified, it became but a matter of induction to continue their analogy to the seven functional planes of vibration as interpreted through other planets, and formulate those doctrines which have been handed down to posterity. Indeed the Egyptians were so apt in their knowledge regarding the vibratory force of light that they applied it with great facility in the cure of diseases.

To the materialistic scientific concepts of that era (as well as our own), this was pure hogwash—occult gobbledegook—without experimentation; and this remains the prevailing opinion of orthorox textbooks of that day and this. Yet it has been recently discovered scientifically that humans are not only psychologically influenced by various colors—often predictably—but also physiologically. British studies and experiments at the Delawarr Laboratories in Oxford and elsewhere give positive indications that, in certain combinations, various wavelengths of the visible spectrum can stimulate growth, healing, or the opposite.

According to McCormack:

> Every material particle gives a vibratory response according to the color value of the rays impressed upon it. The vibration thus induced manifests itself in the atmosphere, hence the energetic and stimulating red rays engender heat and drought in the Earth which react on the atmosphere, and elevate the temperature. The blue ray, cool and moist, on the contrary, decreases temperature, increases moisture and produces decomposition. The luminous principle is everywhere—that of life itself and being unified in the Sun—source of life and heat. The solar orb then is the centre of attraction through which magnetic vibrations of the planets manifest themselves. And so, as the tiny ray of light is reflected to us, do we find blended and fully capable of analyzation the astral principles of the Universe.

With more mundane terminology, he called Mars "the celestial spark plug." When the Red Planet is at major stations, statistically significant numbers of fires (pine trees, for example, have been observed to start burning from their *tops*) caused by spontaneous combustion due to the intense Martian-induced heat and drought.

Oddly enough, when Mars is at its apogee (greatest distance from the Earth), which can be almost 250 million miles, there is a definite decrease in the thermal effects of this close celestial neighbor. Conversely, heat and drought *increase* with Mars' perigee (1.88-year) periods.

Mars' closest possible perigee (roughly 35 million

miles) occurs at approximate 15-year intervals and coincides with prolonged heat, drought and increased danger of forest and other fires, both natural and manmade. The next *super*-perigee of Mars, in July, 1986, will coincide perfectly with the return of Halley's comet. Rational minds detest the idea of specious catastrophism, particularly for the sake of sensation alone. Still—the concept of learning everything humanly possible about the cosmic environment is to enable us to anticipate future possibilities and avoid or prevent the worst. Heuristically, then, the correlations between comets and terrestrial events coincide in the most remarkable way. At this writing, although some personal natal astrologers do it, there are no reliable rules for including and interpreting the influence of comets in solstice and lunation charts for astro-weather forecasting.

Mars' last three super-perigees occurred in August, 1971, September, 1956 and October, 1941. These periods are also related to inflammatory, eruptive diseases in human beings. These epidemics (measles, for example) are like the atmospheric dryness and heat, i.e., they are more intense in northern sectors when Mars is in northern declinations, and vice versa. The most pronounced effects occur when (in solar, cardinal ingresses and lunation charts) Mars is either ascending or descending in terrestrial longitude, when it is southing or occupies the lower meridian.

At perihelion (nearest to the Sun), Mars indicates higher than average temperatures for that season. Planets on the lower meridian in key celestial maps indicate maximum intensity at that terrestrial longitude. The points where weather originates under Mars are the longitudes where the Red Planet forms aspects to the meridian. Make careful observations of the time when either Mars, Mercury, Venus or the Moon form aspects to the Sun—the exact dates and times are important.

The influence of Mars is extremely dry in the hot sign of Leo, particularly when forming configurations with the Sun or Jupiter, but is more humid in the water signs—Cancer, Scorpio and Pisces. By itself, Mars induces acute, powerful atmospheric activity, and is most turbulent of all in conjunction (or other negative aspects) with Mercury, Saturn, Uranus, Neptune and—in some cases—Pluto. Mars on the celestial equator stirs up intense storms on the western coastlines because of marine westerly winds.

With Mars-Venus relationships at maximum strength, there are local showers and warm temperatures in spring and summer and sudden temperature increases in cold seasons. This combination also raises temperatures during winter months. If either Mars or Venus is contra-parallel (in opposite declination) to the Sun, the potential for destructive, windy storms is increased. During spring and summer months, the greater the degree of heat, the more intense and destructive are the storms that follow. Mars in Aquarius makes for very warm weather in the south and extreme heat in the summer months if Mars is retrograde; in the winter, greater amounts of snow and rain in northern regions. In Pisces: rain in spring and summer, and extreme snowfall and rain in winter. In Capricorn: hot and humid in southern areas, and heavy snows in the north during winter months. Either way, Mars in Capricorn is one indicator of rain and snow generally. In Sagittarius: moderate snow and rain, with more pleasant balmy atmosphere in southern regions.

Mars–Sun: In any configuration, rising temperatures, with relative strength in the following order: conjunction, sextile, trine and semisextile (0°, 60°, 120° and 30°). The most upsetting angles to the terrestrial atmosphere are the opposition, square and semisquare (180°, 90°, and 45°) angles. Mars in parallel of declination with the Sun causes atmospheric influences like the conjunction, but more intensely. In *contra*-parallel of declination (i.e., Sun 5° south and Mars 5° north, for example), storms with destructive gale-force winds can occur. With Mars in northern declination, oceanic currents in the northern hemisphere are usually disturbed; in southern declination, vice versa. Also, Sun-Mars conjunctions and oppositions affect the currents of the Earth's mantle of water, and *all* Sun-Mars configurations should be considered in view of the Sun's position by zodiacal signs to help forecast the overall *character* of the season.

Mars-Jupiter: Unusually dry and seasonably high temperatures during these configurations, especially when they're both in northern declination, occupying (or in configuration to) the meridian in ingress and lunation charts. Mars-Jupiter conjunctions, which happen roughly every two years, increase thunderstorms and atmospheric electricity—even during cold winter months. Those rare strokes of lightning you see in the northern hemisphere in January or February can usually be traced to Jupiter-Mars conjunctions. In the fire sign, Leo, the conjunction of these planets corresponds to parching drought and heat. In direct proportion to the heat, electrical storms of great intensity accompany or follow these conjunctions.

Equal declination, 60°, 120°, 30°, and 150° configurations, indicate dry, rising temperatures, heat waves and sometimes drought, particularly so for the sextile (60°) aspect. Without the addition of aspects by Mercury, Saturn, Uranus or Neptune, there is less likelihood of storms and other disturbances with Mars-Jupiter aspects. However, the most intense breeders of storms in aspects between these planets are the negative opposition (180°), the 90°, 45° and 135° aspects. Even the parallel of declination coincides with northwest winds.

Carefully observe "cold" planets—i.e., Mercury, Saturn and Uranus—and their aspects to Mars-Jupiter—and how they broaden and intensify storms.

Mars-Saturn: All configurations between these planets, particularly when in aspect to the meridian, stir up windy weather. The 60°, 120°, 30° and 150° angles are conducive to windy, cloudy weather. As noted before, Saturn, according to astro-weather tradition, reflects *negative* electricity and the blue part of the solar spectrum. Ordinarily considered "malefics" in natal astrology, Mars and Saturn are mutually exclusive opposites in nature and character. Saturn causes a falling barometer, atmospheric upheavals, lowered temperatures and condenses or crystallizes atmospheric humidity. Mars, on the other hand, symbolizes friction and heat. Result: a tremendous clash of atmospheric forces and destructive, gale-driven storms when these planets orbit into conjunction, parallel, opposition, or square aspects to one another. The most intensive of these vast turbulences of air occur when these aspects, particularly the conjunction, occur in late spring and summer.

Mars-Uranus: When *positively* aspecting each other (the 60°, 120°, 30° and 150° aspects), there is breezy, occasionally gusty weather, with lower temperatures, stratus clouds and sharp drops in the temperatures of inland elevations. *All* Mars-Uranus aspects presage strong, erratic, often unpredictably variable and acute wind velocities. The locations of storm emergencies and severe damage from hurricane-force winds may be determined from solar ingress charts where the conjunctions and oppositions occur on the upper or lower meridians (or square to them).

The following negative configurations tend to rip up the atmosphere at altitudes above 10,000 feet—the conjunction, opposition, parallel, square and the lesser 45° and 135° angles. In late spring and summer, when temperatures are high, there are more likely to be scattered electrical storms in the afternoon or evening as falling, cold, dry air masses meet rising masses of moist warm air. At these times damage from thunderstorms and high winds occurs along narrow pathlines in low-lying areas and valleys. Mainly during April and May, these configurations breed tornadoes in the lower central and southwestern states, but are by no means confined to these areas. During truly anomalous planetary configurations, tornadoes, like earthquakes and (in extremely rare cases) even volcanoes, can happen almost anywhere on Earth, including areas where such things were previously unheard of.

If Mercury forms aspects to Mars-Uranus configurations, it causes sleet in winter months and the danger of driving hailstorms in summer, during which heat waves are usually dissipated. These turbulences are more intense near rivers, streams, and to the leeward of hills and mountains, yet they often completely bypass some areas, making it hard to know exactly where the storms will strike.

Mars-Neptune: Neptune in Scorpio, in the parlance of G.J. McCormack and John Hazelrigg, is the "pluvial planet par excellence." The maximum effect of this configuration centers over the area where—in lunation and ingress charts—Neptune occupies or is in quadrature (90°) to the meridian. *All* Mars-Neptune aspects are usually accompanied by or closely followed by rising temperatures. Under harmonious configurations, winds range from southerly to variable, often encouraging hazy, humid and static atmospheric conditions, with lowered barometric readings. During summer months, muggy, sticky, uncomfortable weather and high temperatures. During winter, fogs and thaws.

Although some astrometeorologists have (historically) experimented with the following hypothesis (sans definite conclusions so far), it should be interesting to students of future seismic events to observe Neptune's role in the production of earthquakes. The eighth planet of the solar system seems intimately related to all liquid and gaseous phenomena, both in the Earth's atmosphere and its interior! This means that it may conceivably have some influence on the Earth's molten core and the lava and gases that interact with tectonic movements.

Watch therefore, for Mars-Neptune conjunctions, oppositions and parallels as possibly partial triggering elements of anomalistic earthquake activity.

16

THE INFLUENCE OF JUPITER

THE GIANT PLANET of the solar system—more than twice as massive as all other solarian planets together—may be a relatively small, dark star in its own right, with a retinue of 13 "planets"—the Jovian satellites. Two of Jupiter's moons are bigger than Mercury. Its churning, ever-changing atmosphere is forever roaring with electrical and radio storms whose intensity and violence are beyond human comprehension. At perihelion, Jupiter is almost 460 million miles from the Sun, yet it radiates 2½ times as much heat as it receives. At aphelion, it is about 507 million miles from our star.

Aside from the fact that when seen through a good telescope something unusual, new, and unexpected is always happening to its astoundingly detailed, silver and cream-colored surface, Jupiter's size is simply staggering—about 85,750 miles in diameter, 314 times the mass of Earth and 1,312 times Terra's volume.

All the outer (Jovian) planets—Jupiter, Saturn, Uranus and Neptune—are vastly different from the inner or terrestrial worlds. Although astronomers know a little more about them than they did before the days of satellite telescope observations, the mysteries outnumber the known data by several orders of magnitude. Whether they contain extensive rocky cores is problematical; they seem composed mainly of gases, chiefly methane and ammonia.

It's no longer fashionable to regard Jupiter's Great Red Spot as something fixed and tangible. Pioneer 10 revealed its internal structure as a pinwheel-like vortex whose superviolent pattern of circulation (the "scar" from the eruption of Venus?) displaces the clouds of the south tropical zone. The Spot rises five miles above the surrounding bands of clouds, often gaining or falling back as much as 90,000 miles compared to its environment, and has a strange red tail trailing to its right, which often wraps itself completely around the Red Spot. This is one of the greatest mysteries of the solar system.

Intriguing as the physical details of Jupiter may be, they're readily available from any of the astronomical magazines—one of the best of which is *Astronomy,* "the world's most beautiful astronomy magazine." Or, better yet, *Larousse Encyclopedia of Astronomy* (Prometheus Press, New York). We're concerned here, though, with the impact of this giant on the Earth's weather.

The largest planet of our solar system rotates on its axis faster than any other; Earth's day is nearly three times longer, for Jupiter spins on its axis once every nine hours 58 minutes and 41 seconds. At apogee (when its node is at 9° 54′ of Cancer) its distance from the Earth is "only" 365 million miles. At this range or any other—Jupiter is one of the brightest and most impressive "stars" in the night sky. When it is thus favorably situated, Jupiter's light is strong enough to shine through fairly thick clouds and cast a shadow on a light surface.

Jupiter symbolizes the indigo ray of the solar spectrum; its action on the terrestrial atmosphere is generally of a moderate nature. It inclines toward producing northerly winds, fair-weather cumulus clouds and an increase in the ozone layer through gravitational and other action on the Sun. Jupiter symbolizes positive electricity, and its chief characteristic is to cause moderate elevations in temperature and barometer. This is a fair-weather planet, with minimum humidity due to encouraging moderately descending flows of air.

When in Taurus, Leo, Scorpio or Aquarius (the "fixed" signs) and in the Earth signs (Capricorn and Virgo), Jupiter seems to influence statistically higher numbers of earthquakes. When you find Jupiter on the meridian (the mid-heaven at your point of observation) during spring or summer ingresses, this is a significator of good growing weather for crops except when that meridian happens to be Gemini, Virgo or Leo, in which case the season will tend to be dryer than usual (depending, as always, on *total* synthesis of all solarian elements). Moisture is above average when Jupiter is found in the water signs (Cancer, Scorpio and Pisces). On the meridian in a winter solstice (ingress) chart, Jupiter indicates a temperate season.

When Jupiter forms the 60° angle with the Sun, invigorating, warm temperatures are exceptionally noticeable; similarly but slightly less so when Jupiter is at the north tropic, on the celestial equator, stationary, near perihelion in Aries, and when it forms the conjunction, parallel, sextile or trine aspects to the Sun. These aspects help generate (or they coincide with) increases in atmospheric ozone, rising temperatures and healthful, stimulating air flows. By nature Jupiter is temperate, but its character can vary, depending on the number and strength of aspects formed with other planets. In northern declinations with Mars, Jupiter inclines toward thunder, drought and heat. With negative Saturn, humidity and cloudiness, generally. But when in *negative* aspects with *Saturn,* extended atmospheric depression and low barometric pressure. With Uranus, especially conjunctions, oppositions and parallels, intense electromagnetic disturbances, high wind velocities, sudden *abnormally* high-pressure areas and low temperatures—all of which have a profound influence on human health and disease conditions.

With Neptune, the atmosphere tends to become stagnant, with oppressive humidity, freakish types of moist weather and often widespread sickness from such extended negative atmospheric conditions. In spring and summer, when Mars and Jupiter form conjunctions, squares and other negative aspects, sudden increases in temperature are often succeeded by high cumulus clouds and sudden thunderstorms. Clear, fresh atmospheric conditions, however, quickly follow. Jupiter-Neptune aspects (because of the fact that Jupiter tends to increase, intensify and *expand* the influence of the planet with which it falls into configuration) are indicators of seismic activity.

When Jupiter is closest to the Sun (perihelion)—*particularly when the former is in Aries*—there is usually a major period of sunspot activity. Roughly, there's a 111-year cycle of especially great sunspots that coincides with the approximate culmination of Jupiter, Saturn and Uranus —i.e., ten orbital periods of Jupiter, four of Saturn and one and a half of Uranus. This is about 12, 30 and 84 years each.

There also seems to be an *intermediate* period of sunspot activity timed at 55 years, which is equal to five Jovian and two Saturnian orbits of the Sun. According to a New York-based economic-solarian cycle corporation, this coincides with vast changes in mass human psychology, extended drought cycles, the condition of the economy and epidemic diseases. Three 18.6-year cycles of the north lunar node are slightly more than 55 years; three 18-year, 11-day saros eclipse cycles are a bit more than 54 years. At the very least, these are interestingly close "coincidences." Multiples of the cycles of these three planets bring them into orbital conjunction at the same longitudinal juncture in cycles of 1,351 years.

Under Jupiter, you'll detect rising temperatures for long periods, southerly winds, but no extremes of heat. Throughout most of Europe and in the Soviet Union, Jupiter often inspires northerly winds and some drought. When in aspect to Mars and the Sun, Jupiter inclines toward extreme heat, and when in configuration with Mercury and Venus at the same time, oppressive humidity and thunderstorms.

In Aries—bad for agriculture, generally; windy and dry. In Taurus: balmy breezes, lovely weather and clear skies. In Gemini: windy, the atmosphere hot and dry. In Cancer: extremely fertile and fruitful, with soothing, comfortable temperatures. In Leo: pleasantly warm, but dry, with very high summer temperatures (under southerly surface winds, cloudy weather).

Jupiter-Saturn: Until the year 2080, Jupiter-Saturn conjunctions occur approximately every 20 years in the Earth signs: Taurus, Virgo and Capricorn. A most unusual "fall-out" of these 19.85-year Jupiter-Saturn conjunctions occurs in 1980, when they meet (incidentally, during the November Presidential election) in *Libra, an air sign!* Because the death or the assassination of American presidents during these Jupiter-Saturn conjunctions has always occurred in Earth signs since 1840, many astrologically minded people, not aware of the change of element in which the conjunctions occur in 1980—have predicted the repetition of a John F. Kennedy-type assassination sometime during the term of the President-elect of 1980.

This is rather like the eyewitness observation that beating tomtoms during a solar eclipse always "causes" the Sun to reappear. First, not only will the 1980s President-elect survive his term in office, he will overcome unprecedented obstacles to become one of the most universally popular American leaders in national and world history.

Here's why: Most mundane (state) astrologers base their predictions on a horoscope of the United States using 7°, 35′ of the sign Gemini as its rising sign or ascendant. For some unfathomable reason they believe (or were taught) that the U.S.A. radix of July 4, 1776, was at 2:13 A.M. *This timing is off by about ten hours!* But the astrologers like it because this puts the Moon in Aquarius in the tenth house (the Mid-heaven position), with Uranus (ruler of Aquarius) almost exactly on the ascendant (8°, 50′ of Gemini).

This is purest bull. According to the rules of astrology, the actual character of an individual (or any other entity, be it a corporation, a nation, or group of nations) is profoundly influenced by the exact moment it becomes *an independently functioning entity:* In spite of all the arguments and guesswork (and contrary to the idea that the United States is a Gemini ascendant), proof that the American horoscope has Libra rising comes from no less an authority than the *Journal of Congress* for July 4, 1776 (it's available for anyone to check):

> Agreeable to the order of the day, the Congress resolved itself into a committee of the whole, to take

> into further consideration the Declaration and after some time the President resumed the chair, and Mr. Harrison reported that the Committee had agreed to a Declaration which they desired to report. . . . At a little past meridian,* on the Fourth of July, 1776, a unanimous vote of the thirteen colonies was given in favor of declaring themselves free and independent states.

The horoscope of the Declaration of Independence for July 4, 1776, therefore, was approximately at zero hours, 20 minutes *post* meridian, giving the fledgling government at Philadelphia 14° 42′ of Libra ascending, with the Sun, Jupiter, Venus and Mars in the ninth house and Saturn on the ascendant—in *Libra!*

The ascendant of a chart denotes the *outward* personality (as opposed to the inner character). Here's an apt description of Libra rising from my book *Write Your Own Horoscope* (Signet Books, The New American Library (revised), New York, 1975):

> *This is one of the most likeable and harmonious Ascendants* [don't laugh yet]. *You are sensitive and strongly influenced by your surroundings as well as existing conditions. Libra rising gives you an innate sense of fairness, makes you honest, courteous, compassionate and kind. You are optimistic, candid, and have a good deal of willpower, but very little perseverence. One of your chief drawbacks stems from the fact that you will weigh first one side of a question and then the other—and then perhaps wait to see what someone else will do—before making a decision of your own.*
>
> *Your talents include constructive and inventive ability . . . you learn quickly and can master almost any branch of business. The difficulty lies in the fact that you may, while engrossed in any avocation, suddenly change your mind and follow an entirely different line of interest.*

*"Meridian"—the Mid-heaven, when the Sun is directly overhead—in other words, *slightly after 12 o'clock noon!*

> *Social and personal pleasures are matters of great absorption to you with Libra ascending. This is the natural sign of partnership and harmonious relationships; unfortunately, too many of these connections are more disruptive than amicable. . . . You'll take some long trips, but the chief source of your profit and success will be in your own country. . . .*

Has there in recorded history ever been a more novelty-loving nation or country with more natural resources than the United States? (Figure 39 is the correct horoscope of the United States, with the Sun, Venus, Mars, Jupiter and Uranus all in close north parallel declination.)

Although the man elected as President of the United States in 1980 has already been proved capable of overcoming great obstacles, he will achieve unparalleled success and previously unheard of diplomatic victories. He'll be the first great world leader to crystallize the ideal of a united human species and may begin by working toward the abolition of passports and the arbitrary concepts of national borders, toward a workable solution to unilateral disarmament and the establishment of a globally operative series of large, fully equipped and prepared disaster relief squads.*

Despite this man's warm, human appeal, innate honesty and integrity, his apparent willingness to make unpopular compromises in order to promote future world harmony, he has powerful determination, a virtually indomitable will and an intuitive grasp of the precise nature of future national and world problems during the decade of the 1980s—and beyond.

Saturn will be in Libra until December 1982, roughly the time suggested by Drs. Gribbin and Plagemann in *The Jupiter Effect* for the earthquake they claim will destroy large portions of California. To the uninitiated, the alleged "alignment" of planets on the other side of the Sun is pictured (even illustrated as such in popular magazines and newspapers) as *a straight line*—with the Earth and Moon on one side of the solar system, and Mercury,

* This was written *before* Jimmy Carter was considered a serious candidate for the Presidency.

Venus, Mars, Saturn, Uranus, Neptune and Pluto strung out straight as an arrow on the other side of the Sun, making it impossible for Earthbound (even lunar-based or orbiting) telescopes to see them.

Much as one hates to throw cold water on a seemingly neat theory, the fact is that all these planets will—*at their closest*—not only *not* be in conjunction, they'll be scattered across 85° of celestial longitude—*almost one fourth of the zodiacal circle!* Don't, however, misinterpret this wide, almost random, spread of the planets as inconsequential. Their angular positions, their configurations to each other and to the Earth will be intensified during the bitterly cold winter of 1981, particularly in the Northeastern and Northwestern and border states of the U.S.A., throughout the Canadian northwest, and especially in Europe and the Soviet Union. The Deep Freeze of 1981 will last from the time of the winter solstice of December 21, 1980, through January, February and March of 1981, more intensely so during Saturn's stationary position centering on January 25, 1981. This promises to be the most bitterly cold week of the most bitterly cold winter within living memory.

Moreover, it will be intensified by the Jupiter-Saturn parallel of declination throughout the winter months, then extending to mid-August, which will make 1981 the most memorable year ever for unseasonably cold blasts of Arctic air, blizzards and every variety of below-normal temperatures during spring and summer.

The winter of 1981 could be the record-breaker since weather record-keeping began. With Jupiter-Saturn again in conjunction from July 24 to about August 10, the southern hemisphere will receive the full brunt of *its* winter—this time centering about 43° west of the worst intensity of the northern hemisphere's winter.

(*Under these circumstances, it is almost certain that large-scale destruction of crops will result in extreme worldwide shortages of food. The prospect of the ensuing famine and probability of mass starvation, epidemic disease, economic and political chaos should be warning enough to begin preparations* now *to avoid the worst of what is yet to come.*)

Jupiter and Saturn's relatively slow orbital velocities make their configurations long-lasting—slow to form and slow to separate. While Jupiter symbolizes and typifies the principle of *expansion,* Saturn relates to *contraction.* In ingress and lunation maps (particularly for the years 1979–1986), the focal points of intensity will be found to relate to the Jupiter-Saturn meridian positions and the negative angles formed to and from them. Thunderstorms, hailstorms, blizzards—any kind of precipitation—tend to become more violent and widespread during most Jupiter-Saturn configurations, more intensely so during the conjunction, opposition or parallel of declination (or when the conjunction and parallel occur at the same time, *as during January, February and March 1981*).

This kind of chronic cold and damp weather is disastrous to public health. The *positive* aspects of 60°, 120°, 30° and 150° bring fair weather and gentler breezes. The negative aspects are extraordinarily conducive to gravitational/electromagnetic disturbances that result in sunspots; this is accentuated with the conjunction, opposition and square or quadrature (90°) aspects. These configurations (to which you can add the parallel of declination) cause increased precipitation in southern areas, powerful winds, ionization of the atmosphere, strong magnetic disturbances and intense cold fronts. In the highest atmosphere, where winds are strongest, the air most rarefied, and the lightest gases (hydrogen and helium) most prevalent, there is a great tendency—under adverse Jupiter-Uranus configurations—for the Northern Lights (Aurora Borealis) to manifest.

Jupiter-Uranus conjunctions occur on the average at about 14-year (13.82) intervals, although the oppositions repeat at about 8.90-year cycles. If both planets are at the meridian (directly overhead for any point of observation in lunation or ingress charts) that season (or month or fortnight) will be characterized by extremely powerful winds. It is not unusual for 80-to-90-mph gales to be clocked at these times. This also applies to *all* other Jupiter-Uranus aspects to the meridian.

But in the more positive 60°, 120°, 150° and 30° aspects—in that order of descending intensity—these two planets are conducive, particularly in northern areas, to cooler, dry weather and a high barometer with a noticeable lack of magnetic disturbances. Below-normal coolness predominates in southern locations when Uranus is southing in lunation and ingress maps, and precipitation will be well below normal.

Jupiter-Neptune: Oddly enough, the most potent aspect between these two planets is the *parallel of declination,* which affects the atmosphere more intensely than either the conjunction or opposition! Conjunctions occur about every 13 (12.82) years. The quarterly cycles of Jupiter and Neptune take about 3.20 years, with double that increment (6.40 years) between oppositions and conjunctions. These are negative in every respect and promise dominating low-pressure, high relative humidity downslope, stagnant damp weather, mists and fogs in valleys and low-lying areas, and above-normal precipitation, particularly near rivers, streams and lakes.

These conjunctions and oppositions promise cloudbursts in narrow, isolated areas. Torrential downpours breed flash floods, particularly when Neptune is at the lower meridian or in opposition or quadrature to it. During summer, the 45° and 135° configurations (which occur approximately 20½ months before and after the square aspects) breed altocumulus clouds with oppressively humid and muggy air. The positive configuration of Jupiter-Neptune (60°, 120°, 30° and 150°) breed higher temperatures and generally clear skies and fair, quiet weather. In winter these aspects bring on slow thaws that melt snow and create muddy conditions in rural areas.

17

THE INFLUENCE OF SATURN

THE CONTINUATION OF our fragile life-supporting environment depends on an all-out scientific study of how terrestrial weather corresponds so exactly to the angles formed among planets. Whatever the (presently) undiscovered forces that govern the potency of those angles may be, we can see this principle operating here on the Earth. Although no two snowflakes have ever been found to be alike, they always conform to the "crystallizing" (sextile) or hexagonal shape. All superior metals crystallize at this 60° angle of a regular polygon.

All the so-called "non-living" crystals form exact angles in their natural state. These angular relationships are also detectable in the way leaves, twigs and branches of various trees grow: a relatively simple form in the pairing, i.e., when two grow exactly opposite (180°) from each other, while the next pair above and below grow in opposition to the mother branch, stem or twig, but *at right angles* (90°) to the original pairing. In this, as in all such branching techniques, nature's intent is to permit maximum dispersion so the leaves can receive maximum sunlight. The same quadrature and opposition of leaves and branches is found in maple trees, horse chestnuts, dogwoods and ash trees.

The trine, or 120° angle, is found in the distribution of the leaves of beech trees. Apple trees, oaks and cypress leaves have a distribution angle of 144°—*a dozen times a dozen,* or two-fifths of a turn for each succeeding pair of leaves. Holly and spruce leaves spiral on their branches at three-eighths of a turn—at angles of 135° each. In large trees these turns also occur at five thirteenths, about 140°, and so on.

These are not random or chaotic. Each numerator and each denominator is the sum of the two immediately preceding it. Both numerical sequences form a regular and simple progression; like this: 1, 1, 2, 3, 5, 8, 13, 21, 34, 55, 89, 144, 233, 377. It is called the Fibonacci series after its thirteenth-century Italian discoverer. According to Guy Murchee, in "The Realm of the Tree" (*Diplomat* magazine, August 1966), these sequences not only form the basis of tree design, they are also *"part of the same ubiquitous music of the spheres that builds harmony into atoms, molecules, crystals, Suns and galaxies and makes the Universe sing—as Pythagoras taught in 500 B.C."*

The ambience of these forces is also manifested in our close physical relationship to the trees and plants. We may have more in common with a pine tree or a sequoia cactus than with the most intelligent beings from far-off worlds in the Galaxy. Chemists, for example, recently discovered that green chlorophyll in trees and plants is almost identical to the red blood that courses through our veins. If *a single atom* of magnesium is detached from a molecule of chlorophyll and replaced by an atom of iron, it becomes *a molecule of red blood!*

Mars "rules" iron *and* human blood (how could ancient men have known that?) and is also the ruling planet of Aries and Scorpio (some astrologers now say Pluto, too), whose constellation, Scorpius, is most notable because of the red giant sun called Antares ("against Aries"). Compared to our local star, which is about 865,000 miles in diameter (several Earth-sized planets could easily be dropped into a moderate-sized sunspot), the diameter of the red giant, Antares, would engulf the Sun, Mercury, Venus and Earth, and reach *several million miles past the orbit of Mars.* Antares, therefore, is *approximately 375 million miles in diameter,* or 450 times the size of the Sun.

Still another gigantic star (of the spectroscopic type M2) is called VV Cephei A. If placed in our solar system, the diameter of this colossus would reach far beyond the orbit of Jupiter (engulfing it along with the Sun, all the inner planets *and* Antares!) VV Cephei A is 1,200 times the diameter of the Sun—over *1 billion, 200 million miles in diameter.* And then there's ϵAurigae B, a K5 type supergiant that would swallow up the Sun, all the planets (including the other two supergiants, Antares and VV Cephei A) and reach past the orbit of Saturn—halfway to the orbit of Uranus. ϵAurigae B is two thousand times the diameter of our Sun, or 173^8 miles in diameter. The time it would take for light, flashing at 186,000 miles per second, to cross the two-billion-mile diameter of this superduper giant is about two hours and 13 minutes!

Then there's Betelgeuse, or Alpha Orionis, the Red Supergiant only 60,000 times the size of the Sun, which is slightly smaller than Antares. Yet the outer cloud or shell of potassium gas of Betelgeuse is 400 times the diameter of the entire solar system—i.e., the staggering radius of 1.6 trillion miles, or over three trillion miles in diameter. Betelgeuse is not a nova or a supernova, yet it is blowing off its mass at the rate of our own Sun every year. And the mysterious quasars and other cosmic bodies whose mass and density, if not size, equals that of entire galaxies composed of hundreds of billions of stars—all these cosmic bodies interacting through gravitational, electromagnetic and yet undiscovered forces and energies whose complexities are beyond present human comprehension.

It isn't hopeless however. We could have a good leg up on such understanding if we start with the relatively simple study of intercorrelations among the planets of our local system.

Saturn, the most beautiful planet, with its veils of gossamer rings, is roughly 80,000 miles in diameter, second in size to Jupiter. Saturn has nearly a thousand times the mass of Earth and a sidereal cycle of nearly 30 (29.46) years. Its axial rotational period is close to that of Jupiter—ten hours, 14 minutes and 24 seconds. Saturn crosses the celestial equator at intervals of about 15 (14.73) years. Conjunctions with the Sun occur 10 to 11 days later each year.

Normally, Saturn's influence is slow-acting, ponderous, heavy and concentrative. Like all others, the ringed planet combines with and reflects the nature of the zodiacal sign in which it happens to be located—either transiting in direct motion, stationary, or in apparent retrograde movement. Negative electricity is under the nominal signature of Saturn and related to the "cold" blue part of the visible spectrum. Where Saturn is at the meridian in solar ingress and lunation maps (or in quadrature to this Mid-heaven position) for any specific spot on the globe, the season for that area will be characterized by cold centers and maximum moisture, with major low barometric pressure.

Rising warm, moist masses of air with counterclockwise flows from every direction toward the center are characteristic of Saturn's negative configurations, i.e., when stationary, in conjunction, opposition, parallel, 90°, 45° and 135°. Relative humidity becomes more intense when moist air rises and condenses in the colder regions of higher altitudes. Various downfalls become more intense, cloudiness increases, temperatures rise and prevailing westerly winds follow low barometric pressure eastward.

Storms influenced by Saturnine aspects tend to be widespread and of long duration. But when these storms transit eastward of your point of observation, the temperature drops and northwest winds coincide with clearing weather. When such disturbances cross, or even approach, bodies of water their intensity builds to near-cataclysmic proportions. Under *negative* Saturn configurations, additional power is added to all other planetary indicators of the storm.

Saturn in the crystallizing 60° aspect is the most effective angle to induce sharply falling temperatures. Sixty degrees is a positive aspect for *any* planetary body. The 60°, 120°, 30° and 150° configurations, with relative strength in that order, bring generally fair weather accompanied by variable cloudiness and gradually lowering temperatures. When on the lower meridian, Saturn is inclined to push storms in a more northerly direction, while temperatures will rise in the south and southeastern sectors. In direct relation to the intensity of the storm, temperatures drop in southern or southward areas, adversely affecting crops. Heaviest storm damage centers over southern areas when colder air sucked in from the northwest stabs far to the south as Saturn is southing, i.e., when the ringed planet orbits toward the meridian or Mid-heaven (the M.C.) position in lunation and ingress charts. The importance of Saturn's position at the cardinal angles (from 0° to 30°, 90° to 120°, 180° to 210° and 270° to 300°), the first, fourth, seventh and tenth channels, should never be overlooked—not even in lunation charts.

To time weather changes for any other longitude, check all transits and aspects to the M.C. and nadir of the chart. In other words, the exact degree of the Midheaven and that of the nadir position (*under* the Earth). For example, low-pressure areas and/or storms don't always coincide with the exact date of a Sun-Saturn conjunction. I don't know why, but if it's ever possible to learn why our long-range astrometeorological forecasts (six months in the science-fact section of *Analog* magazine) were only 93 percent accurate, even though we dealt only with the most significant, often catastrophic, atmospheric events (it just didn't seem worth bothering with inconsequentialities such as "degree days, average precipitation, averages of temperature . . ." and the like), it might be possible someday to render extremely detailed long-range weather forecasts with an *average* accuracy above 98 percent—consistently.

The further south (in declination) Saturn is, the colder the seasonal frosts and freezes become. These below-normal temperatures are intensified by Saturn's transits of the Tropic of Cancer, the celestial equator, when it is stationary, or is on the meridian of ingress charts or in quadrature to that meridian.

One of the coldest of all astronomical-weather indicators is the long-lasting crystallizing 60°-sextile aspect between Saturn and Uranus, particularly when one or the other planet occupies the meridian of the ingress or lunation chart. When Saturn adds its influence to storm-breeding angles among other planets, the atmospheric effects are more concentrated and prolonged.

It may seem paradoxical, but under conflicting or contradictory influences, Saturn will often intensify a season of drought or increase the severity and intensity of winter storms. Saturn in Leo, especially at or near the nadir, increases snow and rain. In Virgo: in northern declination, pleasantly seasonal rainfall; in southern declination, extended periods of drought. In Libra: when direct in motion, better agricultural conditions, more food and lower prices. When retrograde, drought in localized areas and possible near-famine conditions. In northern declination, dryness; pleasantly moist weather if in southern declination. In Scorpio: scant rainfall if in southern declination; in northern declination, abundant moisture. In Sagittarius: northern declination, plenty of rainfall; southern declination, considerably less moisture. In Capricorn: in southern declination, coldness and dryness; in northern declination, seasonal precipitation and moderate temperatures. In Aquarius: in southern declination, dry cold atmospheric conditions; in northern declination frequent wintry blasts and cold storms. In Pisces: in southern declination, thunderstorms over bodies of water; in northern declination, cold, windy, stormy and wet. In Aries: generally easterly winds, but cold. When aspected by the Moon, wet and freezing in winter; in summer seasons, rainy and windy. In Taurus: prolonged cold, wet periods. In Gemini: in southern declination, often dry and pleasant, but windy weather. In northern declination, particularly in winter, bitter coldness. In summer seasons, cool and windy with atmospheric electricity and thunderstorms. In Cancer: in southern declination, the weather tends to be seasonally cold and wet. In northern declination, cold and dry.

Saturn-Uranus: These slow-moving outer planets form configurations that last intermittently for months at a time, thereby impressing more than one season during their aspects. *In 1988, for example, there will be three successive conjunctions of Uranus and Saturn in the last degrees of Sagittarius. They will also be in close parallel of south declination at the same time, so severe drought can be expected centering in February, June and September and during the growing seasons in both the northern and southern hemispheres.*

The quadratures of Saturn with Uranus occur about 11½ years (11.37) years apart (their conjunction cycles happen every 45.5 years). Their semisquare (45°) configurations happen every 5.69 years. Extremes and prolonged disturbances of the atmosphere occur during their conjunction, parallel, opposition, square, semisquare and 135° configurations, with relative strength of the angles formed in that order.

"Saturnine" diseases are characterized and correlated to electrical conductivity of the atmosphere, radical changes in temperature and barometric extremes that tend to lower the physical resistance of large populations. These diseases can reach epidemic proportions and spread from *east to west* around the entire globe. This is contradictory to the normal direction of weather movement. Abnormally high northeast and easterly winds usually coincide with Saturn-Uranus combinations.

Chronically frigid, anomalistic temperatures accompany the most crystallizing (60°) aspect. The trine (120°) configuration is similar, but not as severe or intense. Even the more transitory lunation charts, where Saturn or Uranus are on the meridian (overhead or M.C.) of the longitude of your chart or in quadrature to it, indicate regions of maximum intensity.

Saturn-Neptune: The conjunction cycle of these two planets is about 36 (35.73) years. Their quadratures occur about every nine (8.93) years; both planets symbolize and coincide with a low barometer. Their configurations often last for months at a time and consequently influence whole seasons with abnormally damp weather, particularly under the conjunction, opposition, square, 45°, 135° and/or parallel aspects. When there are prevailing southerly or easterly winds, the greatest extremes of cold, damp weather occur during the conjunctions and oppositions.

With precipitation always above normal during these aspects, the worst downpours occur in low-lying sections, valleys and similar isolated areas, causing disastrous flash floods. Paradoxically, other nearby areas, particularly the highlands, will receive little or no rain or snowfall. Sometimes Saturn forms a major configuration with Uranus, then turns retrograde for a very long time before turning direct in motion once more. When this happens, the faster-moving planet will *repeat* the identical aspects to Uranus, causing the adverse anomalies of weather to be duplicated over the same extensive geographical areas. These aspects may endure as long as two whole seasons!

Flooding is always a danger with Saturn-Neptune configurations because they coincide with periodic, prolonged and very heavy rainfall. In springtime: lowland mists, hazy days and foggy nights. In summer: abnormal rainfall, strange hazes, smog and a generally unhealthy, devitalizing atmosphere. Like Venus-Saturn aspects, the configurations of Saturn and Neptune are characterized by diminished sunshine, but with *saturating* humidity. In the fall, the equinoctial chart with Saturn-Neptune aspects cause chronic, predominating counterclockwise low-pressure patterns, abnormal cloudiness and heavy, lasting rainfall, followed by sharply dropping temperatures, with frost at night. In wintertime, extremes of snowfall and hail over inland areas and higher elevations. On the average, temperatures are well below normal for this season, particularly when the Saturn-Neptune aspect is also joined by Uranus and/or Mercury.

Under the favorable weather configurations of 60°, 120°, 30° and 150°, Saturn and Neptune (particularly when they're activated by the transits of faster-moving inner planets) induce dull, misty weather in lowland areas, and in the interior and at high altitudes, variable temperatures with stimulating showers. At those points in geographic longitude where Saturn is on (or squaring) the meridian, the trend is toward lowered temperatures. With Neptune at (or quadrature to) the meridian, isolated squalls are intensified, there are more southerly winds, storms, cloudbursts and—in the so-called "tornado belt," but *not always* confined to these areas—twisters, especially in the springtime. Whatever Sign concentrative Saturn happens to occupy, the nature and character of that Sign is consequently crystallized.

18

THE INFLUENCE OF URANUS

THE NOMINAL "RULER" of the sign of Aquarius happens to be one of the enigmas of the solar system. Although classified as a giant planet, Uranus is considerably smaller than its closest inner neighbors, Jupiter and Saturn. (Incidentally, if you have trouble recalling the order of the planets after you reach Jupiter, simply remember SUN—Saturn–Uranus–Neptune.)

The diameter of Uranus is 29,300 miles—more or less. Its vast distance from the Sun, roughly 1,783 million miles, makes the details of this strange world and its rings faint and difficult to discern, even through powerful telescopes. While Saturn has nine satellites (*a tenth one discovered twice, but in vastly different orbits, may not be a natural moon*), Uranus has five (perhaps six) moons.

The solar orbit of this oblate, faintly ringed world takes 84 years and seven days. One rotation of Uranus on its axis is closer to that of Saturn and Jupiter than to any of the inner terrestrial planets, just ten hours and 41 minutes. But the chief peculiarity of this world is the tilt of its unique axis of rotation, which is inclined at an angle of 98° to the perpendicular to the plane of the solar system. The Earth, for example, is tilted only 23° from the "vertical."

Uranus travels at a mean velocity of only 4¼ miles per second along an orbit that is not very steeply inclined to the plane of the ecliptic. In fact, the angle between them is only 46 seconds of arc (0° 46′). Because of the fact that Uranus "lies on its side," in its orbit, each of its seasons averages about 21½ years. As a consequence, its northern hemisphere is in total darkness for over two decades; its equatorial region is exposed to sunlight for a total of about 42 years; then the southern hemisphere is plunged into 21 years of unimaginable darkness and cold.

Some planet.

Uranus croses the celestial equator once every 42 years and takes seven years to transit one zodiacal sign. The north node of Uranus is at 13° 43′ of Gemini, and its conjunctions with the Sun (in geocentric longitude) occur 4½ days later each year. Uranus is related to the highest barometric pressure; it triggers incredibly cold air in the highest reaches of the atmosphere and activates descending cold air masses from the Arctic.

The influence of Uranus on terrestrial weather is to encourage high-pressure areas and descending masses of cold, dry air with winds circulating in *clockwise* motion outward from the center. East of these centers, temperatures are lowest with prevailing northwest winds and cloudless, clear blue skies. Winter thaws and summer heat waves frequently unfold on the western edges of these highs. Unless Uranus happens to be in one of the three water signs, dry weather with windy drought conditions are the rule.

In hot weather, sudden wind shifts from the northwest (under cold fronts) trigger line squalls downslope and scattered thunderstorms with extraordinary amounts of atmospheric electricity. During the coldest months in the northern hemisphere, Uranian winds create blizzards, especially along the southern shores of the Great Lakes. Quickly following all major configurations, particularly where Mercury, Saturn or the Sun are involved, temperatures drop sharply. As usual, the crystallizing sextile aspect serves to intensify frigid air. Deep freezes are more intense when Uranus is making an important aspect to Saturn (especially 60°) and when it is at or close to its deepest south declination. In conjunction with, or in opposition to, Jupiter or Mercury, Uranus is responsible for truly violent winds. Conjunctions with other planets in water signs, as well as the opposition, square and semi-square (45°) aspects, create penetratingly cold, humid weather and bleak overcast skies.

It usually takes two or three days for adverse aspects of the Sun to Uranus to culminate at any given observational point. This is when blustery, variable cold winds are indicated by stratus clouds that look like horizontal brush strokes stemming from the western skies.

Under negative aspects to Venus, Uranus induces cold, drizzling or freezing rain or (in winter) light snowfall. With Jupiter, electromagnetic disturbances, strong to powerful winds and increased sunspot activity. With Saturn, enduring cold waves and unseasonably low temperatures.

It is about 45 years between conjunctions of Saturn with Uranus. The next one is scheduled for February 10th, 1988, with Neptune and Mars in *southern parallel of declination.* Because these aspects culminate so closely to the degree of the *preceding* winter solstice of 1987, the chart for *that* Arctic-type deep freeze will be even more intense than for the winter of 1981!

When Uranus is near or on the nadir, the meridian, southing, or *squaring* the meridian, it causes unseasonably low temperatures, dominating northwest winds, highest barometric pressures and high-gale velocities with unpredictably erratic weather changes.

At the nadiar of ingress, lunation, eclipse or other key charts, the high-pressure areas caused by this position of Uranus result in isolated droughts in northern sections and low average temperatures for the season or period you have calculated and are interpreting. Because of cold fronts in the south and southeast, abundant rainfall is likely in narrowly defined sections; droughts will be more pronounced in the more highly elevated areas. Cold, dry masses of air center southward when Uranus is southing, and lows will be drawn northward. Wherever Uranus is in quadrature to the meridian, high- and low-pressure areas come into violent juxtaposition; storms and winds become stronger and more intense. Thunderstorms predominate during summer months under this aspect.

Blasts of gusty winds occur when Uranus is aspected by the Sun, Mercury, Mars or Jupiter. Although solar configurations influence the weather constitutionally those of the planets govern organic changes. as the *functional* arbiter, the Moon's position provides exact timing at your required point of observation. The aspects of *all* planets to the meridian (upper or lower) are extremely important. The effects of descending cold air masses when Uranus is stationary take about three days to reach your meridian. Every 42 years, when Uranus crosses the celestial equator, the dominating windy, cold, intermittent patterns of weather will often last for months at a time.

When a New Moon, a Full Moon or an eclipse coincides with a Jupiter-Uranus conjunction (especially in charts depicting planetary positions at a solstice or equinox), and *particularly* if Mercury is one of the multiples of 15° or 18° to any of these bodies, wind intensity can reach hurricane proportions. In maximum declination, i.e., when Uranus enters Capricorn or Cancer (its solstitial colure), you can interpret bitterly cold seasonal weather, particularly under adverse aspects from Saturn.

February 1899, one of the most bitterly cold winters in Florida's history, was surpassed when Saturn's quadrature (from Libra) was repeated on January 28, 1951. Pensacola's temperature then dropped to below freezing, and lakes in Mobile, Alabama, were frozen so solidly that crowds of people went ice-skating.

The most intensely cold winter seasons are indicated by Uranus' most southerly declination, *augmented* when Saturn also reaches its deepest southerly declination. Again, the warning that Saturn will conjoin Uranus on February 10, June 30 and September 21, 1988, in the final degrees of Sagittarius, is the most concrete indication possible that all existing cold weather records will be smashed, perhaps not to be equaled or surpassed for decades. Even the summer months will be so anomalistic (particularly in Eastern Europe and throughout the Soviet Union) that by their very freakishness they will become legendary.

It would be provident for meteorologists and other scientists to put these rules to the acid test of crucial experimentation. Both 1981 and 1988 are periods to which we should give serious attention while there is still sufficient time to prepare for what is to come.

Sun-Uranus: In equal declination or any other configuration, barometers rise, temperatures fall and cold dry masses of air flowing *clockwise* descend from the highest reaches of the atmosphere. As always, when northwest winds blow eastward downslope, the coldest temperatures are first felt most strongly in the higher elevations. Daily long-range predictions can be determined by comparing each day's planetary configurations to the celestial map of the last cardinal solar equinox (or solstice, depending on the season). This ingress map must then be transposed to your chosen point of geographic observation. When Uranus is *angular,* i.e., the first, fourth, seventh or tenth channels of the chart, that center of terrestrial longitude is where this eccentric planet's maximum intensity will originate.

If, for example, Uranus approximates its nadir position—that is, if it norths toward the midnight (directly below the Earth) or 00:00 o'clock position, the more intense cold fronts and dominating high pressure areas will stem from the north. When Uranus souths—comes into close approximation to the Mid-heaven (overhead) in the northern hemisphere or 12:00 position, the M.C. of your chart—masses of cold air will move in eastward direction over the most southern regions. In square or quadrature (90°) from the meridian, the predominating weather pattern will be variably windy with great storm potential.

In conjunction with the Sun, in parallel of declination, or at 60°, 120°, 30° and 150°, Uranus breeds cool, fair, dry weather—the single exception being during the heat of summer. But even following hot temperatures under these aspects, erratic cold fronts from the northwest trigger scattered thunderstorms downslope from higher elevations and eastward through low-lying areas and valleys. During winter seasons, sudden, unexpected drops in temperature. Winter snows, frequent cold drizzling and sporadic cloudiness, high winds and high humidity accompany the 90°, 180°, 45° and 135° angles between Uranus and the Sun.

Storm emergencies, up to and including erratic changes in the atmosphere and the EEC (electrical Earth currents), with possible tectonic implications, occur when Uranus is on the M.C. of any solar ingress chart. By combining the character of the Sign from which the Sun forms its configurations to Uranus (and vice versa), your interpretations will become more facile, and with experience, your forecasts will be increasingly more accurate. All the foregoing weather conditions become more complex when Sun-Uranus configurations culminate at the time of New or Full Moon or aspects by Mercury, Venus, Mars, or Saturn.

Uranus-Neptune: Aspects formed between these planets are extremely rare because of Neptune's nearly 165-year orbital period. All configurations between these extremely slow-moving outer worlds are characterized by freakishly contrasting atmospheric conditions that manifest over periods ranging from months to entire seasons. Such weather conditions return intermittently when the inner, faster-moving planets form their transitional aspects.

The next conjunction of Uranus with Neptune will take place (in *geocentric* longitude) in February and March, and again throughout September, October and November of 1993 in the late degrees of Capricorn. This may be the tail end of an intermittent cycle of extremely cold and stormy wintry deep freezes, but world conditions will by then have changed so radically that the rules presented here will probably be regarded as the most elementary, archaic, perhaps crude understanding of the cosmic energies that interact among all celestial bodies.

Uranus-Pluto: The most recent conjunction—the first in about 1¼ centuries—between these two planets took place in October 1965, in the middle of the sign Virgo. Pluto is believed to influence terrestrial weather in somewhat the same way as Mars, but with more intensity. To me, this seems extremely unlikely because there simply hasn't been enough time or anywhere near enough dedicated astrometeorologists to accumulate the vast number of observations and correlations on which to base statistical data to be extrapolated. For this reason, I tend to discount the *characteristic* influence of Pluto, but not its potency in the production of sunspots or its influence on the Earth's weather.

There's a great deal yet to learn—and not very much time left in which to do it.

19

THE INFLUENCE OF NEPTUNE

TRYING TO PROVIDE detailed, new descriptions of a planet that has been referred to and often analyzed through recent chapters might seem a bit redundant. Yet Neptune's influence is one of the most important elements studied for nearly a century and a half (since its discovery, which was based on calculations of perturbations in the orbit of Uranus by Le Verrier on September 23, 1846—by the presence of the unseen Neptune, as it turned out).

Due to the close similarity in the sizes of Uranus and Neptune, astronomers have often mistaken one for the other, but Neptune is just barely the smaller of the two, with a diameter of 27,700 miles as compared to 29,300 for Uranus. Neptune probably has three (or more) moons, only two of which have been discovered, the smaller one, Nereid, in 1949 by Kuiper. The larger satellite, Triton, is about 3,300 miles across (considerably bigger than our own Moon's 2,160 mile-diameter), and was discovered in 1846 by an astronomer named Lassell.

Neptune's average distance from the Sun is 2,793 million miles and rolls around its nearly circular solar orbit at a speed of about 3½ miles per second; it takes 164 years and 280 days to complete one of its nearly circular orbits of the Sun. Not until the year 2011 will Neptune return to the point where it was discovered! Although details of this far-off world are faint—even with powerful telescopes—like Uranus it has a greenish-blue color and there seem to be dark belts of clouds composed mostly of methane. Because of Neptune's low temperature (—170°), it's very likely that much of this methane has become liquid instead of being in a gaseous state as it is in the atmospheres of Jupiter and Saturn. Most of the other (presently known) gases are probably frozen solid, with oceans of liquid methane yanked around into surging tides by the powerful gravitational tug of huge Triton.

The length of Neptune's day is figured by spectroscopic analysis to be about 15 hours and 40 minutes. Its axis is inclined at an astonishing 29° to the perpendicular to the plane of the ecliptic! Insofar as its influence on terrestrial weather is concerned, Neptune indicates variable low visibility, rising currents of air, predominantly southerly airflows, lowered barometric pressures, extreme humidity and stationary pockets of air that, in lower areas, increase fog and smog, and in the higher stratas of the atmosphere often pose serious difficulties for aircraft.

In summer months Neptune causes unexpectedly sudden veering from absolutely dead calms to line squalls or semitropical lows. In fall and winter seasons fog is prevalent under Neptune aspects, but during late spring and summer, there are extremes of humidity, thick ground hazes and a rapidly dropping barometer. Somewhat like Venus, Neptune causes heavy, often short-lived periods of rainfall. In hot spells, the humidity climbs even higher when Neptune is aspected by Venus and/or the Moon. Under Neptune's influence, air rises in vertical columns from the surface, carrying smoke, smog and dust particles into the upper atmosphere so rapidly that it frequently generates a spiral that develops into a devastating tornado, particularly over southern plains states.

Even in wintertime, temperatures usually rise with Neptune's angular impressions on the atmosphere, creating calm, humid and hazy conditions. Winter weather is mild, frequently resulting in thick fogs, thaws and snowslides in mountainous sections. They're more intense during warmer months and tend to follow the paths of rivers and streams. These influences are largely dependent on the nature of other celestial bodies aspecting Neptune. Venus-Neptune configurations relate to flash floods and localized heavy rainfalls. Oddly enough, there's virtually no movement whatever of air masses during Neptune-Venus aspects, particularly the conjunction and declination. Under the negative aspects of Mercury, Mars or the Sun, Neptune's angles in the spring and summer trigger erratic squalls and rough, choppy water where smaller sailing craft may be endangered.

Human health and disease conditions often relate to the conjunctions, oppositions and quadrature configurations of Jupiter, Saturn and Uranus with Neptune—the most "pluvial" planet of them all.

It's usually safe, prudent, or both, to predict extreme atmospheric moisture, extensive rainfall and excessive precipitation when you find Neptune at the meridian during *cardinal* solar ingress charts. This location either threatens or actually results in floods that destroy low-lying farmlands. Loss of sunshine due to extensive overhanging clouds is especially severe in valleys and downslope areas. Extreme dampness creates conditions favorable to the breeding grounds in which crop-destroying insects thrive. This Neptunian dampness can be interpreted, therefore, as disastrous to crops in the affected areas.

At geographical longitudes between 90° and 105° West during spring equinox when Neptune is at the meridian (*the noon, directly above the Earth, or "12 o'clock" position*) during a Mars conjunction, square or opposition —particularly when Neptune occupies the meridian of an ingress or eclipse chart and in line to a potentially volcanic area—the likelihood of closely following seismic activity in that area is intensified.

Neptune remains in each zodiacal sign for about 14 years. At about 42-year periods, this pluvial planet alternately transits the tropics and the celestial equator. When the Sun forms positive or favorable configurations of 60°, 120° or the slightly less favorable 30° and 150° aspects to Neptune, there will be seasonably mild temperatures and generally fair weather. Still, air masses tend to rise when

Neptune is thus aspected; this causes light fogging and ground-hugging hazes followed by variable winds to the leeward of high hills and mountainous areas as well as in low-lying areas near bodies of water.

You'll find that humidity and cloudiness are increased and the barometer falls when the Sun makes the conjunction, opposition, parallel, square, or even the less effective 45° and 135° configurations with Neptune. Truly incredible disturbances will rip up the atmosphere at those locations where Neptune (in the chart for ingresses or lunations) is on the meridian or even when it forms any of the above-mentioned configurations to the M.C. These disturbances become absolutely spectacular when there's a lunation (especially an eclipse!) that occurs in quadrature, opposition or conjunction to Neptune.

To sum up, then: Neptune on the meridian of seasonal solar ingress maps is a sure indication of plenty of moisture and an unusually wet season. In lunation charts (New or Full Moon or eclipses) Neptune at this position indicates a *repetition* of the unusual wetness during the following month. Neptune induces isolated line squalls, abnormally segregated precipitation, extremely low barometer and abnormal humidity.

Depending on the season as well as the angles formed to this planet, downpours under Neptune's influence can result in anything from local flash flooding to huge watery disasters such as the overflowing of the banks of large rivers to engulf hundreds of square miles of home and farmland. Oddly enough, these anomalies are far easier to interpret on an extremely long-range basis than virtually useless short-range predictions if the rules of astrometeorology are mastered and applied with discipline and mathematical exactitude. (Rules for the correct calculation of celestial maps for any point on the globe are included at the end of the book.)

Although Jupiter's tendency to expansiveness was once regarded as meaning inordinately wet seasons when found on the meridian of ingress and lunation charts, Neptune has been found to be the most saturating celestial influence of all. These low barometers, excessive humidity, hazes, fogs and abnormally long-lived rains are even worse when Neptune forms the square (90°), semisquare (45°), or 135° angles to the meridian in key charts. There will be cooler temperatures dominating northern locations when (in lunation or ingress maps) Neptune is southing —i.e., approaching the meridianal position or topmost portion of the chart.

This situation in a winter solstice chart is the classic pattern for anomalistic snowfall in extreme southern areas, and when (always in geocentric longitude) Neptune is either changing direction from an apparent retrograde motion or beginning to turn "backward"—that is, when Neptune is stationary—its saturating influence on the atmosphere for that season or month will be spread over a much greater area than that covered for the point of observation in the celestial chart calculated for that area.

Always interpret Neptune on the *lower* meridian as a harbinger of floods.

20

PLUTO, THE MOON, AND DETAILED FORECASTING

USING THE FOUR-METER telescope at Kitt Peak National Observatory, three visiting astronomers from the University of Hawaii discovered methane ice on the surface of Pluto, the outermost known planet.

"This is the first indication we've ever had of solid methane in the entire solar system," said astronomer Dale P. Cruikshank. "We've always theorized that methane was present in the primordial nebula from which the planets were formed, but so far it has only been found as a gas in the atmospheres of Jupiter, Saturn, Uranus, Neptune, and Saturn's large moon, Titan."

In their theoretical early nebula however, methane *couldn't* have frozen solid before it got as cold as —225° C. From this, they now believe that the primorial solar nebula had cooled another 40° while the planets were still condensing. The next colder element to condense beyond methane is neon. But neon is a noble gas and almost impossible to find with remote sensors, so it wouldn't have frozen solid until the temperature of the solar nebula would have dropped to within only 8° above absolute zero—i.e., —273° C.

But then somebody over at Hale Observatory theorized

that Pluto had a *neon* atmosphere. Well, it's possible—*anything's* possible in science—with the exception of those things scientists don't believe in. Neon's molecular weight is high enough to keep it from escaping into space and yet volatile enough to keep it from freezing at such low temperatures. Even Pluto's fantastic coldness isn't low enough to turn neon into a liquid, let alone a *solid!*

If there are indeed neon oceans on Pluto, that world must have an atmospheric surface pressure 20 times higher than that of the Earth. Scientists think this is unlikely because of Pluto's small size (its diameter has been variously estimated at from 5,800 kilometers to over 40,000 kilometers).

Cruikshank thinks that Pluto's diameter may turn out to be considerably less than our own Moon's 3,500-kilometer diameter, but who knows? They're still trying to measure the moons of Uranus and Neptune (Oberon and Triton) to find traces of methane in those closer satellites of the giant gaseous planets.

It seems perfectly obvious that anyone can see that Pluto is an escaped moon of Neptune. Why not? Consider *this* scenario: The entire solar system became temporarily unhinged (perhaps, as Velikovsky claims), just a few thousand years ago—maybe longer. It just might have happened as all his evidence indicates. Let's say that for some unknown reason a larger-than-Earth-sized world that once orbited between Jupiter and Mars either blew itself or *was* blown to bits and became what is now known as the asteroid belt. The meteoric debris from this titanic destruction (to use the analogy of an atom again) split into component "subatomic" particles—meteors—that bombarded every world in the solar system. The surfaces of Mars, Venus, Mercury, our own Moon and Earth all bear traces of this terrible punishment. In all likelihood, so do the inner cores of the outer planets.

More important, there was probably a displacement of Mars and the eruption of a planet-sized mass (Venus) from Jupiter. The moons of Saturn and Uranus must bear the scars of that terrible explosion, too. But they were probably not as displaced as the *third* Neptunian moon, Pluto—which may account for the fact that Pluto's orbit (except for those of a few large asteroids and meteors) is the most eccentric of any in the solar system. At aphelion, Pluto can be well over 4½ billion miles from the Sun, while at perihelion, it comes to within 2,766 million miles of our local star. At certain times this brings it well inside the orbit of Neptune. Moreover, Pluto's orbit is inclined at an angle of 17° 6′ to the plane of the ecliptic—an enormous orbital tilt.

Since Pluto's revolution around the Sun, discovered in 1930, is 247.7 years, it won't return to the location at which it was first seen until 2177. But in 1989 Pluto will be at its perihelion station, enabling space-age astrometeorologists to make precise determinations of Pluto's combined influences on the Sun, the Earth and other planets.

It's also conceivable that because Pluto appears to be a "terrestrial"-type planet (small and dense, compared to the outer gas giants), rather than the most distant planet, it may be the first of a whole new series of terrestrial-type worlds—in which case I will have to eat some astrological crow because I've always criticized the Uranian astrologers —with their eight (undiscovered) planets—as being outright crackpots.

Although at this writing, Pluto is suddenly a vastly more interesting world than ever before, its size, extremely low temperature and vast distance are such that NASA isn't quite sure it can build space probes capable of reaching it.

That's what they *say*. What the engineers do will be far more spectacular and exotic. The spaceships of today are the "gasbag balloons" of early space travel (as balloons may be compared, say, to the Boeing 727, the Concorde or the Tupolov 114). In the early, exciting days of dirigible flight, when the imagination of the world was captured by Count Ferdinand von Zeppelin's fantastic feats, young George J. McCormack very nearly saved America's greatest entry in world airship competition—the mighty *Shenandoah*—the greatest American dirigible every constructed. If the officials had heeded his long-range astrometeorological warning, "The Daughter of the Stars" might have been saved.

Steerable, lighter-than-air craft began before the American Civil War. Naturally, nobody listened to the "crazy" fifty-six-year-old Dr. Solomon Andrews in 1862 when he told President Lincoln that his airship could easily swing the course of the war.

By 1900, Count Zeppelin gave the world the first look at his own device at Lake Constance. A floating hangar swung open its doors and revealed an airship with the awesome dimensions of 425 feet and driven by two Daimler marine engines. A much-heralded 12-hour flight in 1908 was Zeppelin's next-to-last triumph—a full 24 hours in the air—a lovely scenic cruise down the Rhine.

Unfortunately, a sudden, freak wind smashed Zeppelin's magnificent LZ-4 to the ground, where it lay in shredded ruins. But the Germans, and others throughout the world, came to his aid, and personal financing poured in to help him rebuild. One of Zeppelin's first allies was Dr. Hugo Eckener, who became his partner in the world's first airship passenger line. By 1913, five German airships had flown over 100,000 miles without a single injury. During the war years, 86 great flying ships were built in German factories to terrorize the population of Great Britain. Some of these leviathans grew as long as 750 feet and could climb as high as 25,000 feet!

After the war the entire world caught the airship fever and wartime flyers quickly picked up the art of flying for fun. When the Americans caught the fever, the first native American airship, the *Shenandoah,* was built in 1923, and did more for American pride than winning the war against Germany. The mighty *Shenandoah* was lifted by helium—much safer than the hydrogen used by the Germans. And instead of the prohibitively expensive hangars, Americans designed mooring masts.

But when a huge American dirigible, the *Los Angeles,* was caught in a gale that sent it somersaulting from a right angle to a vertical position and then settling into a left angle, McCormack wrote to the American ship commanders stressing the necessity of accurate long-range forecasts to safeguard the flights of these huge and mighty, but fragile, ships of the skies.

At first he was ignored. Instead, the commanders and the ships' owners decided to put the mast idea to the crucial experiment. The ultimate engineering experiment seemed to be to test it against the midwinter gales at Lakehurst, New Jersey. So in January 1924, the *Shenandoah* was hooked to a mast for a ten-day trial. After five days, one of the ship's officers looked up and reported that the *Shenandoah* had blown away. But by some fantastic good luck, a former Zeppelin officer happened to be in the control car when the huge airship went blowing off like a huge, uncontrolled kite. He managed to bring the pride of America back safely. His name was Anton Heinen, and he had been brought to America to train U.S. "zeppelin" captains.

Dirigibles flourished, mooring masts sprang up like mushrooms all over the country, just hoping for a visit from a dirigible. Even the Empire State Building in Manhattan later constructed a dirigible mooring mast to the then highest building in the world.

When a great tour of the United States was announced by the *Shenandoah's* owners, and the itinerary published, George McCormack wrote from his Fair Lawn home to Commander Lansdowne advising him to avoid the Ohio segment of the last leg of his 9,000-mile triangular Odyssey during the late summer of 1925. In the spring issue of his self-published *Astrotech Weather Guide,* McCormack cited detailed planetary patterns for the solstice at several Ohio meridians along the *Shenandoah's* scheduled route. Even though McCormack ignored the airship's flights through fogs, deserts, storms, winds and mountains, he wrote a letter of warning when he learned the *Shenandoah* was ordered to make a tour of state fairs in the Midwest. Directly because of McCormack's forecast, plus his proven record of accuracy, Commander Lansdowne objected to and then balked at making the flight into that area.

The "Daughter of the Stars" had thrilled the nation and had become a *living* legend, proving beyond doubt that the United States could not only construct and fly great dirigibles, but also train great crews to pilot them as well. The *Shenandoah* had logged about 25,000 miles by the late summer of 1925 when she was summarily ordered to tour the state fairs of the American Midwest.

Citing McCormack's record and current seasonal forecast, Commander Lansdowne barked, "Christ, I'd rather take four straight trips to the North Pole and back than one to the Middle West during this particular season." Authority, however, prevailed and Lansdowne faced his duty, prepared for the worst.

It came. While Henry Ford built his own mooring mast in Dearborn, eagerly awaiting a visit from the great ship *Shenandoah,* the eccentric and vicious sudden summer storm McCormack had predicted and Commander Lansdowne had feared, destroyed the beautiful vessel over Ohio and her commander as well. Young McCormack took the loss almost personally. He wrote scores of angry letters—all to no avail. After all, he was a "nut" who openly admitted that he used ancient metonic eclipse and synodic planetary cycles in his forecasting.

Although these cycles were known to the ancient Chaldeans, they're very likely to be rediscovered scientifically, as is a tenth planet—*and possibly an eleventh.* But it should end at that. Here's why:

Logically, there should be 12 celestial bodies to correspond to the 12 signs of the zodiac. As it now stands, both Venus and Mercury double as "rulers" of Taurus-Libra and Gemini-Virgo respectively. It may be that the discovery of two more planets beyond Pluto will help to increase the accuracy of astro-weather forecasting. At this stage, though, that's sheer speculation. But when scientists begin the study of our natural satellite from the viewpoint of its various influences, they're bound to discover some basic truths among the old "superstitions" about the Moon.

At this point in its history, the Moon's mean daily motion is 13° 10′ and it makes a complete circuit of the zodiac (geocentrically, of course) in 27 days, seven hours and 43 minutes. It functions as the barometric indicator and distributor of atmospheric moisture. When (in lunation or ingress charts) it transits either the north meridian, the nadir (or the south meridian), or is in quadrature to those points, it causes the culmination of atmospheric conditions that were generated *west* of the meridian.

As one NASA physicist, William Corliss (who spends all his spare time compiling and publishing books of weird, wonderful, but unexplained "Fortean"-type phenomena), recently put it, "When science is unchallenged by the 'impossible' matters of fact and observations of the unexplained, it becomes increasingly dogmatic and degenerate." In *Harper's Weekly* (No. 3158, April 5, 1976, page 16) Corliss observed, "Almost anything can be correlated with one astronomical phenomenon or the other."

So the Moon's minor 45° aspects to the meridian are nearly as effective as its others. There's no other way than these lunar cycles to explain the 3½- and seven-day cycles that so often coincide with major planetary phenomena. All the Moon does is to *reflect* changes in weather already determined by the positions and aspects of the major planets and to indicate the time these atmospheric changes will happen; when the Moon transits the Mid-heaven, the dominating weather patterns focus *due south.* When transiting the fourth sector or channel (90° to 120°), the dominating patterns center *northward.*

At certain times the Moon will trigger upcoming combined configurations of two (or more) planets—sometimes as long as several days before their actual culmination, so all transiting planetary aspects to the local meridian must be examined with great care and synthesized accordingly. It's supremely important to observe those times when the Moon is in perigee and on the celestial equator and *at the same time* happens to coincide with planetary and/or solar aspects that produce atmospheric disturbances. This is when (all other pertinent celestial factors considered) the *least* reaction will be abnormally high tides, coastal flooding and unbelievably powerful, intense storms.

Planets in the third (60° to 90°) and ninth (240° to 270°) sectors affect weather conditions directly *westward* of your point of observation. The character or nature of the sign on the cusp of the fourth (90° to 120°) channel must always be seriously studied. All configurations of the Sun and other planets make definite impressions on the atmosphere and then move eastward.

The following series of charts has been calculated by computer for the ultimate in mathematical precision, then simplified and redrawn to make them easily understandable, and yet, with the aid of the key of all the symbols for the signs, planets and aspects, as accurate as necessary for the intelligent beginner to interpret astronomic weather and seismic charts.

I said previously that it was simple, but I didn't say it was easy. Nothing worthwhile ever is. You could not just read a book and become a doctor, even if that book were written by Hippocrates himself. There isn't enough here to make you an expert astrometeorologist. You might—just might—become a good *local* astrometeorologist by absorbing, testing and experimenting with the data given in the preceding pages. It helps to know something about the topography of your local environment. All the charts here are set up for the meridian of the city of Los Angeles (it would require millions of charts just to cover most of the major metropolitan areas of the United States for the next decade or so), but you can easily transpose these charts any number of degrees east or west of that meridian (as well as north or south of it) to your own location by following the rules in Chapters Six, Ten and Eleven.

I've chosen the meridian of Los Angeles for a number of reasons, the first being that three great "faults" run through or nearby that location. The second is that most seismologists believe that the greatest disaster of modern times will be the slippage of the San Andreas and/or Great White Wolf faults, which will probably spell the destruction of westernmost California (in the opinion of these experts) and the formation of a new land mass in the Pacific Ocean—a mass several times the size of Long Island in New York.

The evidence has been presented in preceding chapters. The "tools" (i.e., the solstice and equinox charts from March 20, 1978, to December 21, 1990)—with the *precision* aspects for each season—are given in the following pages. The 38 solar ingress charts from 1978 to 1985 include spring and autumn equinoxes, and summer and winter solstices. From 1986 to 1990, I've presented only the astronomical New Year (spring equinox) charts for each year.

For obvious reasons, I'm making no bald "predictions" here. If you've followed me this far, you know the series of charts that follows indicates the course of future natural events and their timing. Of interest should be the New Year (spring equinox) chart of March 20 for the year 1980. For more detailed seasonal interpretations, study the summer, fall and winter charts for that year. And for even more precise timing, examine the 18 lunation charts from March through December 1980. (Inasmuch as the changes will not be confined to purely local phenomena, transposition of these charts to your local meridian is imperative.)

Apply the foregoing planetary-solar indicators to the years 1980–1984 (to whatever your local meridian may be) and you'll have a more complete understanding of atmospheric and geologic events from 1980 through 1986.

Before drawing any conclusions about the future, however, be sure to apply these data to as many *past* events as possible. Once you become seriously convinced, I'll be happy to direct you to more advanced studies.

The first step is to learn how to calculate astronomical charts for any geographic point in space and time. For this you need ephemerides and a teacher or a good book. For either of the foregoing, write to the American Federation of Astrologers in Tempe, Arizona, or to me. The use of logarithms makes it so simple that you can learn the mathematics of chart calculation in less than two hours on your own. Mastering the process of precision chart erection shouldn't cost any more than the price of this book.

EPILOGUE

The National Aeronautics and Space Administration (NASA) has more data on planetary interaction than any other official American agency. Now, according to the National Oceanic and Atmospheric Administration, there is increased interest in, and study of, the mechanics of extraterrestrial influences on weather.

Inertia, lack of enthusiasm and authoritarianism, however, continue to block free, open presentation of astronomic weather forecasting techniques—particularly by researchers outside duly accredited, recognized bodies such as the American Meteorological Society.

To be "willing to face the rigors of technical refereeing," according to Dr. Donald L. Gilman, Chief of the Long Range Prediction Group of the National Weather Service, is simply a euphemism for rejection without serious consideration of the theory and practice of astronomic weather forecasting.

This system, in rudimentary form, is passed on—unencumbered by bureaucratic red tape—in these pages so that the intelligent scientist or layman may use the rules and compare his or her results with any orthodox long-range weather-predicting group.

The results, free of the artifices of technical refereeing by biased experts, should prove very interesting indeed.

KEY TO SYMBOLS

ZODIACAL SIGNS	SYMBOL	BODY OR PLANET	SYMBOL	ASPECT	SYMBOL	ANGULAR DEGREES
Aries	♈	Mars	♂	Conjunction	☌	0°
Taurus	♉	Venus	♀	Semisextile	⚺	30°
Gemini	♊	Mercury	☿	Semisquare	∠	45°
Cancer	♋	Moon	☽	Sextile	⚹	60°
Leo	♌	Sun	☉	Quintile	☆	72°
Virgo	♍	Mercury	(☿)	Quadrature (*Square*)	□	90°
Libra	♎	Venus	(♀)	Trine	△	120°
Scorpio	♏	Pluto (*Mars*)	♇ (♂)	Sesquiquad	⚼	135°
Sagittarius	♐	Jupiter	♃	Biquintile	±	144°
Capricorn	♑	Saturn	♄	Quincunx	⚻	150°
Aquarius	♒	Uranus	♅	Opposition	☍	180°
Pisces	♓	Neptune	♆	Parallel	∥	0°
		North Lunar Node	☊	Retrograde	℞	
		Moon's South Node	☋	Mid-heaven	MC	
				Ascendant	ASC	

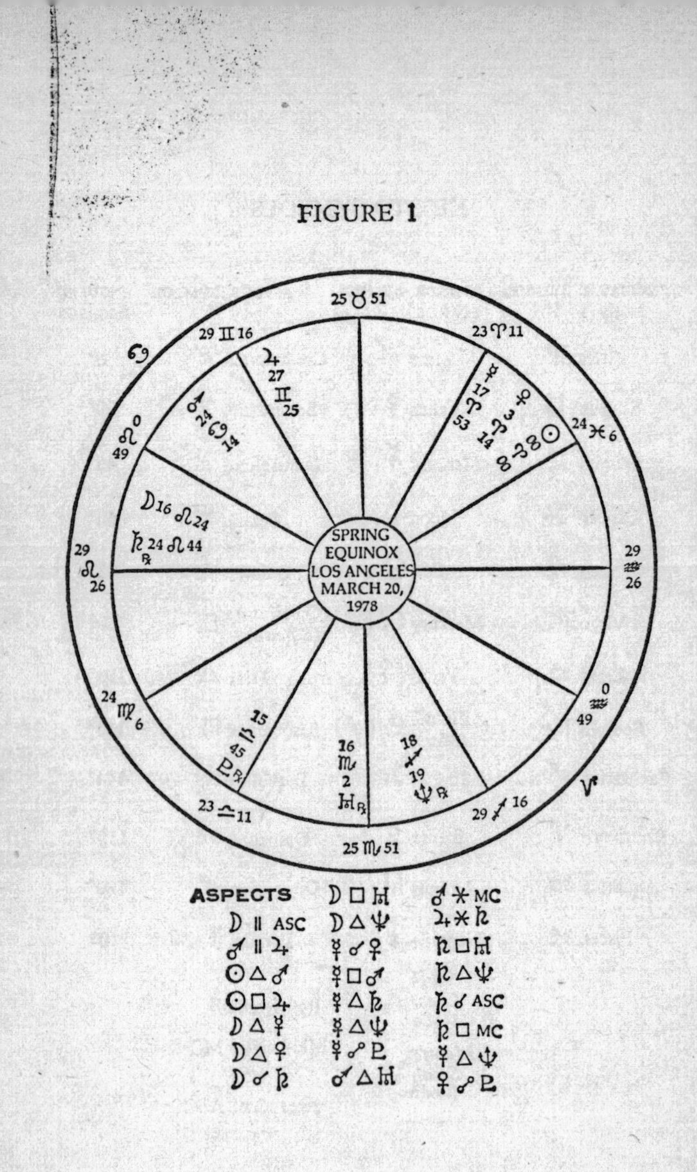

FIGURE 1

FIGURE 2

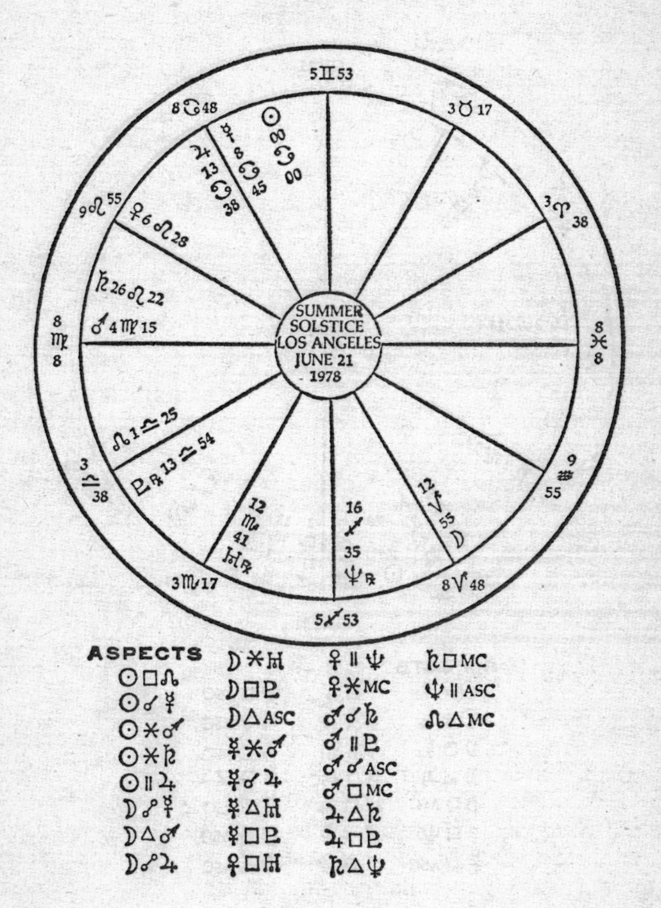

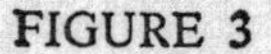

FIGURE 3

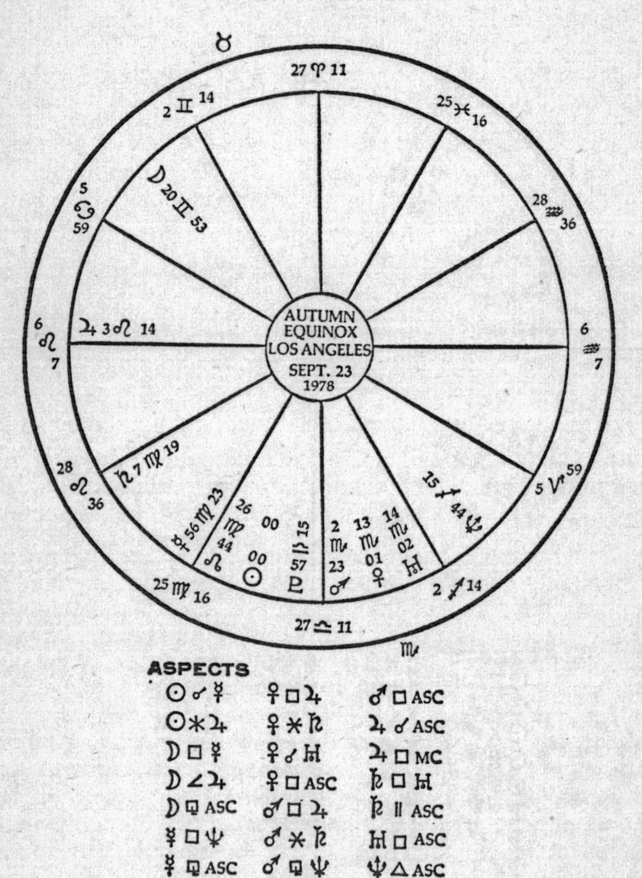

FIGURE 4

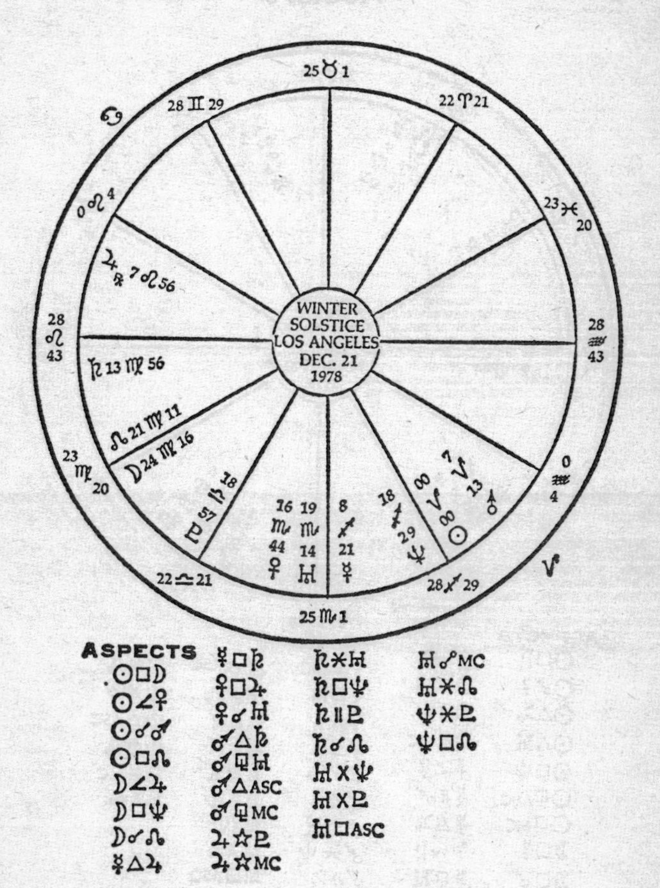

FIGURE 5

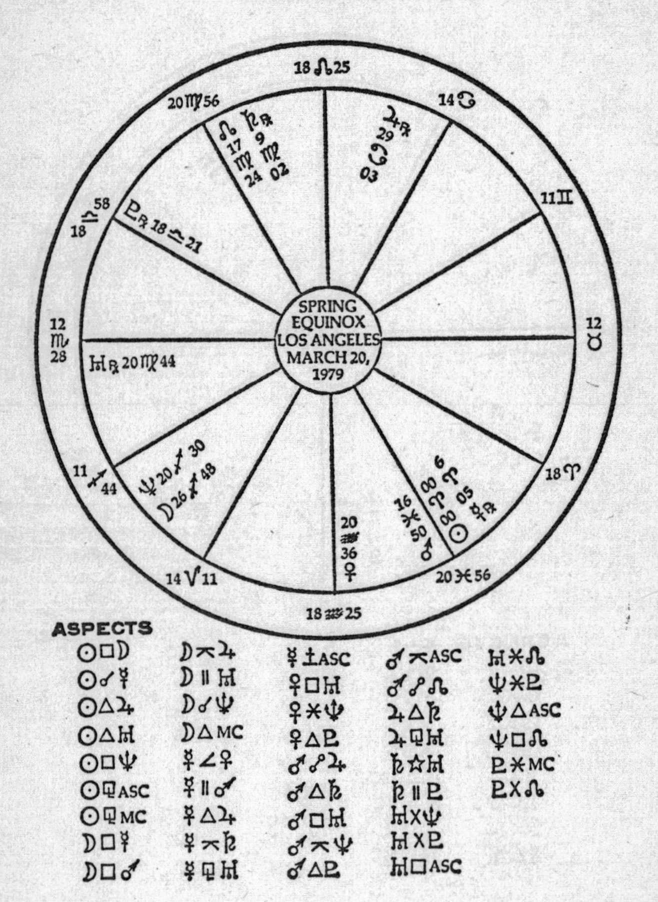

FIGURE 6

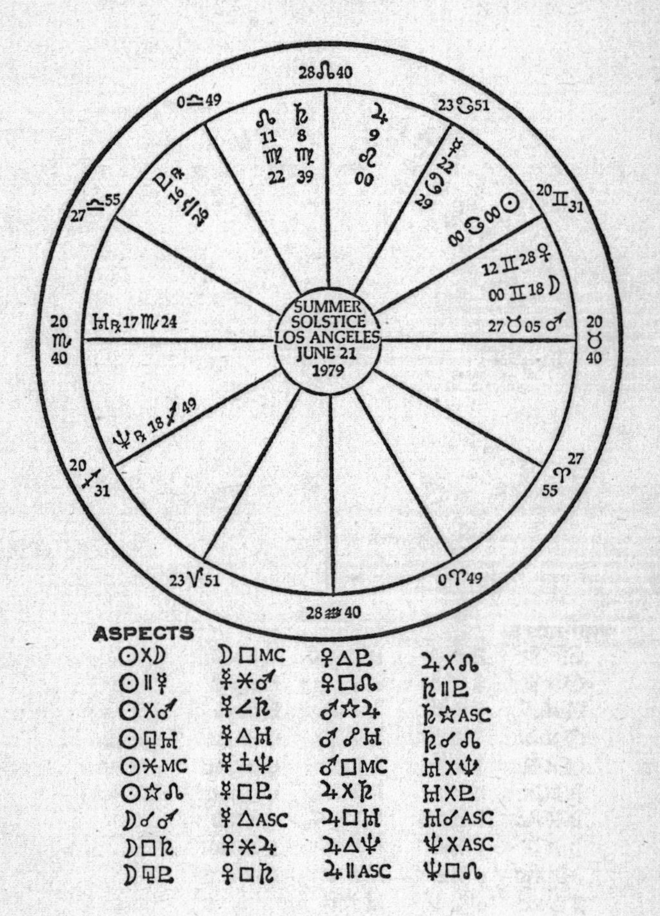

FIGURE 7

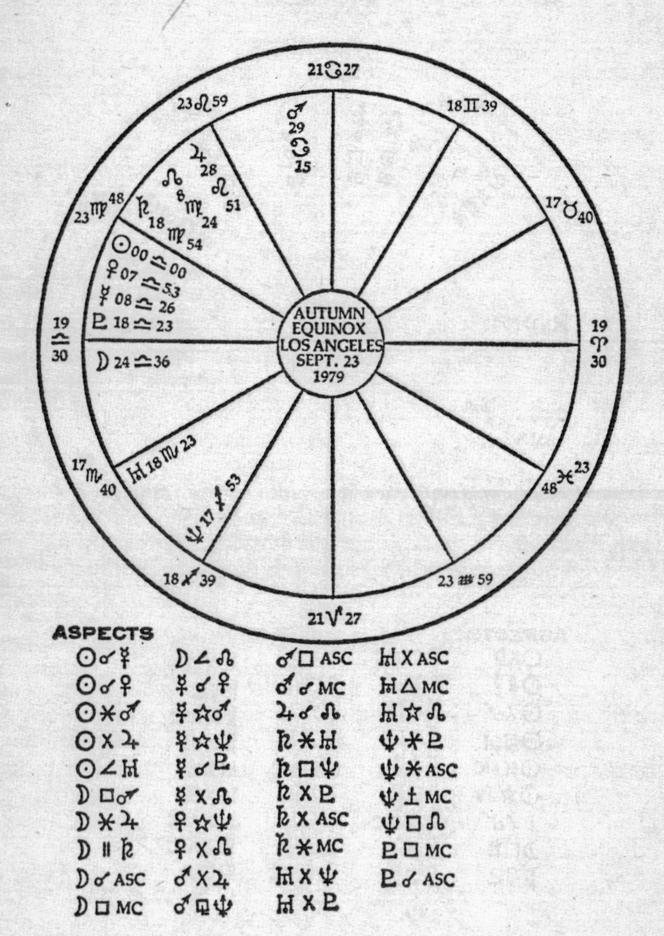

21♋27
18♊39
17♉40
19 ♈ 30
23♓48
23♒59
21♑27
18♐39
17♏40
19 ♎ 30
23♍48
23♌59
♂ 29 ♋ 15
♃ 28 ♌ 51
☊ 8 ♍ 24
♄ 18 ♍ 54
☉ 00 ♎ 00
♀ 07 ♎ 53
☿ 08 ♎ 26
♇ 18 ♎ 23
☽ 24 ♎ 36
♅ 18 ♏ 23
♆ 17 ♐ 53
AUTUMN
EQUINOX
LOS ANGELES
SEPT. 23
1979
ASPECTS
☉☌☿
☉☌♀
☉✶♂
☉X♃
☉∠♅
☽□♂
☽✶♃
☽∥♄
☽☌ASC
☽□MC
☽∠☊
☿☌♀
☿☆♂
☿☆♆
☿☌♇
☿X☊
♀☆♆
♀X☊
♂X♃
♂⊡♆
♂□ASC
♂☌MC
♃☌☊
♄✶♅
♄□♆
♄X♇
♄X ASC
♄✶MC
♅X♆
♅X♇
♅X ASC
♅△MC
♅☆☊
♆✶♇
♆✶ASC
♆⊥MC
♆□☊
♇□MC
♇☌ASC

FIGURE 8

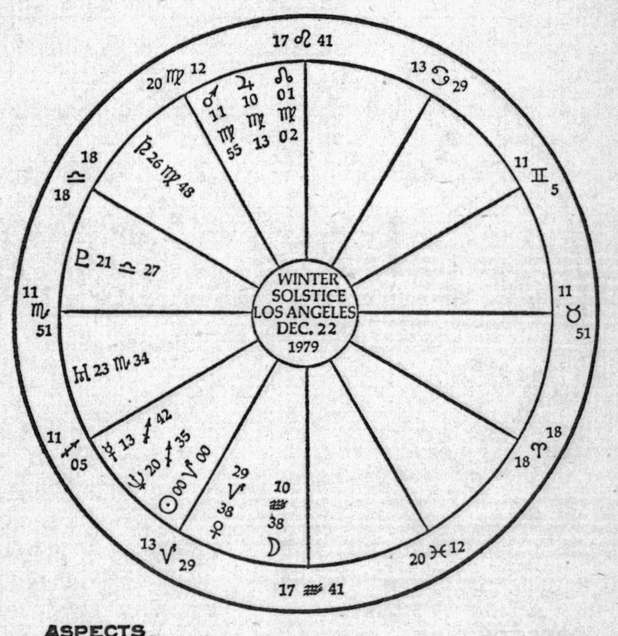

ASPECTS

☉X♀	☽□ASC	♀⚻☊	♄⚹♅
☉□♄	☿∠♀	♂☌♃	♄□♆
☉∠ASC	☿□♂	♂☆♅	♄∠ASC
☉⚼MC	☿□♃	♂□♆	♅X♆
☉△☊	☿XASC	♂⚹ASC	♅X♇
☽⚹☿	☿△MC	♃☆♅	♅□MC
☽⚻♂	♀□♂	♃∠♇	♅□☊
☽⚻♃	♀△♄	♃⚹ASC	♆⚹♇
☽⚼♄	♀∥♆	♃☌☊	♆△MC

FIGURE 9

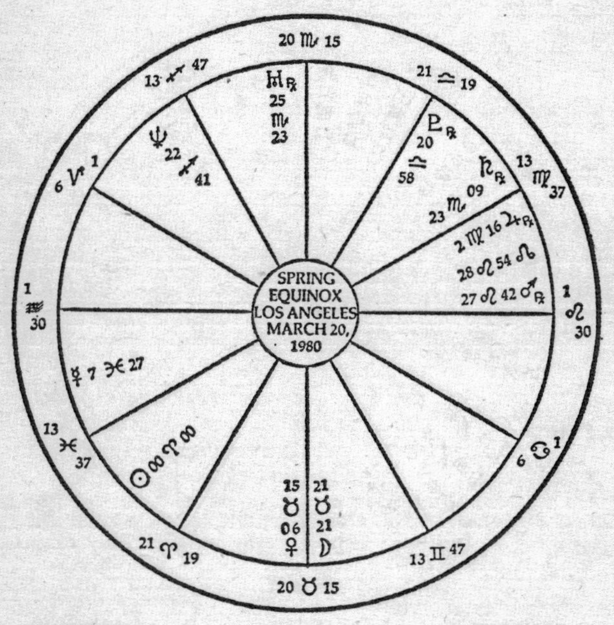

ASPECTS

☉ ∠ ♀	☽ □ ♂	☿ ⚼ ♇	♃ □ ♄	♅ X ♆
☉ ⚻ ♂	☽ △ ♄	♀ △ ♄	♃ △ ♅	♅ ∥ ASC
☉ ⚻ ♃	☽ ☍ ♅	♀ ∥ ♅	♃ ⚼ ♆	♅ ☌ MC
☉ ☍ ♄	☽ ⚻ ♆	♀ ⊥ ♆	♃ ⚻ ♇	♅ □ ☊
☉ △ ♅	☽ ⚻ ♇	♀ ☍ MC	♃ ☌ ☊	♆ ✶ ♇
☉ □ ♆	☽ ☍ MC	♂ ☌ ♃	♄ ✶ ♅	♆ X MC
☉ ✶ ASC	☽ □ ☊	♂ □ ♅	♄ □ ♆	♆ △ ☊
☉ ⚻ ☊	☿ ☍ ♂	♂ △ ♆	♄ X ♇	
☽ ☆ ☿	☿ ☍ ♃	♂ □ MC	♄ △ ASC	
☽ ☌ ♀	☿ ☆ ♆	♂ ☌ ☊	♄ ✶ MC	

FIGURE 10

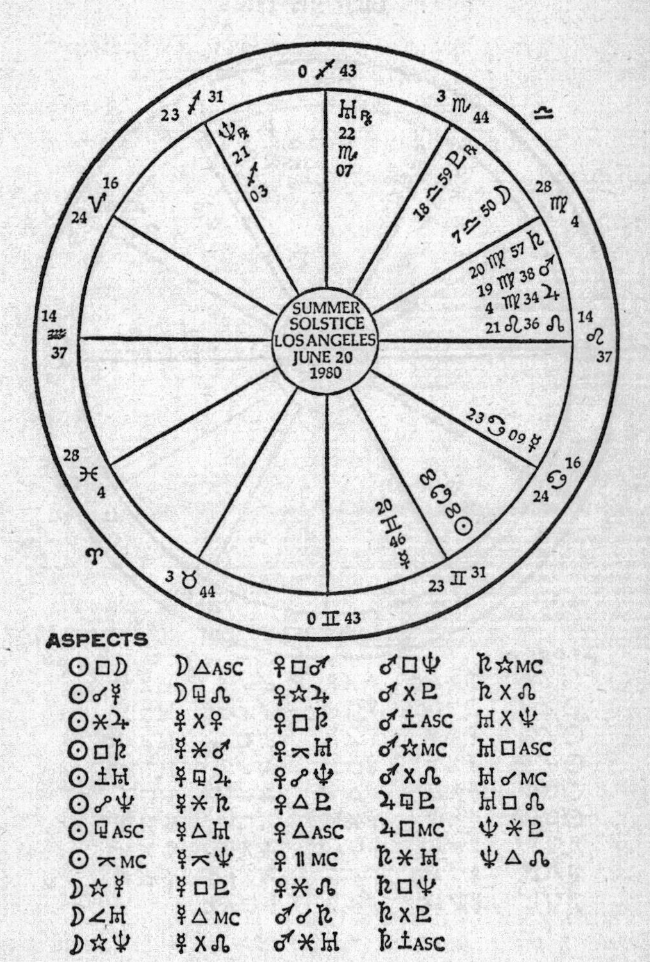

FIGURE 11

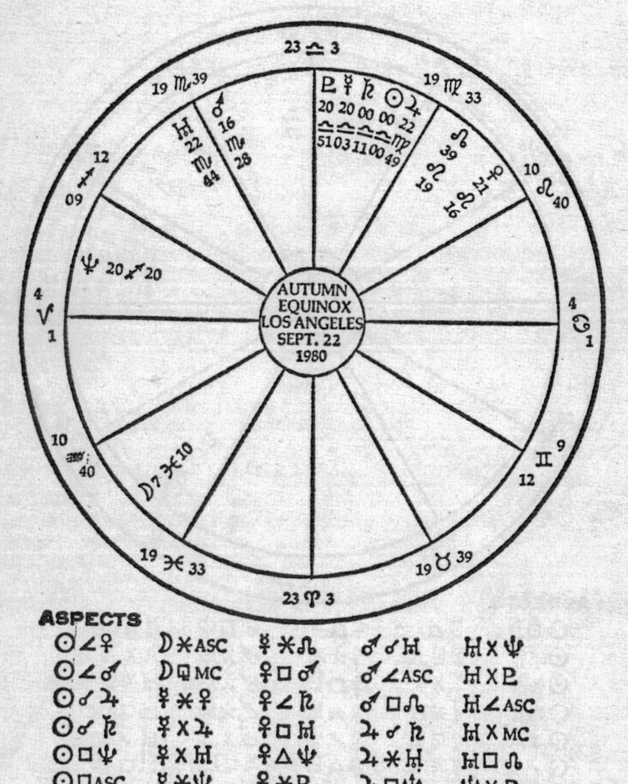

ASPECTS

☉∠♀	☽⚹ASC	☿⚹☊	♂☌♅	♅X♆
☉∠♂	☽⚻MC	♀□♂	♂∠ASC	♅X♇
☉☌♃	☿⚹♀	♀∠♄	♂□☊	♅∠ASC
☉☌♄	☿X♃	♀□♅	♃☌♄	♅XMC
☉□♆	☿X♅	♀△♆	♃⚹♅	♅□☊
☉□ASC	☿⚹♆	♀⚹♇	♃□♆	♆⚹♇
☽⚻☿	☿☌♇	♀⚻ASC	♃X♇	♆⚹MC
☽△♂	☿☆ASC	♀☌☊	♃XMC	♆△☊
☽⚻♇	☿☌MC	♂∠♄	♄□ASC	

FIGURE 12

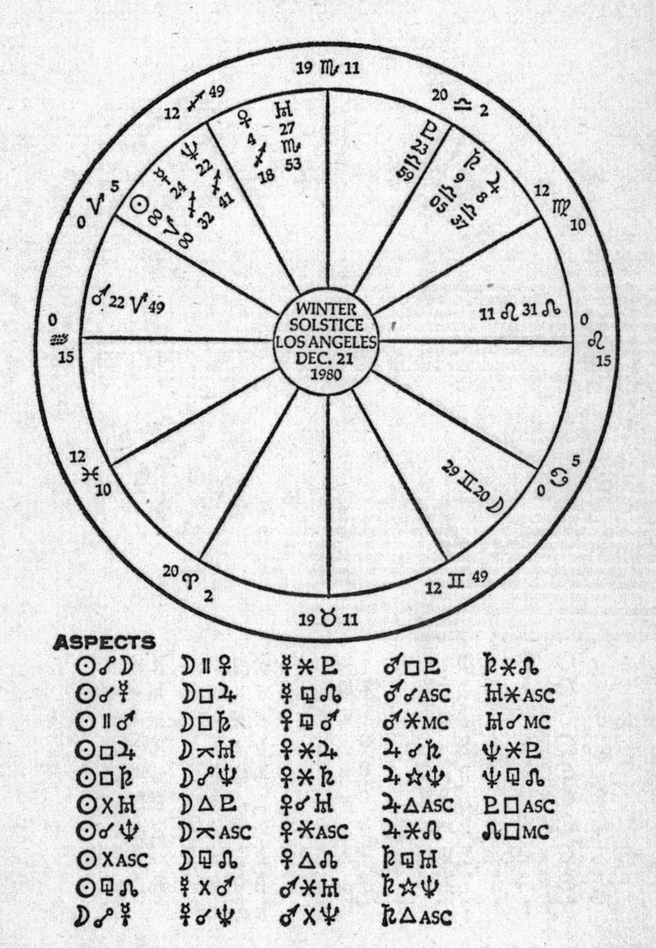

FIGURE 13

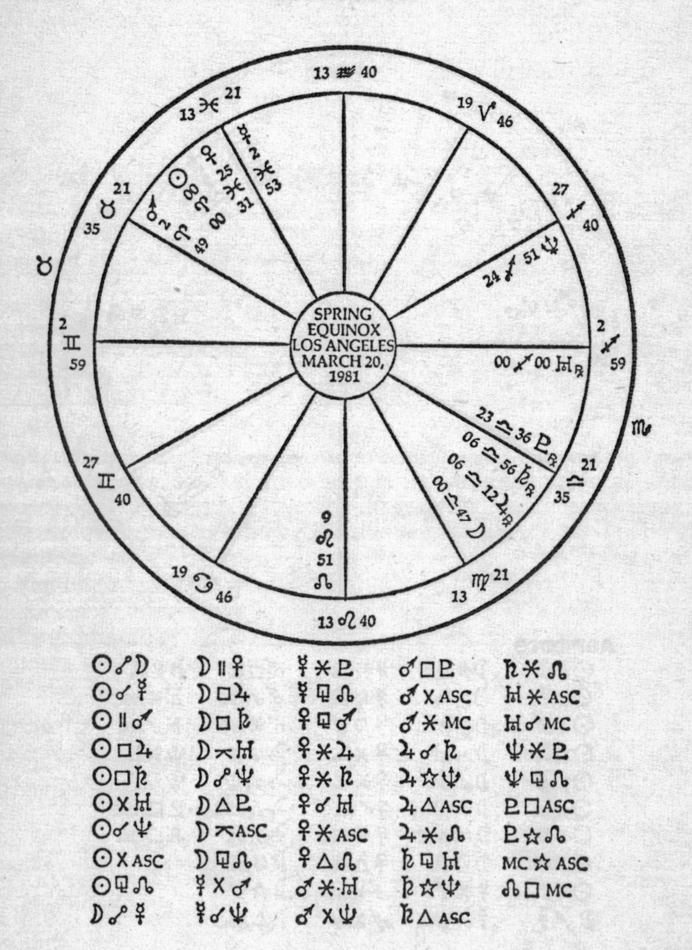

FIGURE 14

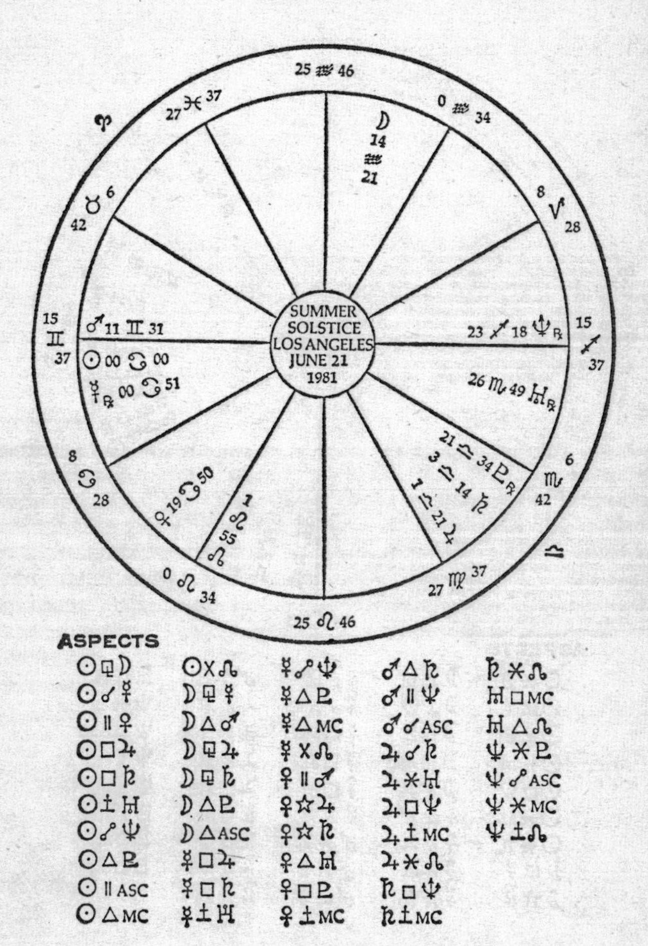

FIGURE 15

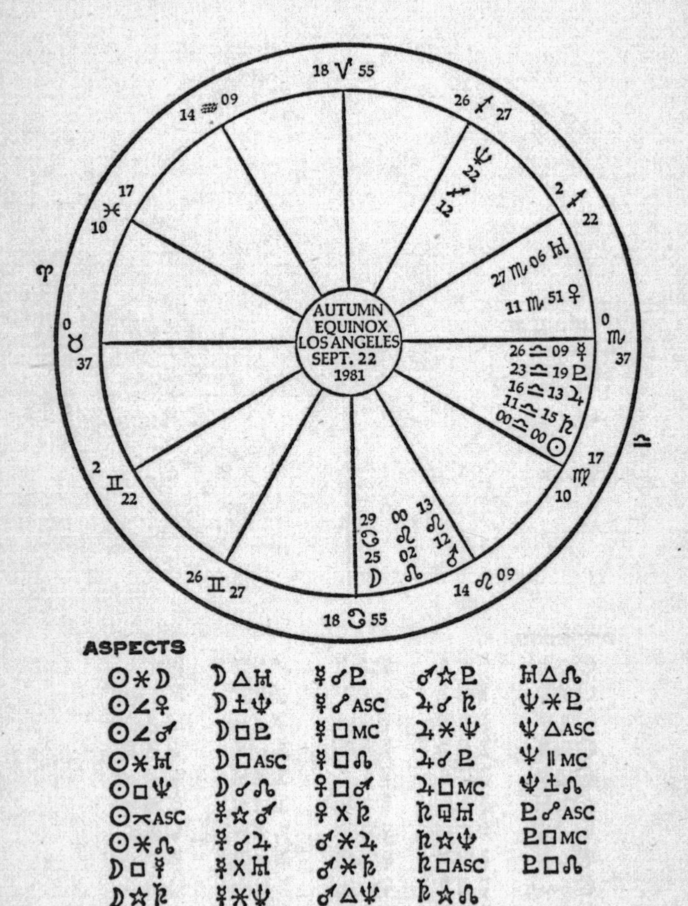

FIGURE 16

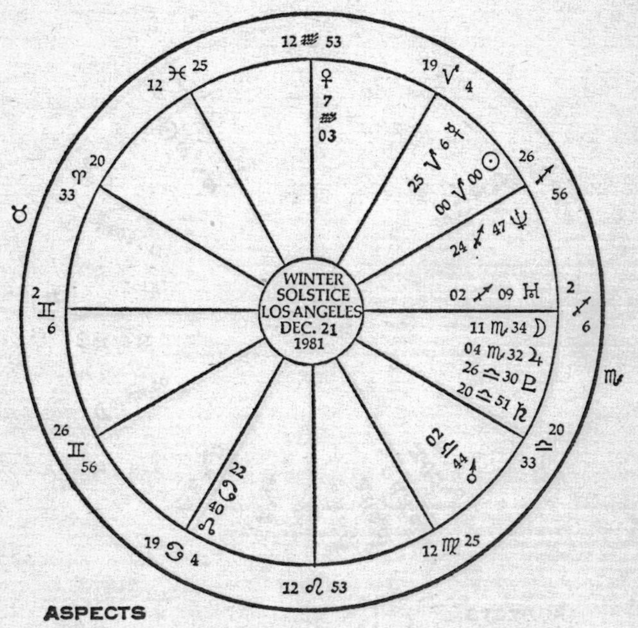

ASPECTS

☉⚼☽	☽⚹☿	♀△♂	♂☆☊	♄□☊
☉☌☿	☽□♀	♀□♃	♃X♅	♅☌ASC
☉□♂	☽☌♃	♀⚹♅	♃☌♇	♅☆MC
☉⚹♃	☽⚼♆	♀X♆	♃⚻ASC	♅△☊
☉☆♄	☽□MC	♀△ASC	♃□MC	♆⚹♇
☉X♅	☿X♀	♀☌MC	♄∠♅	♆⚼MC
☉☌♆	☿□♂	♂X♃	♄⚹♆	♆⚻☊
☉⚹♇	☿⚹♃	♂⚹♅	♄☌♇	♇±ASC
☉⚻ASC	☿☆♇	♂□♆	♄⚼ASC	♇□☊
☉⚼MC	☿±ASC	♂△ASC	♄△MC	

FIGURE 17

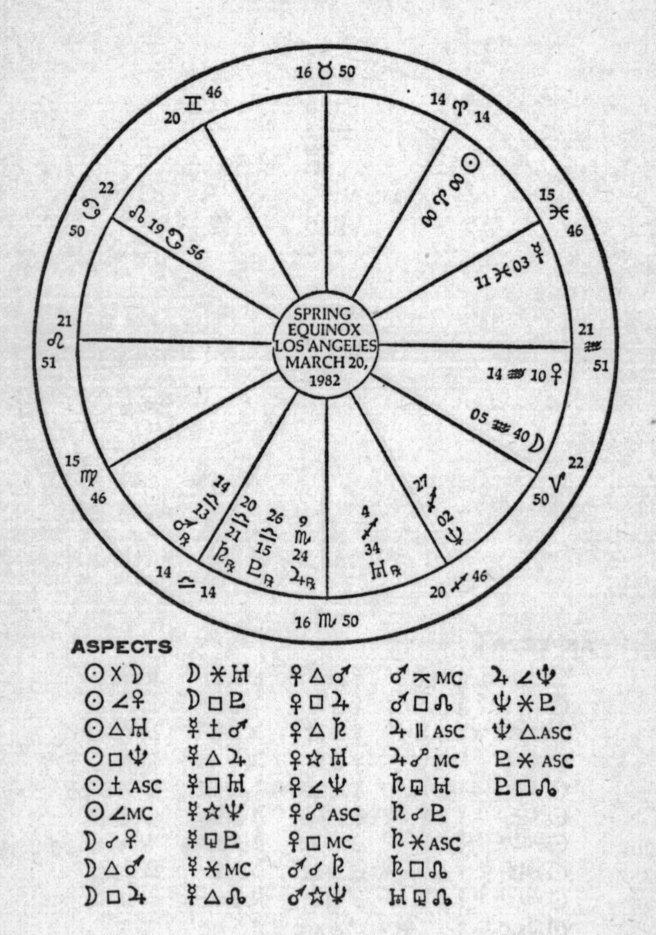

FIGURE 18

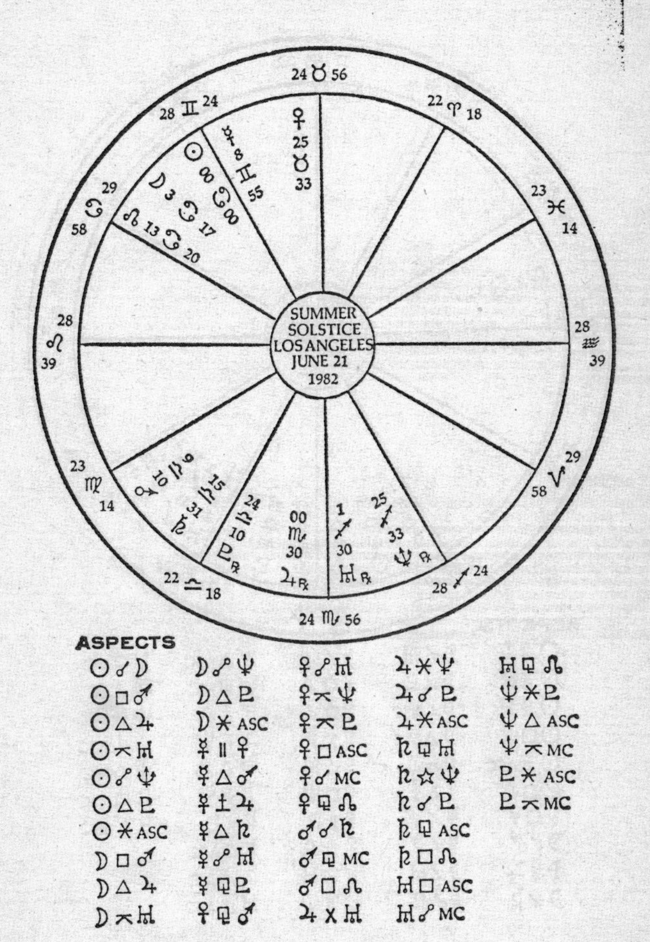

FIGURE 19

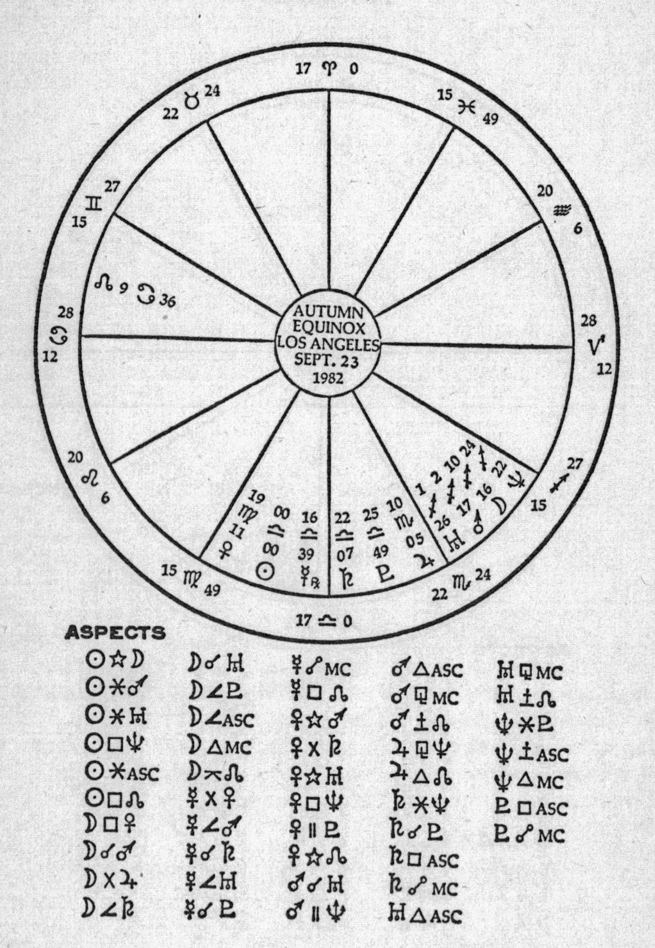

FIGURE 20

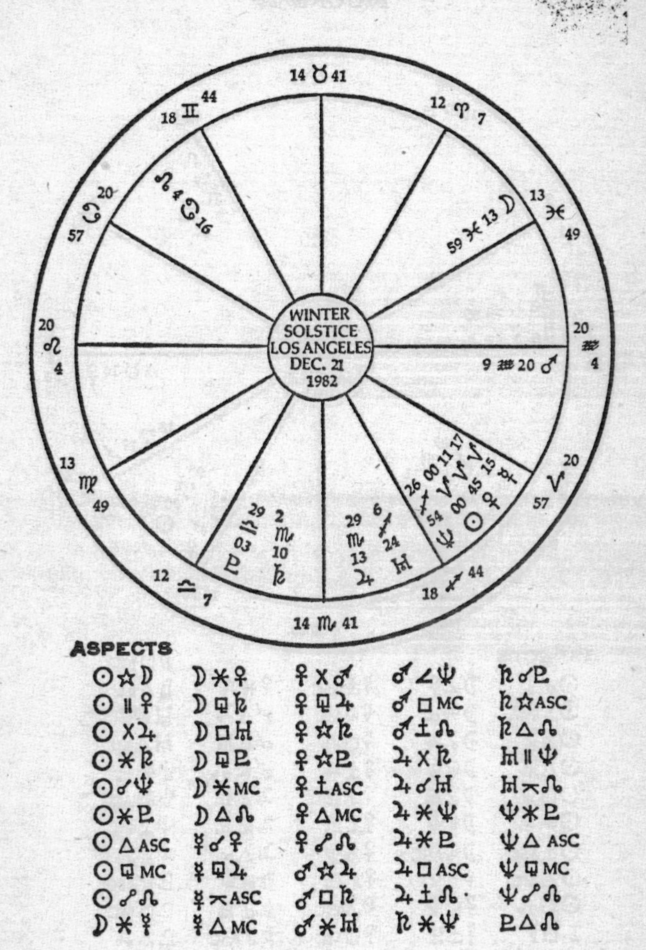

FIGURE 21

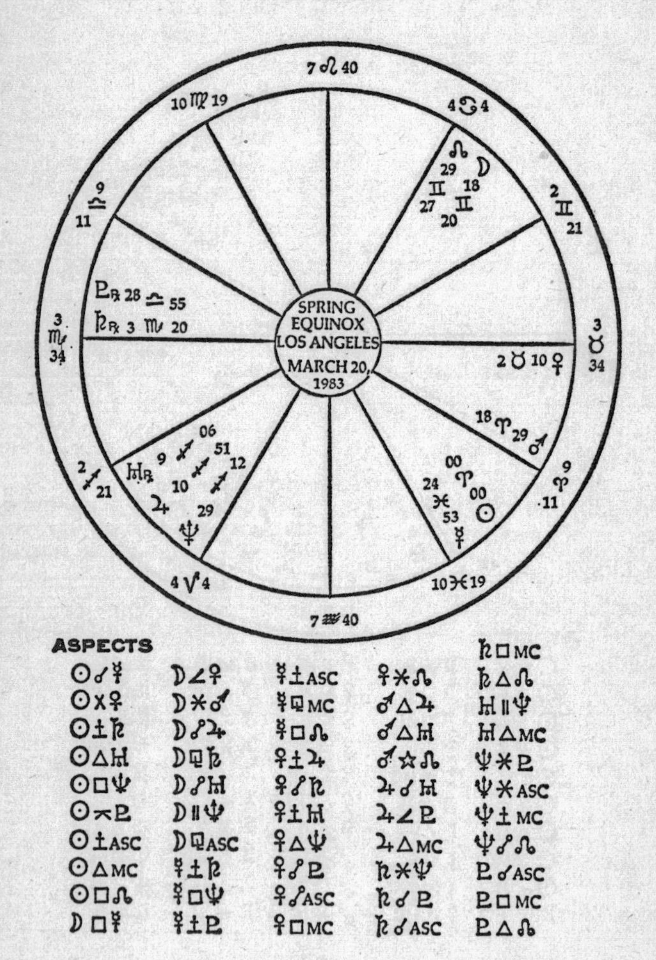

FIGURE 22

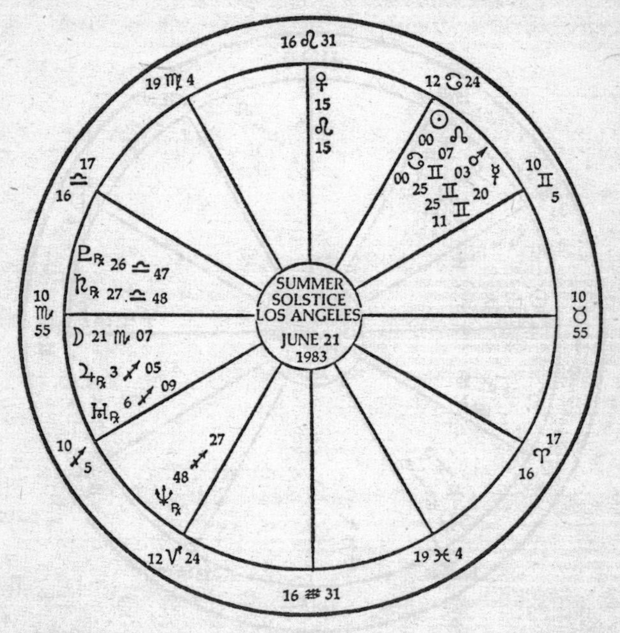

ASPECTS

☉±☽	☽±♂	☿⚻ASC	♂☍♆	♅∥♆
☉∠♀	☽∥ASC	☿⚹MC	♂△♇	♆⚹♇
☉☌♂	☽□MC	♀☆♄	♂⚼ASC	♆ ASC
☉△♄	☽±☊	♀△♅	♂☌☊	♆⚼MC
☉☍♆	☿⚹♀	♀⚼♆	♃☌♅	♆☍☊
☉△♇	☿☍♃	♀☆♇	♄⚹♆	♇☆MC
☉∠MC	☿⚼♄	♀□ASC	♄☌♇	♇△☊
☉☌☊	☿☍♅	♀☌MC	♄☆MC	
☽□♀	☿⚼♇	♂△♄	♄△☊	

FIGURE 23

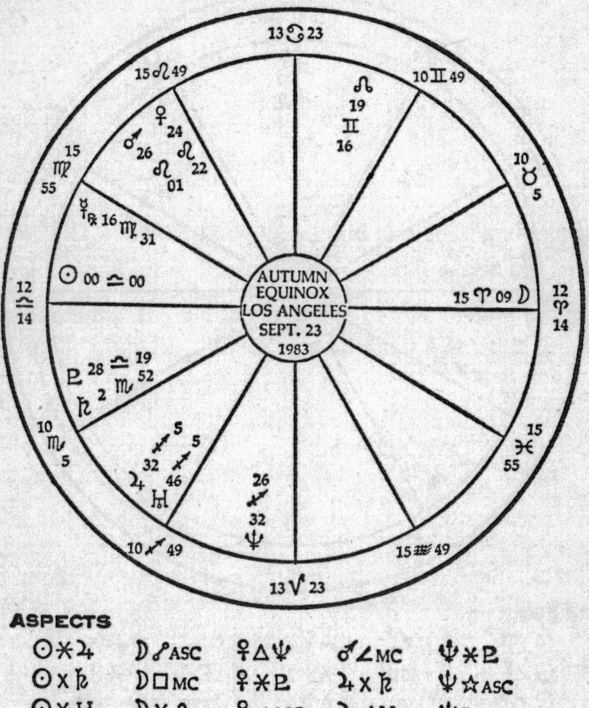

ASPECTS

☉⚹♃	☽☍ASC	♀△♆	♂∠MC	♆⚹♇
☉x♄	☽□MC	♀⚹♇	♃x♄	♆☆ASC
☉⚹♅	☽⚹☊	♀∠ASC	♃☌♅	♆∥MC
☉□♆	☿∠♄	♀⚹☊	♃±MC	♆☍☊
☉x♇	☿∠♇	♂□♃	♄x♅	♇∥ASC
☽⚻☿	☿∥ASC	♂□♅	♄☌♇	♇△☊
☽△♀	☿⚹MC	♂△♆	♄⚼☊	
☽△♃	☿□☊	♂⚹♇	♅∥♆	
☽△♅	♀☌♂	♂∠ASC	♅±MC	

FIGURE 24

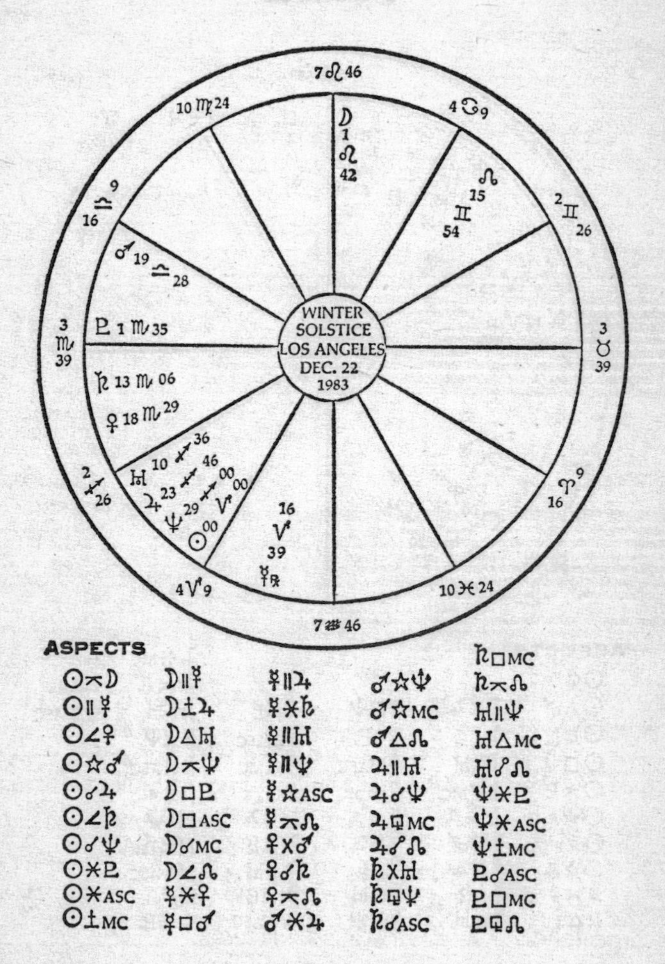

FIGURE 25

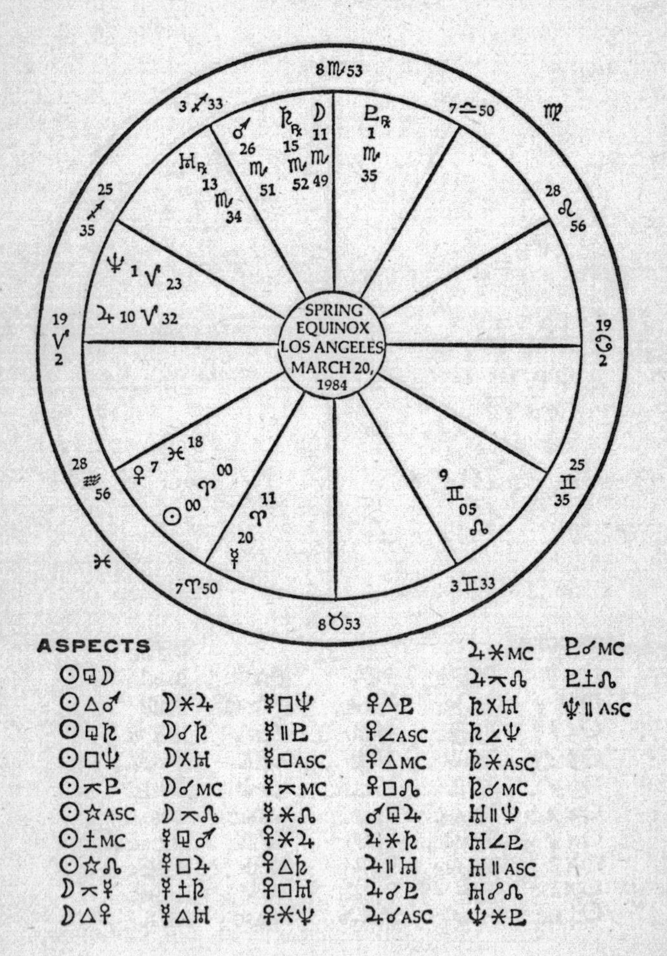

SPRING
EQUINOX
LOS ANGELES
MARCH 20,
1984
8 ♏ 53
7 ♎ 50
28 ♌ 56
19 ♋ 2
25 ♊ 35
3 ♊ 33
8 ♉ 53
7 ♈ 50
28 ♒ 56
19 ♑ 2
25 ♐ 35
3 ♐ 33
♇℞ 1 ♏ 35
☽ 11 ♏ 49
♄℞ 15 ♏ 52
♂ 26 ♏ 51
♅℞ 13 ♏ 34
♆ 1 ♑ 23
♃ 10 ♑ 32
♀ 7 ♓ 18
☉ 00 ♈ 00
☿ 20 ♈ 11
☊ 9 ♊ 05
ASPECTS
☉⚼☽
☉△♂
☉⚼♄
☉□♆
☉⚻♇
☉☆ASC
☉±MC
☉☆☊
☽⚻☿
☽△♀
☽⚹♃
☽☌♄
☽×♅
☽☌MC
☽⚻☊
☿⚼♂
☿□♃
☿±♄
☿△♅
☿□♆
☿∥♇
☿□ASC
☿⚻MC
☿⚹☊
♀⚹♃
♀△♄
♀□♅
♀⚹♆
♀△♇
♀∠ASC
♀△MC
♀□☊
♂⚼♃
♃⚹♄
♃∥♅
♃☌♇
♃☌ASC
♃⚹MC
♃⚻☊
♄×♅
♄∠♆
♄⚹ASC
♄☌MC
♅∥♆
♅∠♇
♅∥ASC
♅☍☊
♆⚹♇
♇☌MC
♇±☊
♆∥ASC

FIGURE 26

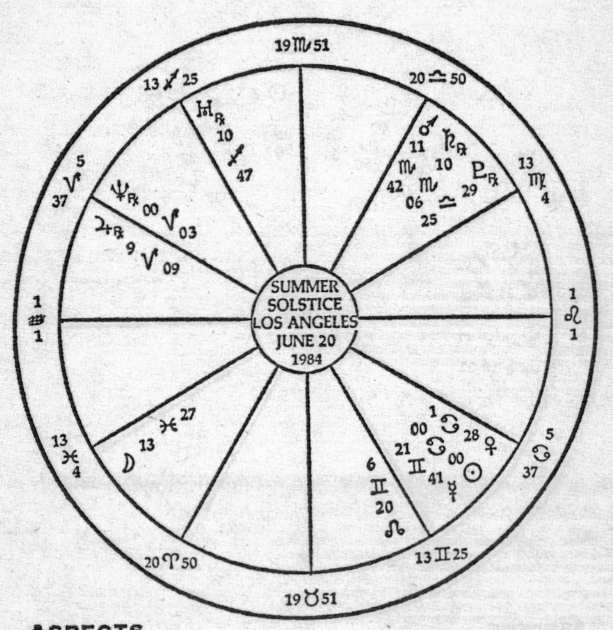

ASPECTS

☉□☽	☽⚼♂	☿☍♆	♂⚹♂	♄X♅
☉☌☿	☽⚼♄	☿△♇	♂☌♃	♄□ASC
☉☌♀	☽□♆	☿⊥ASC	♂X♄	♄☌MC
☉⚼♂	☽⚻♇	☿⊥MC	♂⚼♅	♅∥♆
☉☍♃	☽⚹MC	♀☍♃	♂☌MC	♅⚼♇
☉☍♆	☽△ASC	♀△♄	♃⚹♄	♅☍☊
☉△♇	☽☆☊	♀☍♆	♃X♅	♆⚹♇
☉⚻ASC	☿☌♀	♀△♇	♃☌♆	♆XASC
☽□☿	☿⚼♂	♀⚻ASC	♃☆♇	♇□ASC
☽□♀	☿⚼♄	♀⚼MC	♃⚻☊	♇⊥☊

FIGURE 27

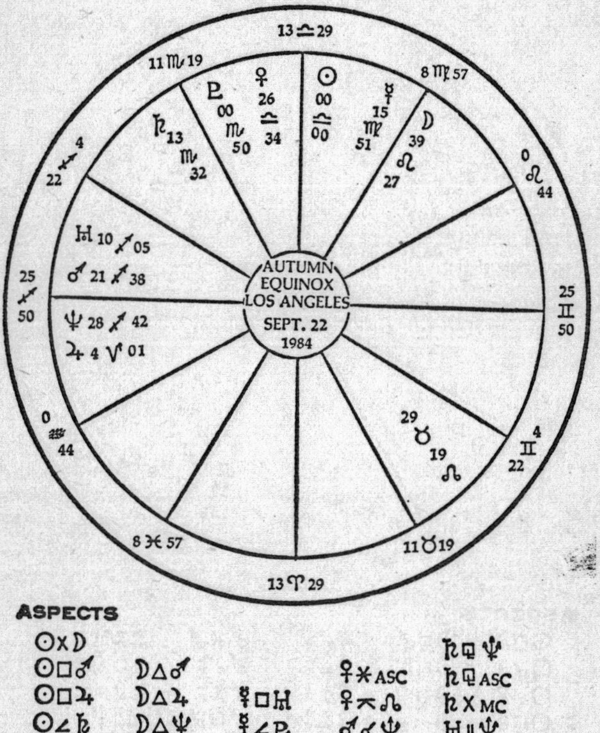

ASPECTS

☉X☽				♄⚼♆
☉□♂	☽△♂		♀✶ASC	♄⚼ASC
☉□♃	☽△♃	☿□♅	♀⊼☊	♄XMC
☉∠♄	☽△♆	☿∠♇	♂☌♆	♅∥♆
☉☆♅	☽✶♇	☿□MC	♂☌ASC	♅✶MC
☉□♆	☽△ASC	☿X☊	♃☌♆	♆✶♇
☉X♇	☽∠MC	♀✶♂	♃✶♇	♆☌ASC
☉□ASC	☽□☊	♀⚼♅	♃☌ASC	♆⊼☊
☉△☊	☿□♂	♀✶♆	♃□MC	♇✶ASC
☽✶♀	☿✶♄	♀☌♇	♃±☊	♇⊼☊

FIGURE 28

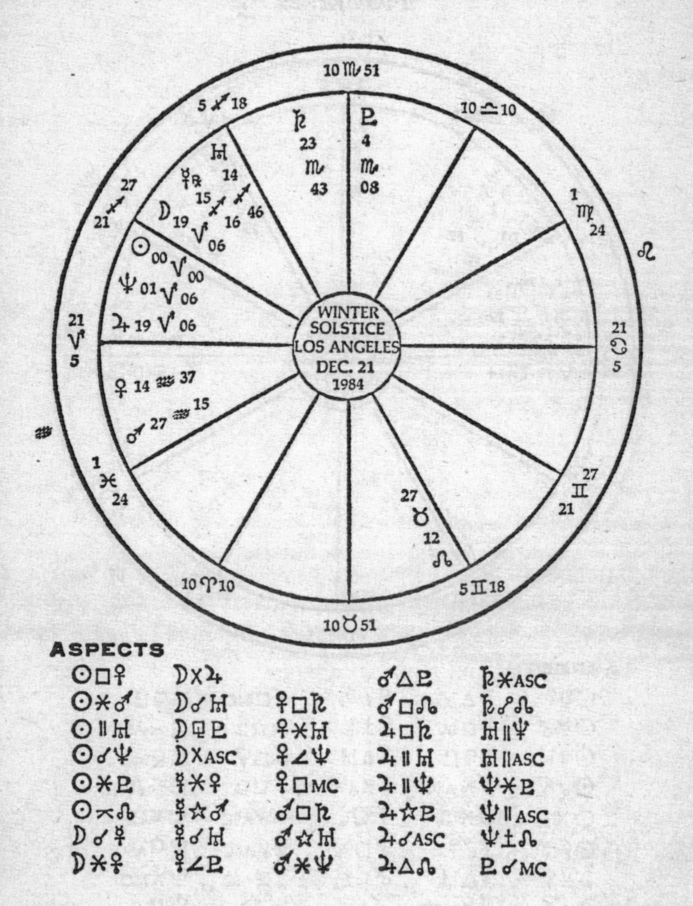
WINTER
SOLSTICE
LOS ANGELES
DEC. 21
1984
ASPECTS

FIGURE 29

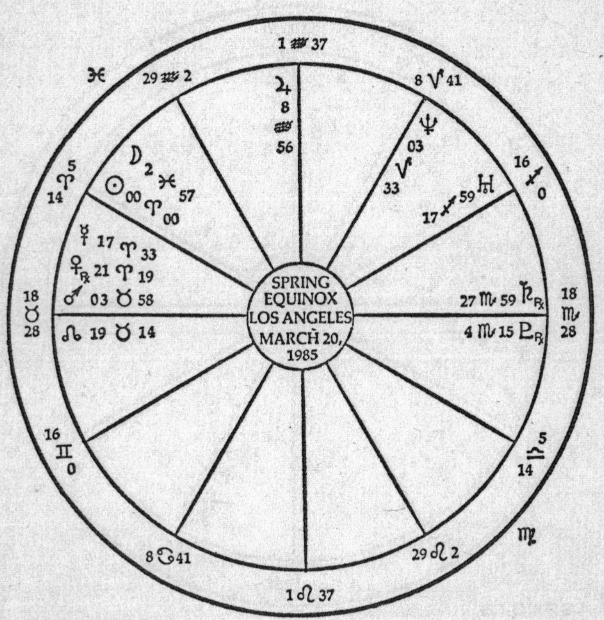

ASPECTS

☉⚼♀	☽△♅	♀☆♃	♂□MC	♅⚼♇
☉✶♂	☽□♅	♀±♄	♃☆♄	♅⚻ASC
☉∥♅	☽⚼♇	♀△♅	♃□♆	♅⚼MC
☉☌♆	☽✶ASC	♀XASC	♃□♇	♅⚻☊
☉✶♇	☽✶☊	♀X☊	♃☌ASC	♆✶♇
☉⚻☊	☿☌♀	♂□♃	♄☍ASC	♆⚼ASC
☽✶♀	☿△♅	♂⚼♅	♄✶MC	♆XMC
☽∠♂	☿✶ASC	♂△♆	♄☍☊	♆⚼☊
☽∠♃	☿✶☊	♂☍♇	♅∥♆	♇□MC

FIGURE 30

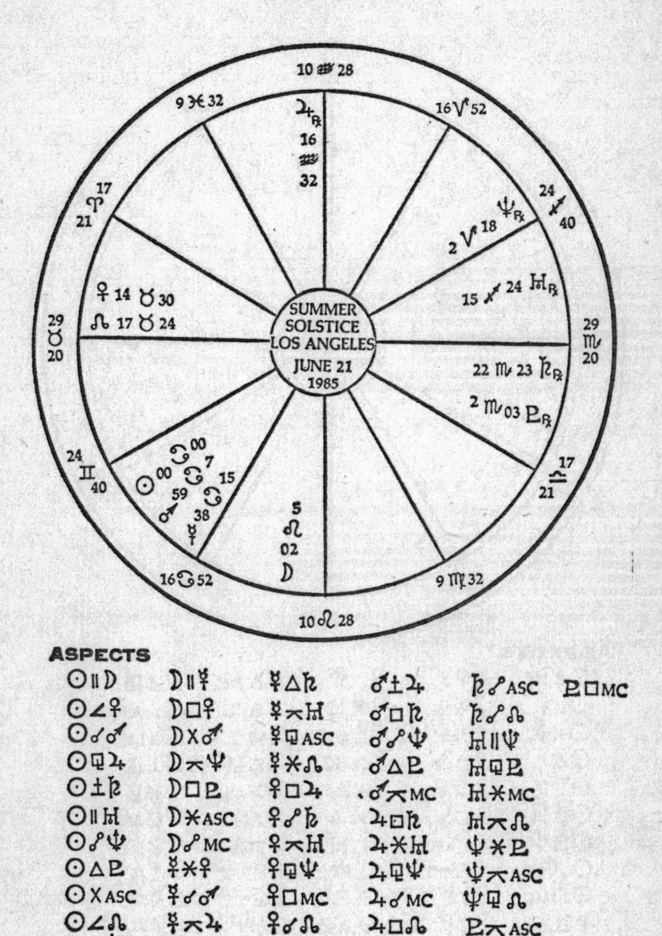

10 ♒ 28
9 ♓ 32
16 ♈ 52
♃℞ 16 ♒ 32
17 ♈ 21
24 ♐ 40
2 ♑ 18 ♆℞
15 ♐ 24 ♅℞
♀ 14 ♉ 30
☊ 17 ♉ 24
29 ♉ 20
SUMMER
SOLSTICE
LOS ANGELES
JUNE 21
1985
29 ♏ 20
22 ♏ 23 ♄℞
2 ♏ 03 ♇℞
24 ♊ 40
☉ 00 ♋ 00
♂ 7 ♋ 59
☿ 15 ♋ 38
17 ♎ 21
5 ♌ 02 ☽
16 ♋ 52
9 ♍ 32
10 ♌ 28
ASPECTS
☉∥☽ ☽∥☿ ☿△♄ ♂±♃ ♄☍ASC ♇□MC
☉∠♀ ☽□♀ ☿⚻♅ ♂□♄ ♄☍☊
☉☌♂ ☽X♂ ☿⚼ASC ♂☍♆ ♅∥♆
☉⚼♃ ☽⚻♆ ☿✶☊ ♂△♇ ♅⚼♇
☉±♄ ☽□♇ ♀□♃ ♂⚻MC ♅✶MC
☉∥♅ ☽✶ASC ♀☍♄ ♃□♄ ♅⚻☊
☉☍♆ ☽☍MC ♀⚻♅ ♃✶♅ ♆✶♇
☉△♇ ☿✶♀ ♀⚼♆ ♃⚼♆ ♆⚻ASC
☉X ASC ☿☌♂ ♀□MC ♃☌MC ♆⚼☊
☉∠☊ ☿⚻♃ ♀☌☊ ♃□☊ ♇⚻ASC

FIGURE 31

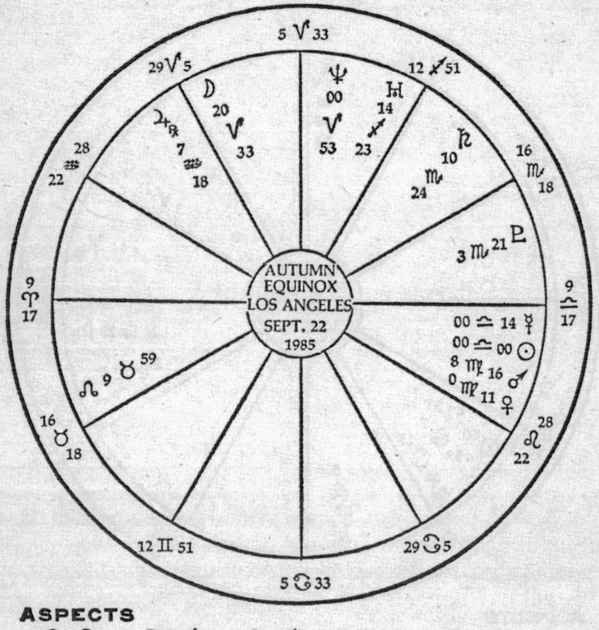

ASPECTS

☉△☽	☽⚼♂	♀△♆	♂△MC	♅∠♇
☉☌☿	☽⚹♄	♀⚹♇	♂△☊	♅△ASC
☉⚹♀	☿⚹♀	♀±ASC	♃☆♄	♅∥MC
☉△♃	☿△♃	♀△MC	♃□♇	♅±☊
☉⚹♄	☿☆♅	♀△☊	♃⚹ASC	♆⚹♇
☉☆♅	☿□♆	♂⚻♃	♃XMC	♆□ASC
☉□♆	☿☍ASC	♂□♅	♃□☊	♆☌MC
☉☍ASC	☿□MC	♂△♆	♄⚼ASC	♆△☊
☉□MC	♀☌♂	♂⚹♇	♄∠MC	♇⚹MC
☽△☿	♀□♄	♂⚻ASC	♅∥♆	♇☍☊

FIGURE 32

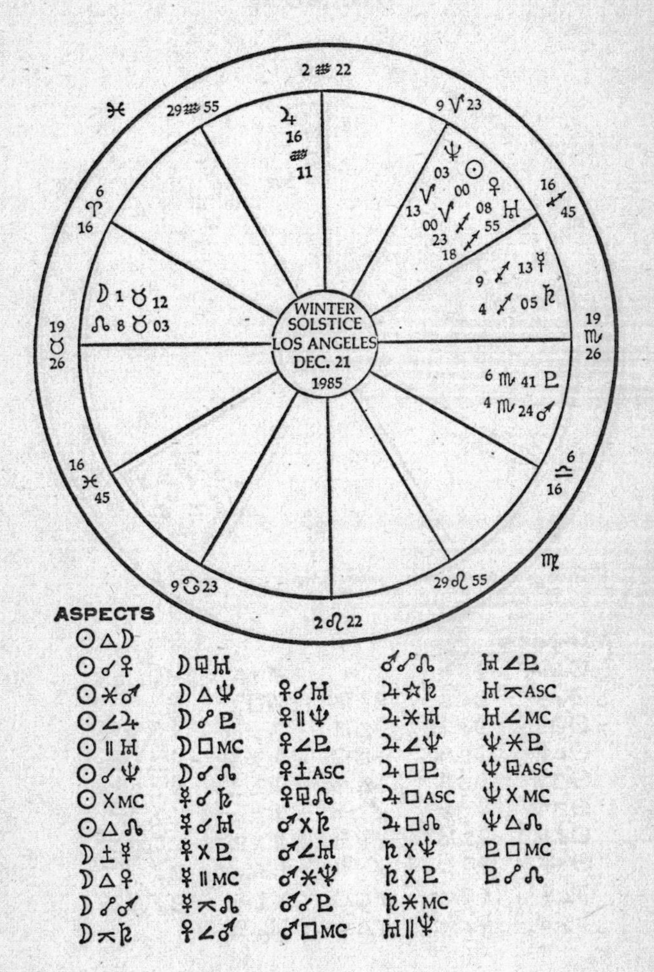

FIGURE 33

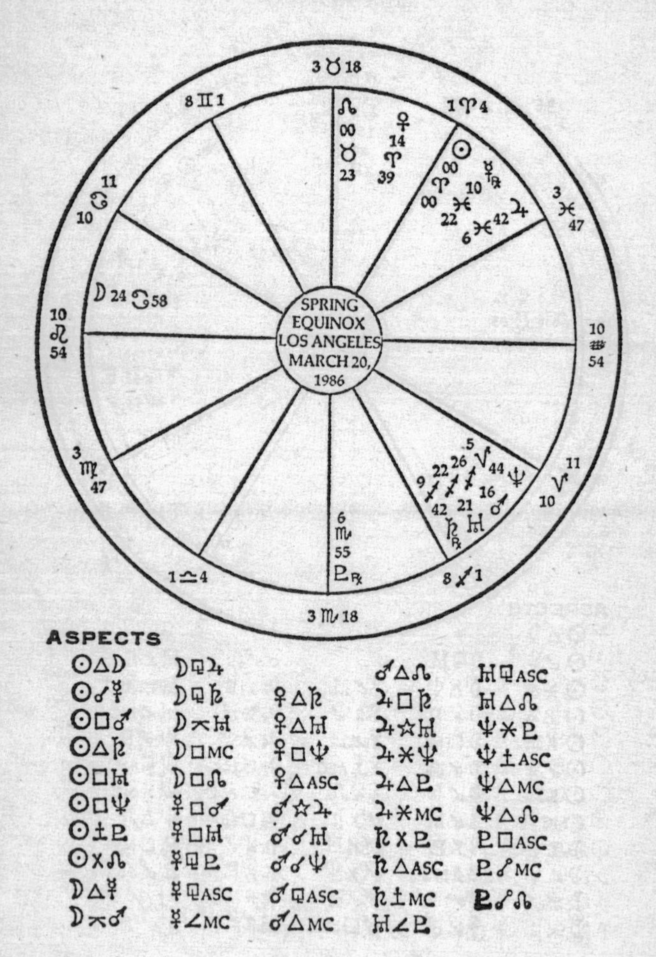

FIGURE 34

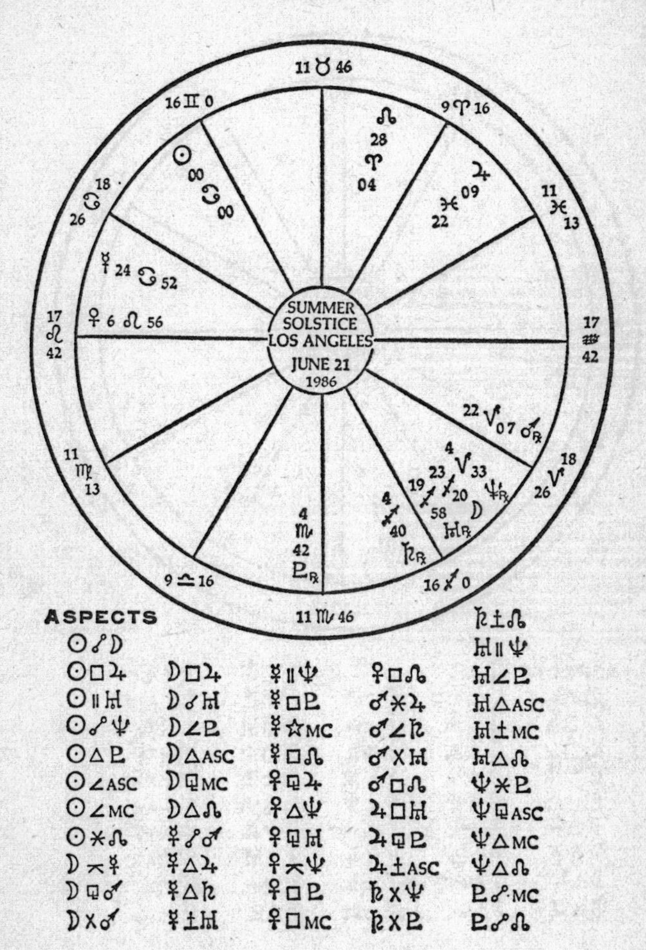

FIGURE 35

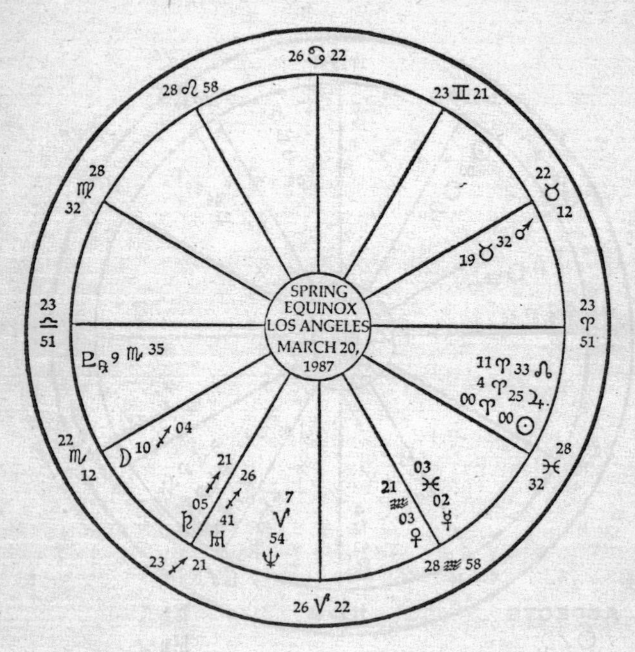

ASPECTS	☽X♇		♂⚼♆	♄⚹ASC
☉☌♃	☽∠ASC	♀□♂	♂☍♇	♄⊥MC
☉□♄	☽⚼MC	♀∠♃	♃□♅	♄△☊
☉□♅	☽△☊	♀⚹♄	♃□♆	♅⚹♇
☉□♆	☿X♃	♀⚹♅	♃⊥♇	♅∠ASC
☉△MC	☿☆♄	♀∠♆	♃△MC	♅⚻MC
☽□☿	☿⚹♆	♀△ASC	♃☌☊	♆⚹♇
☽☆♀	☿△♇	♂∠♃	♄☌♅	♆☆ASC
☽△♃	☿△ASC	♂⚻♄	♄∥♆	♆□☊
☽X♆	☿⊥MC	♂⊥♅	♄∠♇	♇⚻☊

FIGURE 36

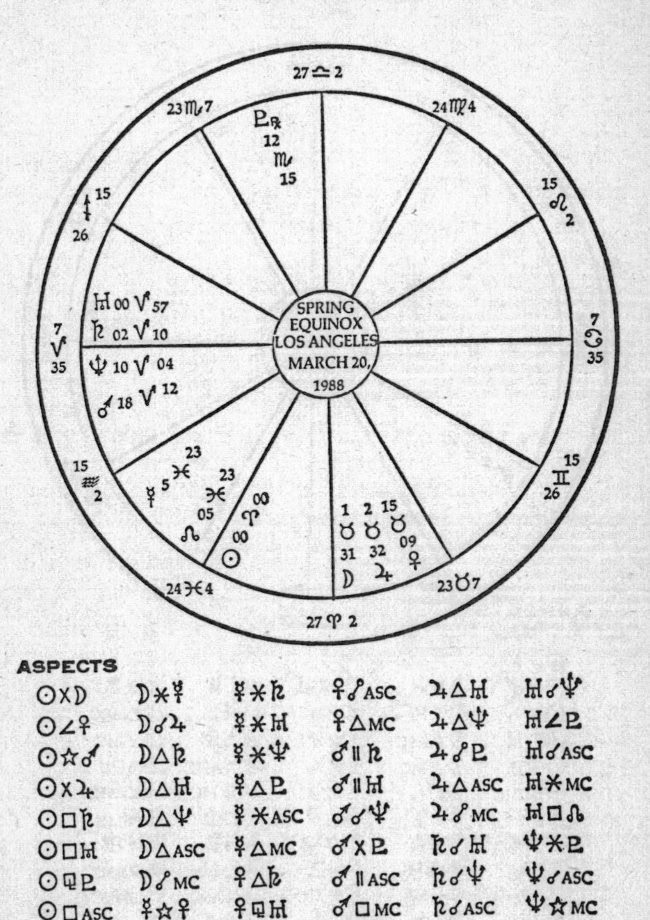

ASPECTS

☉x☽	☽⚹☿	☿⚹♄	♀☍ASC	♃△♅	♅☌♆
☉∠♀	☽☌♃	☿⚹♅	♀△MC	♃△♆	♅∠♇
☉☆♂	☽△♄	☿⚹♆	♂∥♄	♃☍♇	♅☌ASC
☉x♃	☽△♅	☿△♇	♂∥♅	♃△ASC	♅⚹MC
☉□♄	☽△♆	☿⚹ASC	♂☌♆	♃☍MC	♅□☊
☉□♅	☽△ASC	☿△MC	♂x♇	♄☌♅	♆⚹♇
☉⚼♇	☽☍MC	♀△♄	♂∥ASC	♄☌♆	♆☌ASC
☉□ASC	☿☆♀	♀⚼♅	♂□MC	♄☌ASC	♆☆MC
☉⚻MC	☿∠♂	♀⚼♆	♂⚹☊	♄⚹MC	♆☆☊
☉☌☊	☿⚹♃	♀△♇	♃△♄	♄□☊	♇⚹ASC

FIGURE 37

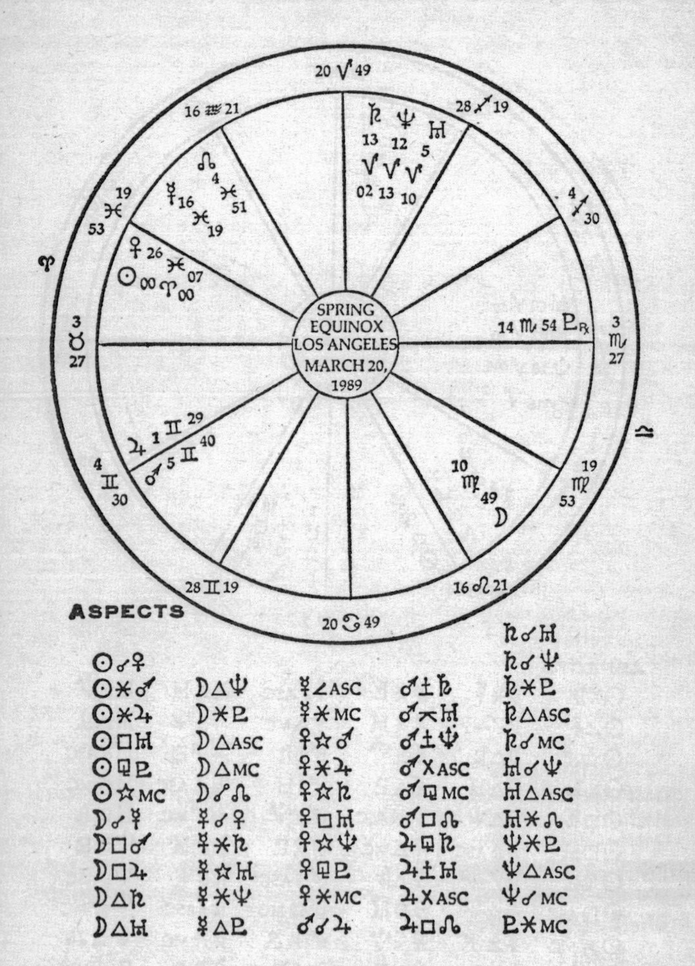

FIGURE 38

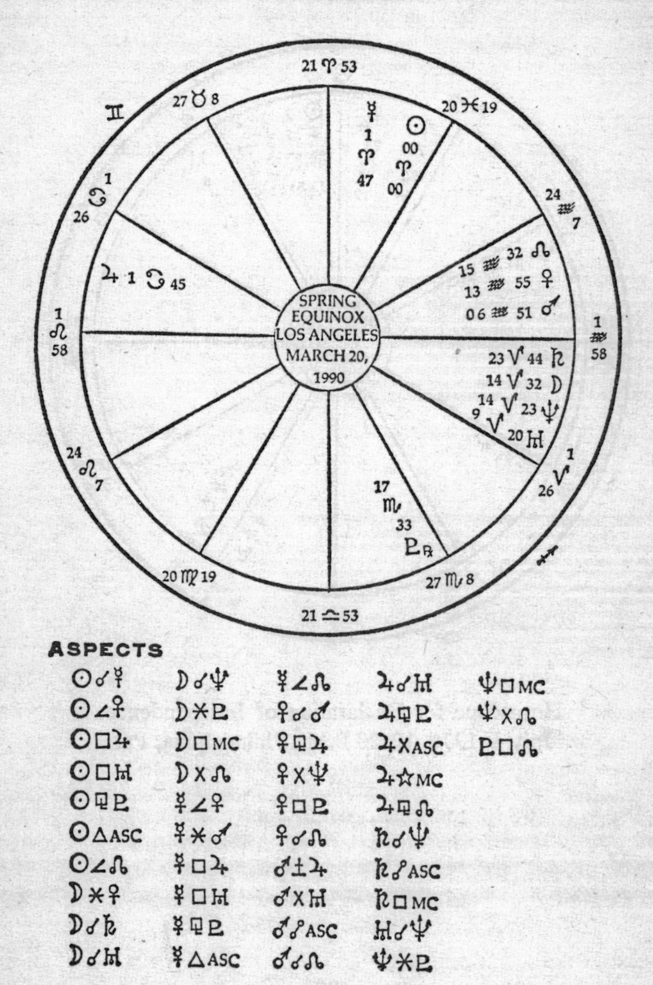
SPRING
EQUINOX
LOS ANGELES
MARCH 20,
1990
21 ♈ 53
20 ♓ 19
24 ♒ 7
1 ♒ 58
26 ♐ 1
27 ♏ 8
21 ♎ 53
20 ♍ 19
24 ♌ 7
1 ♌ 58
26 ♋ 1
27 ♉ 8
ASPECTS

FIGURE 39

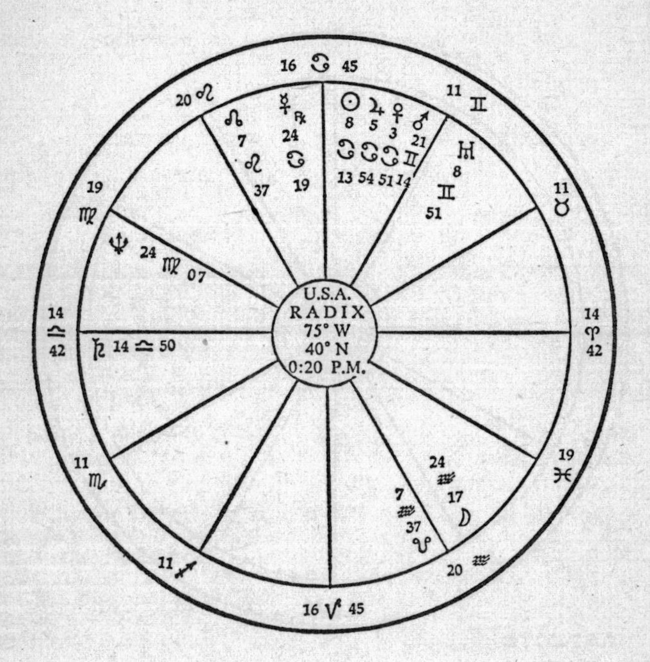

Horoscope for Declaration of Independence
July 4, 1776, 12:20 P.M., Philadelphia, Pa.

INDEX